Writings
of Lion's Lair

Volume 1

The Lord and his
End Times Servants

Writings of Lion's Lair, Volume 1, The Lord and his End Times Servants. Published by My Soul Does Wait. Centennial, Colorado.

My Soul Does Wait Publishing is a trademark of Leo R. Lewis. My Soul Does Wait logo design by Leo R. Lewis (Canva stock images).

All full scripture quotations are from the Holy Bible, King James Version, Thomas Nelson Publishers, Thomas Nelson Inc., 1989. Online sources referenced for these same scripture quotations include biblegateway.com and biblehub.com. In several cases where deeper meaning of terms or specific words within these quotations are explained, Strong's Concordance at biblehub.com was referenced.

No Artificial Intelligence (AI) was used for the development of written content in this book. All written content in this book is currently available online for an indefinite time at mysouldoeswait.com.

First paperback and hardcover editions: December 2025

Author contact information: leolewis@gmail.com

Paperback Book ISBN: 979-8-9936812-0-7

Hardback Book ISBN: 979-8-9936812-1-4

Ebook (kindle) ISBN: 979-8-9936812-2-1

Ebook ISBN: 979-8-9936812-3-8

Audiobook ISBN: 979-8-9936812-4-5

Library of Congress Control Number (LCCN): 2025923861

BISAC: REL067060

Book design by Leo R. Lewis

Cover design by Leo R. Lewis

Cover design: Copyright © by Leo R. Lewis

Cover images: Canva stock photo and design elements

Yea, all kings shall fall down before him:
all nations shall serve him. (Ps. 72:11)

Table of Contents

Introduction

Several years back, due to personal circumstances and continuing worldwide anomalies, pondering the possibility that the end of the age was upon us was of great intrigue to me. As of February, 2020, I had recently taken a few trips through scripture in an attempt to increase my understanding of God's Word. I began to study and then share my findings online in the form of written posts. In the course of my studies, I was particularly struck by numerous topics that either inform or directly speak to the biblical end times scenario. I was even more struck that I was finding a story that was different than that I had previously thought was the case.

In fact, I found myself writing about topics that I had never heard discussed form the pulpit. Chief among these was the existence in scripture of end times biblical characters, not the least of which is the person representing the Lord's Spirit in the midst. I also discovered an anointed lost sheep remnant who will proceed into the Millennial Kingdom. So, here, I ask: If you thought that we were living at the end of the age and that biblical figures similar to Moses in his day or Elijah in his could be spiritually "birthed" for the coming Kingdom, would you be interested?

I could only process so much at a time. So, I shared findings of my focused studies one-at-a-time on my site entitled, Lion's Lair (mysouldoeswait.com). Over time, my content grew to the point at which I realized I had a larger story to tell. This story for which my early writings were the foundation is told in my books, *Biblical End Times, Volumes 1 and 2*. I would recommend these for a reader who would like to explore the story for remnants of Israel and Gentiles who will proceed through coming end times events and arrive at the doorstep of the Kingdom.

While these scripture-supported teachings will likely be new to you and are not reflected in popular discussion, if they are accurate, generally speaking, then it would be a reflection on the current state of our society as to whether truth can prevail. The fact that there is virtually no discussion of topics that are covered by a multitude of scripture would certainly suggest that this story has been deliberately quieted. This means that the kingdom adversary is in control of the narrative. We can logically infer that current day rulers do not want an informed populace that becomes aware of coming judgment and that watches for the Lord's deliverance and return. As a result, false teachers and prophets temporarily prevail with misleading and deceptive messages. Of course, this fulfills prophecy too.

Like I was, I believe that you will be amazed at how an understanding of a last days anointed remnant opens up the meaning of scripture. This integrated story in the context of the spiritual kingdom war that still rages is fitting and consistent from the beginnings of God's Word in the Garden of Eden through the end of his Word with a manchild "birthed" in the midst of the "woman" and her seed (Revelation, Chapter 12). Jesus' parables also have significant meaning for this remnant's story. In the course of categorizing these parables accordingly, I describe the full meaning of the Parable of the Mustard Seed in detail and as supported by additional scripture. This Parable relates to the last days anointed remnant being instrumental branches of the 'tree' that represents the Lord's coming Kingdom.

Overall, in this book, *Writings of Lion's Lair, Volume 1*, I provide original passages from online posts of mine (with slight edits for book format) that are related to the Lord's Holy Spirit in the midst along with his anointed remnant at the end of the age. Passages are categorized into broad topic areas, sometimes presented in series, that exist independently of one another. Having said that, I commonly reference other series or passages throughout, where applicable, for the benefit of any reader who desires to enhance their holistic understanding. Some of these cross references may be found in *Volumes 2 and 3. Volume 2* describes prophecy and signs for Israel and Gentile believers within the context of last days world Babylon's kingdom. *Volume 3* contains an analysis of Old Testament scripture and provides insights about prophecy and patterns for the same last days scenario that will play out. This end-of-the-age scenario will usher in the Lord's Millennial Kingdom.

Chapter 1.

Being Awake and Watching in the Last Days

Passages from Lion's Lair provided in this chapter include:

1.1 Being 'Awake' and 'Watching' for the Soon Coming of our Lord and Savior

1.2 Components of Watching and Waiting

1.3 Watching and Warning

1.1 Being 'Awake' and 'Watching' for the Soon Coming of our Lord and Savior

Jesus instructed that we are to be aware, awake and watching. It naturally follows that I might address the general biblical concept of 'watching.' As you might expect, this concept is presented differently in the scripture, depending on the context in which it is used.

Ancient Roots of Modern Day Surveillance and 'Watching'

At the darkest, highest spiritual level the most evil characters (fallen angels and their Nephilim offspring) were originally labeled as "Watchers" by Enoch. This kind of surveillance-nature evil has always existed, some might say since the original serpent in the Garden, and it certainly continues even to this day. Now it is enhanced by intrusive high-tech spying methods. It looks to "catch" us in our wrongdoing, and then hold us falsely accused or condemned (via age-old methods such as blackmail, shakedown, extortion, etc.).

We know from scripture that the Pharisees, priests and scribes many times followed and tried to catch and accuse even Jesus himself (e.g. for violating the Sabbath, eating with tax collectors, giving non-kosher responses to their "trap" questions, etc.). This type of continuous 'watching' is done for the purpose of attempting to accuse, condemn, and then to ultimately imprison, control and hold an individual in bondage. This, then, allows the enemy control. As mentioned above, it comes from a very dark, yet highly powerful, spiritual place. Of course, Jesus himself was never going to be fooled by these methods, and repeatedly called out these Pharisees as hypocrites.

[NOTE: I mention this type of 'watching' here, early on in this writing, because this is one primary method, along with intentional deception, used by the modern day Chaldean-/Babylonian-/Pharisee-types in order to gain incredible power and influence as well as to eliminate any threats to that power. This anti-Christ group that operates and schemes in secret will be a very important topic across Volumes 1 through 3 of this publication. I believe the reader's understanding of them will help provide some fresh, new insight for interpreting and explaining various prophetic scripture as well as some assistance in understanding current events.]

Only God Sees All

So now I have the opportunity to contrast the above with the good news. At the highest, brightest spiritual level God watches- the God who we know is all-powerful, all-knowing and omnipresent. His eyes are everywhere (Prov. 15:3), in a way that the evil one cannot counterfeit. And we also know from Jesus' teachings that He is with his people always (Matt. 28:20). God and his angels' spirit is one of love and protection, for our benefit, and even for our own course-correction. God especially watches those who he calls his people and who he enlists to reach the world with his message of love, forgiveness, grace and salvation. We know that Jesus Christ ultimately came to this earth and died for the sake of our souls so that we can call on his name, ask forgiveness of our sins, ask to be delivered from bondage and to be *set free*.

Awake and Watching for the Return of Jesus Christ

With all of that said I finally arrive at the primary, most important, meaning and purpose for 'watching'; that is, *our own watching for*

Jesus Christ's return. In order to watch, we must first be *awake*. When we are spiritually 'awake' we are more likely to be discerning and less likely to be deceived. Children of the light as Paul mentions in First Thessalonians (5:5) are those who are 'children of the day,' and those who are awake and sober in their watching. Jesus stated that servants of a house should be awake and keep watch because they do not know the time at which the owner (He) will return; and so that when he does he should not find them sleeping. In instructing us about the end times Jesus said, "Take ye heed, watch and pray..." (Mk. 13:33). When Jesus instructed his disciples to stay awake and watch in the Garden of Gethsemane, he said that they should remain awake so they should not fall into temptation as a result of weakness of the flesh, fear, etc.

It is interesting that upon his disciples' falling asleep in Gethsemane, against his instruction, Jesus was then, "betrayed into the hands of sinners" (Mk. 14:41). I believe that the modern day application of this is that the Church- as an institution and its leaders- has largely fallen into apostasy and that many individual Christians are being caught by various temptations, deception and lies of the modern day, anti-Christ Chaldeans, the adversary that I will describe in more detail, particularly in *Writings of Lion's Lair, Volume 3*. As a result, *Christ is being abandoned once again.*

Meanwhile, the modern day Chaldean group headed by world leaders and "elites" seeks to ensure that current world systems and processes in place will make for a natural transition for the arising and (initial) acceptance of a world government and its leader (Anti-Christ) who will presumably solve the world's problems and, of course, protect *their* own interests. But we who are awake know that this will usher in even greater troubles and chaos such as that which the world has never seen. This will be the Day of the Lord, which I describe in detail in *Volume 2.*

Those of us who are truly awake clearly see the signs of the times and the time of the signs. The final few decades at the end of the age prior to the Lord's Kingdom to come will be like none other in human history. We should be knowledgeable and informed so that we can be prepared. I firmly believe that we are in that season. You may want to refer to my books, *Biblical End Times, Volumes 1 and 2.*

Remember, in the days of Noah, only he and his family were awake, watching and prepared. And then the flood came...

1.2 Components of Watching and Waiting

In this passage I'll describe the concept of 'watching' a little more and how our act of 'watching' as Christ-believers naturally requires components of waiting and patience. I believe that many Christians in the current day will relate with the context and background presented here in which true believers of Christ are waiting for our Lord's appearance.

While we wait patiently on Christ, many of us do so within the following environment and context:

In Righteousness

In the time of his own waiting and trials King David prayed, "May integrity and uprightness protect me" (Ps. 25:21). In his Psalm (37), David provided a stark contrast between the wicked who pursue and falsely persecute versus those who stand in righteousness, endure and do not stumble. During this period David found it important to, "Wait for the Lord and keep his way" (Ps. 37:34), as well as not to be worried or to fret when the evil ones carry out their "wicked schemes." Jesus and his disciples themselves also warned us against various temptations and trials expected to come in these end times.

King David, in the midst of his own persecution, was joyful and confident that righteousness and justice would ultimately prevail. This sustained him. He recognized that God only was his judge and the keeper of his soul and remarked, "Against you and you only have I sinned" (Ps. 51:4).

In Doing His Work

In our process of waiting we should still be about doing the Lord's work. In the book of Matthew (Chapter 24), Jesus remarked about keeping watch for his coming being like an owner of a house watching for a thief in the night. Jesus remarked additionally about a faithful and wise servant who a homeowner has put in charge to, "give other servants their food." Here, Jesus said, "It will be good for that servant whose homeowner finds him doing so when he returns." The 'food' given by the wise servant here is spiritual food. It is equivalent to Jesus telling Peter several times, "feed my sheep."

Similarly, in the *Parable of the Talents*, we know that the servants who put their resources to work on behalf of the owner were "good and faithful" servants. These benefited even more when the owner returned; thus, demonstrating the general principle that those who desire to enter the Kingdom of God and earn its rewards should be about its work in the meantime.

In Persecution, Hardships, and Affliction

Have you ever found yourself waiting and yearning for our Lord during times of persecution, hardship and spiritual battle? Hardship and persecution necessarily cause us to look up, watch and wait. There is no better example of patience in persecution and affliction than the prophets themselves. The Prophet Jeremiah not only suffered much hardship personally but also witnessed God's divine, devastating judgment on Judah/Jerusalem. In the midst of extremely difficult times Jeremiah still acquiesced, "The Lord is good to those whose hope is in him, to the one who seeks him; it is good to wait quietly for the salvation of the Lord" (Lam. 3:25-26).

The apostles also suffered much. Paul wrote from personal experience when he advised:

Endure hardship as discipline; God is treating you as sons. (Heb. 12:7)

No discipline seems pleasant at the time, but painful. Later on, however, it produces a harvest of righteousness and peace for those who have been trained by it. (Heb. 12:11)

We are 'trained,' at least in part, through our understanding of how personal tribulations ultimately lead us to possess a spirit of hope such as Paul described in some initial chapters in the book of Romans.

In Faith, Trust, and Hope

Our ability to withstand the process of watching and waiting for our Lord over a long period of time is grounded in our faith. We know certain biblical characters of particular "faith-fame" demonstrated incredible patience in their waiting including but not limited to: Noah; Abraham; Sarah; Jacob; Joseph; and David. David said, "We wait in hope for the Lord; he is our help and our shield...for we trust in his holy name" (Ps. 33:20-21).

The ever-faithful Apostle Paul in his day envisioned the glory that is to come when the creation that we inhabit- a creation he observed even at his time as being in decay, groaning, and bondage- will be freed and belong to God and his people. In already anticipating God's Kingdom to come, Paul stated, "But if we hope for what we do not yet have, we wait for it patiently" (Rom. 8:25).

In Prayer and Supplication

Not surprisingly, the Apostle Paul mentioned several times in his writings the combination of prayer and being watchful. After Paul described the well-known 'armor of God' in Ephesians, Chapter 6, he also spoke of perseverance and prayer "on all occasions" along with being alert. In Colossians, Chapter 4, Paul again advised being devoted to prayer amidst being watchful.

On both occasions in these letters Paul asked for prayers for himself and other saints. He made this request as a result of his being in bondage due to what he described as his laboring in revealing the "mystery of the gospel."

I believe that in the present day, given the high level and intensity of spiritual warfare in the ongoing kingdom war, that we should be praying for God's final remnant of believers as a whole. While we observe rampant apostasy, there are still those who are attempting to live a Christ-serving life and proclaim the good news of the Gospel, all while enduring persecution. If you happen to find yourself as qualifying for this distinction Paul advised as part of his bigger message about the topic of love to be "joyful in hope, patient in affliction, and patient in prayer" (Rom. 12:12)

In Perseverance and Endurance

Not surprisingly, the Apostle Paul was also a great example of endurance. In Second Timothy, Chapter 4, Paul spoke of a time in the future when people will "not endure sound doctrine" and will turn away from the truth. As Paul self-proclaimed fighting the good fight he encouraged us to endure and to evangelize during this time. Jesus, likely speaking of this same future (end-time) period as Paul, referred to strong deception and division but that the one who (waits and) endures to the end "shall be saved."

Believers in the end times will find themselves feeling somewhat alienated and lonely in a world that has largely departed from the one true God. Believers will be left with no other choice but to persevere and endure with a servant's spirit through constant headwinds and spiritual attacks.

In Expectancy of our Reward

As practical believers who are watching and waiting in the end times for our Lord who brings us our salvation it is logical that we envision our bright future. Chances are, true Christ-believers in the final days will choose to distance themselves from the things of this world and instead turn their focus to the coming glory of God's heavenly Kingdom. While we look forward to eternal life in heaven as well as any specific rewards such as various crowns to be given, positions in the kingdom, etc., we will also look forward to a relief and an escape from the evil and corrupt world in which we currently live. Our escape from the current oppressive world system means that we are waiting for:

Salvation- *Truly my soul waiteth upon God; from him cometh my salvation.* (Ps. 62:1)

Redemption- *For I know that my redeemer liveth, and he shall stand at the latter day upon the earth.* (Job 19:25)

Deliverance– *And to wait for his Son from heaven, whom he raised from the dead, which delivered us from the wrath to come.* (1 Thess. 1:10)

Justice- *For evildoers shall be cut off: but those that wait upon the Lord, they shall inherit the earth.* (Ps. 37:9)

In the end, having a "new song" (Ps. 40:3) and the opportunity to mount up with "wings like eagles" (Is. 40:31) sounds especially promising and refreshing to those faithful servants who have truly been through the battle and have run the race.

~

[*NOTE: According to much prophetic scripture, there is one particular group of believers who will especially identify with all of the above end-time challenges associated with waiting and watching for our Lord and Savior. They will be highly familiar with suffering and persecution, and as a result, will turn back to God for their ultimate salvation and deliverance.*

God's Word refers to this group as an end-times "remnant" or "vine" that represents Jacob, or the house of Israel. This group is a relatively small part of a larger vineyard (Israel) that God preserves to help accomplish his purpose in finally defeating evil on this earth as well as for fulfilling his promise for a continuation of his people, Israel, in his heavenly Kingdom to come. These will make their faith in Christ known to others.]

In Chapters 4-8, I will address in more detail about this segment of believers, which surprisingly is virtually never acknowledged nor discussed by modern prophecy teachers. I also discuss their story in detail in my books, *Biblical End Times, Volumes 1 and 2,* published in late 2024.

1.3 Watching and Warning

Those who are truly awake and watching in the current day are in a natural position to warn others. A last days 'watchman's warning will generally include three general topics:

1) Jesus Christ is returning soon

2) Man has largely abandoned the God of the Bible

3) God's 'days of vengeance' on the earth will come soon

I address each of these areas, respectively, in separate sections below.

Warning: We are in the Last Days- Jesus is Returning Soon

We are currently living in the last days before Jesus' return. Even the apostles, in their time, observed that the last days were already underway. The Apostle John wrote:

Little children, it is the last time; and as ye have heard that antichrist shall come, even now there are many antichrists. (1 John 2:18)

The apostles even asked Jesus if that time they were with him in person was the time that would usher in his Millennial Kingdom. Jesus' answer was, 'not yet'; but later, through John's vision described in the book of Revelation Jesus himself reassured several times that he is "coming quickly" and that this book should remain 'unsealed'; thus, it should be open for believers to read and see for themselves about those events that are soon coming soon and will take place in the last days.

Warning: Man has Largely Abandoned the God of the Bible

The same factors (i.e. wayward and wicked human behaviors and human-created institutions) that brought God's judgment on his people in the past are those that exist again. The repeating cycles and patterns in God's Word are unmistakable. As we learn from King Solomon, "There is nothing new under the sun."

Man has chosen to worship other, false gods

God's own people, the house of Israel, are always the first place to look. In modern times, the house of Israel remains away from their own God. The modern day Pharisees (worldwide) attempt to 'manufacture' their own Messiah and even the timing of his arrival. They plan for this false messiah's temple in Jerusalem. They are willing to divide their God-given land in a trade deal that gives away land for so-called peace. But then again, from God's Word we know that the Jews would be blinded in part until their eyes are opened by hard truths to come upon them in these last days. Meanwhile, sadly, many remain *completely* blinded due to their oaths to secret society organizations, following other gods, Rabbi-Talmud teachings, Kabbalah mysticism, etc. Also, think "Synagogue of Satan" here.

The anti-Christ Chaldean "mob" holds individuals and institutions in bondage

False institutions, false teachings and false gods (or having no god) are no more than vehicles for individuals to feel comfortable with unrepentant, chronic sinful behavior. These help to cover up, keep secret and falsely justify a multitude of sins. The modern day anti-Christ Chaldean/Babylonian "mob" captures people in their sinful behaviors, makes them slaves, and then systematically promulgates and reinforces misbehavior via institutionalized and highly organized, criminal matrix-style methods. Individuals are held in bondage for their own sins and are collectively enslaved to help cover up sins of entire institutions and even nations.

As a result, this massive army collaborates and coordinates to heavily influence and control major institutions (governments, elected bodies, corporations, media, religions, etc.) across borders, worldwide. In doing so, they cover up the very ugly truth and iniquity that underlies their power. God warned through the Prophet Isaiah:

Woe unto them that seek deep to hide their counsel from the Lord, and their works are in the dark, and they say, Who seeth us? And who knoweth us? (Is. 29:15)

In a 'free' society like the U.S. truth should naturally reign, be transparent for all and win popular support. With all of the overwhelming, unmistakable evidence for Jesus Christ as the one true God (and no evidence to the contrary), only the existence of this Chaldean "mob" can explain how we end up, even in what is supposed to be a 'well-educated' republic like the U.S., with a relatively small proportion of Christ-believers, and among these, even a much smaller proportion who declare themselves to be *true* bible- and salvation-believers (ref. recent survey research). Instead, many aberrations, variations, and alternatives to the Gospel of Jesus Christ have been invented. In Romans (Chapter 1), Paul discussed wicked idolaters who, "...exchanged the truth of God for a lie."

In the time period of grace since Jesus first established his church on this earth the Gentiles have done no better than the Jews in recognizing and serving the one true God of Israel. Multitudes of both Gentiles and Jews, even in the U.S., have traded out and chosen to serve the adversary instead- i.e. that is, the modern day anti-Christ Chaldeans. And if this is the case in the U.S. imagine how powerful this group is worldwide. (Did you ever wonder how a wicked one-world government and Anti-Christ leader will arise suddenly, so easily, and thus how so many will be deceived practically overnight?)

In the midst of increasing lawlessness, Christ-believers should maintain righteousness

Once we understand the Chaldean army as representing the true deceptive anti-Christ spirit then we understand the primary source for all of those behaviors that we are warned will bring God's wrath. Due to this anti-Christ army's continuous coordination, perpetuation and cover-up of wicked activities we are left with:

- *Lawlessness and corruption* (i.e. unjust financial gain, false witness, murder, extortion, bribery, racketeering, institutional lies/cover-ups, etc.)

- *Moral sin and wickedness* (i.e. adultery, other sexual sin, lewdness, drug use, sorcery, witchcraft, etc.).

- *Rebellious attitudes* (i.e. pride, haughtiness, scoffing, mocking, love of money, censoring of the truth, etc.)

Taken altogether, this sin and lawlessness is a result of entire societies/nations that have turned to worship false gods and idols rather than the one true God of Israel.

So, we are to be warned that, for this season in which we expect Jesus to return, we are to be living in *righteousness* and *obeying his commands*. We are warned that we should be found wearing clean, white garments as opposed to being discovered naked and exposed. Might the 'nakedness' described in scripture (i.e. Rev. 3:18, Rev. 16:15, 2 Cor. 5:3) represent those who are left in their corrupt mortal being that is accompanied by wicked, unrighteous, idolatrous behavior, and spiritual shame? For we know that, "There is nothing secret that shall not be made manifest..." (Lk. 8:17).

Jesus Christ will ultimately identify his true children, his servants and his sheep who are wearing clean garments and he will award them with an escape from the wrath that is soon to come upon the earth.

Warning: God's Days of Vengeance on the Earth will Come Soon

The final time period at the end of the age, sometimes referred to as the 'days of vengeance' or the Day of the Lord, is right at the door. According to scripture, this will be a terrible time on this earth like there has never been. It will be a time of unprecedented distress. There will still be just a few bright spots due to God's designated spiritual army and witnesses on earth at this time. As a result, some people will still be able to come to a belated realization of God's truth and salvation in Jesus Christ.

Otherwise, in the book of Matthew (Chapter 24) Jesus foretold that in the end times: false gods will appear in his name; there will be wars and rumors of wars; nation will rise against nation; kingdom will rise against kingdom; there will be pestilence; there will be famines; and there will be earthquakes in diverse places. He called these events the "beginning of sorrows," but not yet the end.

Events and various signs and perils we are seeing now do not begin to compare with the actual terrors of the Day of the Lord that will soon follow. So, the warning here is about events to come. The best way to understand the coming time of God's worldwide 'days of vengeance' is to refer to God's Word itself. The following are just a few verses in scripture about this soon coming time period:

For then shall be great tribulation, such as was not since the beginning of the world to this time, no, nor shall ever be. And except those days should be shortened, there should be no flesh saved: but for the elect's sake, those days shall be shortened. (Matt. 24:21-22)

The earth shall reel to and fro like a drunkard, and shall totter like a hut; and the transgression thereof shall be heavy upon it; and it shall fall, and not rise again. (Is. 24:20)

The Lord is angry with all nations and furious with all their armies. He will set them apart for destruction; He will give them over to slaughter. The slain will be left unburied, and the stench of their corpses will rise; the mountains will flow with their blood. (Is. 34:2-3)

In the course of our 'watching' in these end times the warnings above are related to the most important events of our times or any time up until now for that matter. I trust that these warnings are well-heeded and duly-noted by those who are truly awake and watching along with me. We know that Jesus Christ will provide an escape and deliverance for those whom he calls his own. I discuss the path through the end times for believers in my books, *Biblical End Times, Volumes 1 and 2.*

Chapter 2.

False Prophets and Teachers

Passages from Lion's Lair provided in this chapter include:

2.1 False Prophets in the End Times

2.2 False Teachers in the End Times

2.1 False Prophets in the End Times

When asked about the last days by his disciples Jesus said that many things would occur during this time and among these, he said, "Many false prophets will rise up and deceive many" (Matt. 24:11). False prophets are one major reason Jesus warned several times that we should be sure and not be deceived in these last days. Collectively, deceitful modern day prophets ultimately play a significant role in end-times apostasy and the great "falling away" described by the Apostle Paul (2 Thess. 2:3). Thus, it makes sense that we should be wise and understand key characteristics of these anti-Christ system players and supporters.

As background, put simply, and generally speaking, a (true) prophet is one who God uses to communicate his message to the people and the peoples' leaders; in other words, a spokesperson. The Apostle Peter said, "For prophecy never came by the will of man but holy men of God spoke as they were carried along by the holy spirit" (2 Pet. 1:21). Earlier in the same line of text, Peter likened God's "sure word of prophecy" as to a "light that shines in a dark place." Genuine current day prophets effectively and accurately share God's Word of truth.

Characteristics of False Prophets

In addition to communicating God's truth, a true prophet will also commonly correct moral and spiritual-based mis-truths communicated by others (ref: BibleGateway.com dictionary, "prophet") including those shared by false prophets. For the most part, *false* prophets do the opposite of true prophets; that is, they lie and deceive. False prophets, just like God's true representatives, may be found in any of a multitude of positions, but are especially found in positions of spiritual or religious leadership. Thus, they are typically easily visible, communicating publicly and openly to an audience who may- at least loosely speaking- trust or believe them to be God's messengers.

We should be aware that false prophets largely prey on others who are: not anchored by sound doctrine; naive; lacking pure motives; possessing "itching ears"; desiring only good news and non-confrontational teaching; or, possessing a spiritual foundation that is built on something other than solid rock.

In Jeremiah's day, so-called prophets in Judah did not properly foresee or communicate about the coming destruction and captivity at the hands of the Babylonians. Instead, they communicated what the kings wanted to hear. In direct contrast, Jeremiah told the hard truth that he received directly from God. He was then held captive because his warning was unpopular and not good news. We see this dichotomous pattern elsewhere in scripture. God spoke to this pattern directly, which is highly applicable for the current end times in which we live:

An appalling and horrible thing has happened in the land: the prophets prophesy falsely, and the priests rule at their direction; my people love to have it so, but what will you do when the end comes? (Jer. 5:30-31)

In several places in scripture (i.e. Deut. 18:22, Jer. 28:9, etc.), we are told that the simple test for detecting whether a prophet is truly communicating a word from God is looking to see if the message that they speak comes true.

Motives of False Prophets

So, what specifically should we be aware of so that we are not deceived by these impostor prophets in our current day? Motives of modern day false prophets may be impure due to any combination of the reasons below. Note first however that many, if not all, of the following reasons for deception are merely a *consequence* of so-called God's messengers in our society already serving, "sold out" to, and/or strongly deceived by, the controlling, anti-Christ Chaldean network (See *Writings of Lion's Lair, Volume 3,* especially, about this secretive, underground worldwide organization). The following dark motives of false prophets addressed in scripture are largely a result of their oaths and belonging to this secretive, occult-driven organization:

- **Money-** *Its heads give judgment for a bribe; its priests teach for a price; its prophets practice divination for money; yet they lean on the Lord and say, "Is not the Lord in the midst of us? No disaster shall come upon us."* (Mic. 3:11)

- **Control or enslavement-** *While they promise them liberty, they themselves are servants of corruption: for of whom a man is overcome, of the same is he brought in bondage.* (2 Pet. 2:19)

- **Pride/ego-** *...They like to walk around in long robes, to receive greetings in the marketplaces, and to have the chief seats in the synagogues and the places of honor at banquets. (Jesus speaking of Pharisees)* (Mk. 12:38-39)

- **Traditions and symbolism-** *You neatly set aside the commandment of God to maintain your own tradition" (Jesus speaking to Pharisees)* (Mk. 7:9)

- **Lawless/sinful-** *I have also seen the prophets of Jerusalem an horrible thing: they commit adultery, and walk in lies: they strengthen also the hands of evildoers, that none doeth return from his wickedness; they are all of them unto me as Sodom, and the inhabitants thereof as Gomorrah. (part of and end times prophecy)* (Jer. 23:14)

- **Heretical/deceiving-** *...they will secretly introduce destructive heresies, even denying the sovereign Lord who brought them- bringing swift destruction on themselves...because of them the way of truth will be defamed.* (2 Pet. 2:1)

- **False peacemakers-** *Thus says the Lord concerning the prophets who make my people stray; who chant 'peace' while they chew with their teeth, but prepare war against him who puts nothing in their mouths.* (Mic. 3:5)

- ***Evil spirit**- For such men are false apostles, deceitful workmen, disguising themselves as apostles of Christ. And no wonder, for even Satan disguises himself as an angel of light. So, it is no surprise if his servants, also, disguise themselves as servants of righteousness. Their end will correspond to their deeds.* (2 Cor. 11:13-15)

All of these motives of false prophets still exist in our current times. In fact, false prophets and their deceptive activities will only get worse as the end times get closer. Though their actions will likely become more and more obvious, they will still have power to deceive "even the elect (if it were possible)" in the end times (Matt. 24:24). In discussing this time of tribulations Jesus told us that false prophets will even perform great signs and wonders (Matt. 24:24). There is no greater, obvious and simple culmination of this than the False Prophet himself who will perform "great wonders" and will openly endorse the worship of the beast in the Day of the Lord (Rev. 13:12-14). I describe the effect of false prophets in the end times story told in my books, *Biblical End Times, Volumes 1 and 2.*

~

In our last days, in some places of Christian worship, deception in the church may still be extremely subtle and not completely obvious and transparent. For anyone who may be looking for some practical ways to detect false church leaders, etc. in addition to the above signs, the following (below) are a few quick tests. These are a few very important top-of-mind issues but not an exhaustive list.

Do church leaders openly believe in and communicate fundamentals such as...

- *Jesus Christ as the only Son of the one true God, and the only way to God himself?* ("...every spirit that confesses that Jesus Christ has come in the flesh is from God, and every spirit that does not confess Jesus is not from God..." 1 Jn. 4:2-3). Do leaders and their church openly believe, communicate and strongly reinforce the fundamentals of Jesus' virgin birth, life, crucifixion, resurrection, ascension and final coming?)

- *The commandments of Jesus?* (along with their relation to obedience versus habitual sin)

- *Prophetic events that will soon unfold including those specifically related to the house of Israel?* (i.e. events that we are already starting to see that the Bible tells us will lead to the <u>return of Jesus Christ</u>). Given the current times in which we live, there is no excuse for church leaders to avoid these.

- *God's judgment and the reality of hell?* A prophet/leader who *truly* cares about the people will gently, but sternly, warn of the consequences of facing God's time of wrath and vengeance in the Day of the Lord; and even much more importantly, the perils of one's soul being eternally separated from God.

In the current times the stakes are very high in the midst of heavy spiritual warfare. Eternal salvation of one's soul is on the line. Even those who are saved in Christ still need good spiritual food and teaching that can only come from those with pure motives and pure hearts. To every extent possible don't waste time listening to those who deceive, mislead or represent obvious doctrinal errors in their ministry.

2.2 False Teachers in the End Times

In my last passage- *False Prophets in the End Times*- I covered various motives behind false prophets' deceptive messages as well as some basic criteria to look for in assessing the authenticity and validity behind any single prophet's doctrinal message.

True Apostles and Prophets are Rare

In my last passage I offered a rather broad, generalized definition of a "prophet" (i.e. one who hears and communicates a message on behalf of God (ref: Bible Gateway, "definitions")) so that in talking about a *false prophet* I could, in turn, offer a fairly wide scope of catchall motives. The motives I offered are indeed broad enough to where they can apply to virtually anyone attempting to communicate a false message on behalf of God.

In getting a little more granular, the Apostle Paul separated distinct parts of the holistic "body of Christ" (1 Cor. 12) and gave a rank order of importance with the first three members being apostle, prophet, and teacher, respectively. He described (true) apostles and prophets as the "foundation of the (worldwide) Church (with Christ as the cornerstone)" (Eph. 2:20). These are able to understand the "mystery of Christ" (Eph. 3:4). Apostles are in a league of their own, able to perform signs, wonders and miracles (2 Cor. 12:12) and "having the mind of Christ" (1 Cor. 2:16). Additionally, we know that an obvious way to tell these true messengers of God, both apostles and prophets, is that we find what they prophesy actually comes to fruition (Ez. 33:33).

It is safe to say that *true* apostles or prophets in the sense of a more concrete definition are fairly rare in our current end times period. Do you know of any? Yet *false* prophets are numerous. In fact, the Bible tells us that many so-called prophets in the last days are going to be ashamed (Zech. 13:4) when actual truth is revealed. I describe this end times scenario about prophets within the story told in my books, *Biblical End Times, Volumes 1 and 2*.

The good news, however, is that all of us who desire truth in a day when it is sorely lacking have all we need in the Word of God- the Word originally given to us by God's own apostles and prophets, divinely inspired by, or witnesses to Jesus Christ himself. In the course of our own study of God's Word the Holy Spirit and prayer can help us with our interpretation and understanding.

Teachers of the Word (next in Paul's rank-order behind apostles and prophets as shown above) should also be able to help. Paul and Peter discussed teachers as "overseers" in scripture. We can likely directly associate these with our modern day pastors or heads of the church who preach, teach and shepherd the flock.

Teachers are Common but so is *False* Teaching

So, in speaking about teachers in this writing I am getting slightly more focused and practical as well as detailing a few types of *false* teachings that contribute to the deception we are called to watch out for in these last days. Keep in mind these do not include teachings in numerous other false religions. Instead, these include those that at least loosely purport to be associated with the one true God of Israel (who we know is Jesus Christ). These false teachings reflect obvious impurities and infiltration by the modern day anti-Christ Chaldeans in pastoral-teaching ranks, and thus, have the same dark underlying motivation(s) that I laid out in my last passage.

For the purposes of this passage I divided the topic of false teaching into three categories based on what we are told in scripture: 1) False doctrine and heresy; 2) teaching of the law; and 3) Anti-Christ blasphemy. I address each of these below.

1) False doctrine and heresy: This is the modern day representation of "Greeks seek wisdom"-thinking. It is found in what appears to be a Christian setting but it has a Pharisee-like manifestation due to rules, rituals, traditions and routines. It is similar to a modern day Gnosticism in that there is an appearance of wisdom but no existence of the true Holy Spirit. A primary distinction is that this teaching is not about Jesus Christ who we know came as both God and man and is the only way to the Father in heaven.

Instead, it claims to offer special "mystical" knowledge for one's spirituality and salvation. There is at least a rough parallel here to Jewish Kabbalah teaching, which at its root (no pun intended) goes back to the Tree of Knowledge of Good and Evil and how eating from that tree, figuratively speaking, can bring enlightenment. Like the serpent said, "...you will be like God..." (Gen. 3:5). Again, this teaching is couched as some form of wisdom and intellectualism but it is correctly called out by the Apostle Paul as follows:

- *Old wives' tales and godless myths (and mythological characters) (1 Tim. 4:7)*

- *Godless chatter and opposing ideas falsely called knowledge (1 Tim. 6:20)*

- *Hollow and deceptive philosophy depending on human tradition (Col. 2:8)*

- *Meaningless talk (that they don't understand themselves) (1 Tim. 1:6-7)*

- *Strange teaching (Heb. 13:9)*

2) Teaching of the law: This is the current day Jewish-Pharisee "circumcision group" as referred to by Paul in Titus (1:10). They have rules and laws upon more rules and laws as they have errantly sought to establish their own righteousness. Their Jewish Rabbi teaching and Talmud doctrine takes precedence over scripture. They still teach the law as if one can actually meet its requirements and be justified in God's eyes. As Jesus warned the Pharisees:

…woe to you (experts in the law) because you load people down with burdens they can hardly carry, and you yourselves will not lift one finger to help them. (Lk. 11:46)

Ultimately this Pharisee-ical teaching leads to the opposite of justification; that is, it leads to bondage and spiritual emptiness (i.e. being a "slave to sin" as Jesus said in John 8:34) with no awareness of the grace offered as a result Christ's death and resurrection. You are probably familiar with the shortcomings of the law as expressed below:

- *All who rely on following the law are under a curse (Gal. 3:10)*

- *Written code with regulations was against us and stood opposed to us (Col. 2:13)*

- *Before true faith (in Christ), "we were held prisoners of the law" (Gal. 4:23)*

- *Works-based faith causes stumbling (Rom. 9:30-32)*

3) Anti-Christ spirit and blasphemous teaching: At the root of this teaching is intentional evil deception and a determination to mislead or "hinder" the flock by denying Christ. Peter described how those in this group secretly introduce destructive heresies (2 Pet. 2:1), including denying the Lord. Both Peter (2 Pet. 2:10) and Jude (8) describe how these men slander celestial beings with Jude (11) pointing out that they make the same mistake as Korah's rebellion, which involved a revolt against Moses and the Levites, God's anointed.

These teachers in our day possess or are influenced by the evil spirit of the eternally condemned, fallen angels or false brethren who Jude (4) observed "have secretly slipped in among you," and possibly include those about whom Paul taught, "came in secretly to spy out our liberty in Christ..." (Gal. 2:4). Peter refers to these as the ones for whom "condemnation has long been hanging over" (2 Pet. 2:3), and for whom both Jude and Peter say the "blackest darkness" has been reserved. These infiltrators intentionally deceive, lead astray, divide and cause confusion. They have apparently committed one of the gravest sins possible in that they once knew the true way of righteousness but then willfully turned their backs on God in defiance (2 Pet. 2:21, Heb. 6:4-6).

Due to their overt blasphemy these divisive and destructive traitors were labeled an "accursed brood" and "springs without water" by the Apostle Peter (2 Pet 2:14 and 2:17). They were further referred to as "clouds without rain" by Jude (12). Not surprisingly, these deceivers and those who willfully engage them possess a dark spirit that leads them into destructive, sinful, immoral behavior described as:

- *Shameful ways (2 Pet. 2:2); corrupt desire of the sinful nature (2 Pet. 2:10)*

- *Eyes full of adultery...seducing the unstable...experts in greed (2 Pet, 2:14)*

- *Grumblers and faultfinders following their own evil desires (Jude 16)*

- *Men who divide and follow mere natural instincts (Jude 18)*

In closing, given the rampant deception and lawlessness in these last days, as these last couple passages about False Prophets and False Teachers have discussed in some detail, believers would do well to heed the Apostle Paul's principle of milk versus solid food in Hebrews, Chapter 5. Here, Paul described that solid food is for the spiritually mature who learn to distinguish good from evil. This attribute of discernment is increasingly important for believers in these last days that we do not fall into the deceitful temptations surrounding us.

Chapter 3.

The Lord's Spirit in the Midst

Passages from Lion's Lair provided in this chapter include:

3.1 An End Times 'Comforter' and 'Restrainer'

3.2 The Lord's Spirit with us (Part 1)

3.3 The Lord's Spirit with us (Part2)

3.4 The Lord's Spirit with us (Part 3)

3.1 An End Times 'Comforter' and 'Restrainer'

At this point, it is logical to discuss some end-times biblical characters beginning with those representing the Holy Spirit to whom we can look in these last days for light and truth in anticipation of Christ's glorious return. The Holy Spirit's presence will provide a counterbalance and restraint to the growing darkness and deception that will usher in world Babylon's and the Anti-Christ's rule here on earth for a short time prior to the return of Christ and the establishment of his eternal heavenly Kingdom.

Now that more believers are becoming convinced that we are living in the last days we are witnessing increased chatter and reference to potential key end-times players of the adversary who will come onto the scene. Of course, believers are also rightly anticipating Jesus Christ's return. At the same time, many are also attempting to guess as to what figure will arise onto the international scene as the Anti-Christ to rule in the interim.

Surprisingly, however, there is very little talk about some other key biblical figures mentioned in scripture who must necessarily be present prior to the revealing of the Anti-Christ and prior to Christ's return. While there is some indication that these individuals may actually be kept hidden in the last days, they should still be addressed given the highly significant and important work that God will do through them.

In this passage, I will discuss two of the most well-known end-times figures presented in the New Testament who are likely one and the same individual/Spirit: 1) The Comforter, and; 2) The Restrainer. These complement many verses and indications in the Old Testament that refer to the Lord's Spirit with us as he fights in the end times spiritual kingdom war.

The 'Comforter'

First, the *'Comforter' is* the Holy Spirit according to Jesus (Jn. 14:26). Jesus also referred to this figure a few times as the Spirit of truth (Jn. 15:26). The *Comforter*, referred to as "he," is obviously an extremely important end-times figure because he will be sent directly by Jesus himself (and the Father) (Jn. 15:26). Equally important is the work that Jesus and God the Father will do through the *'Comforter'* in the end times. We are told that he will accomplish the following:

- Testify of and glorify Jesus Christ as the one and only true God (Jn. 15:26, 16:14)

- Serve as a teacher and reminder of the words of Jesus Christ (Jn. 14:26)

- Demonstrate the sin of the world (and unbelief in Christ) in contrast with true righteousness (Jn. 16:8)

- Bring judgment on evil and the evil prince of the world (Jn. 16:11)

- Take from what is of Jesus (and the Father) and make it known (Jn. 16:14-15)

- Dwell in (believers) (Jn. 14:17)

- Abide with believers forever (Jn. 14:16)

There are some who believe that the '*Comforter*' will manifest as an actual individual; that is, in person, just as Jesus did. After all, Jesus did say, "I will send you *another Comforter*" (Jn. 14:16), likely implying one who lives in the natural just like Jesus did. Certainly, some of the duties described above are those that might be accomplished by a person in the flesh, even if he is to be kept behind the scenes or hidden. If the Holy Spirit manifests as a person in the last days, then it is logical to believe that he will be established on earth given the context in which he is described by Jesus in the book of John.

The 'Restrainer'

In Second Thessalonians (Chapter 2) it is clear that, prior to the Anti-Christ being revealed, there will be one who "lets," "holds back," or restrains. And scripture in this chapter states that "*he*" or *the one* who "lets"- i.e. the 'Restrainer'- must first be "taken out of the way" and then the man of lawlessness can be introduced.

Once again, just like the '*Comforter*' discussed above, the '*Restrainer*' is commonly seen as the Holy Spirit. And this appears to fit accurately since Paul mentioned that the one who *now* lets will continue to do so until he is taken out of the way, thereby implying the same Spirit existing in Paul's time that continues through the end times until being taken. And so here many bible prophecy experts describe the Christ-believing church as representing the Holy Spirit or '*Restrainer*' and that it is the Church that will be "raptured" and removed (from earth) before the unveiling of the Anti-Christ. This simply means that the current day version of the Church and Holy Spirit originally set up here on earth at Pentecost and existing within believers will be removed prior to an Anti-Christ figure being revealed. Here, I pose the following questions:

But if the 'Restrainer' is the Church/Holy Spirit, then is it the Church that accomplishes the work of the Holy Spirit/Comforter above?

It could be in a loose sense but it doesn't quite seem to fit, especially considering the level of apostasy that we see in the church today.

*And if the Holy Spirit in the person of the 'Restrainer' in the same person as the 'Comforter,' can he accomplish all of those things listed above if he is removed from the earth and removed **prior to** the unveiling of an Anti-Christ figure?*

I would just interject the possibility, again, of the Holy Spirit existing in the last days as a physical person. In the case of the *'Restrainer,'* scripture does refer to *"he"* or *"the one."* And the *Restrainer could* (emphasis on "could") possibly be a person who is one-in-the-same with the *'Comforter'* described (in #1) above.

I would also add that the meaning for the *'Restrainer'* being "taken out of the way" (2 Thess. 2:7) based on Greek language is similar to one who is "taken out of or from the midst." As a very simple hypothetical example, this is the same meaning such as one who gets taken out of a waiting area to go into an appointment in another area/room. In other words, this meaning for "taken out of the way" appears to be different from the meaning of being "caught up" (meaning a forceful and violent snatching in a Greek translation) when the Apostle Paul talks about believers being raptured and meeting Jesus when he comes in the clouds accompanied by a trumpet blast in the scenario described in First Thessalonians, Chapter 4.

So, my rhetorical question back to the bible prophecy experts and interested readers like yourself is whether taking the Restrainer out of the way is actually a different event than the "catching up" of believers?

I tend to believe so.

~

In conclusion, it seems to be an understatement that both the *'Comforter'* and *'Restrainer'* are highly important end-times figures. This is especially the case given that both could represent the same Holy Spirit and that either or both could be an actual person living among us in these last days.

With the important scripture that we are given in God's Word about the end-times Holy Spirit as a person who precedes or coexists during Christ's return it is shocking how little he is discussed, especially among those who claim bible prophecy expertise. I discuss him as a biblical figure in detail in my books *Biblical End Times, Volumes 1 and 2*.

Meanwhile, I mentioned in my last passage how Zechariah prophesied that many or even all prophets in the last days will be ashamed. I believe that topics such as discussed in this current passage, along with others presented in *Writings of Lion's Lair, Volumes 2 and 3*, are representative examples of content that, for some reason, bible and prophecy teachers do not want to touch or consider. My own opinion is that there is a glaring omission and gaping hole in prophecy discussion that cannot be chalked up purely to mistaken oversight. Surely those who have spent a career in this area should be able to at least openly discuss and provide analysis for these issues-especially in the current times in which we live. At the same time, this omission says a lot about the spiritual kingdom enemy that prevents and denies truth at all costs.

3.2 The Lord's Spirit with us (Part 1)

Passages throughout *Writings of Lion's Lair, Volumes 2 and 3,* will address topics of the ongoing spiritual kingdom war and God's holy children who are "birthed" in these last days. Of course, the most critical player in the Kingdom war and the most important manchild "birthed" in these end times is Jesus Christ himself.

In future passages herein, I will touch upon our Lord's end times role in leading and equipping the last days 'Jacob army' in their battle versus the anti-Christ Chaldeans. I will also describe the *end times* "birth" of 'Immanuel' as well as Jesus the manchild's "birth" in the Revelation (Chapter 12) story. And of course, there will be the final, glorious return of Jesus in establishing the Millennial Kingdom for his reign.

The Lord's Spirit being *with us, in person,* is a primary issue that should be considered in these last days. Many Jews, while they missed Jesus' first coming and still do not believe, have very good reason in scripture for looking for their Messiah in these last days. A remnant of these will finally recognize the truth in Jesus. Meanwhile, we as Christ-believers are told by prophecy teachers to keep watching the skies for our Lord's coming; this will eventually prove to be true.

But in the interim, there are strong indicators in scripture about a Messianic deity (i.e. member of the holy trinity) being *among* us, living here in these last days. So, while Christ-believers discuss the soon coming Anti-Christ and the anticipation of our Lord coming in the air, to provide an escape, should we be looking around us and listening for indications of our Lord *in our very midst*?

As just a few clues, we are told in an end times context: the bridegroom must be "taken away"; the Son of man will be hidden; the 'Restrainer' will be "taken out of the way"; etc. And it follows that perhaps this is why we are instructed:

Seek ye the Lord while he may be found, call ye upon him while he is near. (Is. 55:6)

While virtually never addressed by Christian pastors or prophecy teachers, I believe that this topic at least deserves *some* discussion. If my hunch is right, it would actually deserve nonstop discussion in these last days. In this passage, I will address scripture-based reasons to believe that our Lord may be among us in these last days. Sections in this passage supporting the Lord's presence include:

- His Holy Spirit (Comforter)

- His awakening and arising

- His "work" on earth and presence with the 'Jacob'-Judah "small flock" remnant

- His arms outstretched to his rejecters

I will cover each of these topic areas in this passage. In subsequent passages on this topic, I will show how the Lord is with us in the context of: saving/helping us; fighting alone for us; providing a pillar of righteousness versus rampant corruption; and then withdrawing from his place here for a time.

His Holy Spirit or 'Comforter'

To begin, Jesus himself told us that both he and his Father would send the Comforter, also referred to as the Spirit of truth and Holy Spirit.

Earlier, I discussed this end times person as the third member of the holy trinity who is likely also the 'Restrainer,' and who we are told is "taken out of the way" prior to the "man of lawlessness" being revealed (2 Thess. 2:8). Since I addressed this earlier, I will not go into much detail here other than to re-emphasize that it was Jesus himself who told us this 'Comforter' would be sent. It also bears worth mentioning, while this person represents the same Holy Spirit that dwells *in* believers of Jesus Christ and will abide with them forever (Jn. 14:16-17), he will also manifest *in-person* in the end times kingdom war to:

- Testify of and glorify Jesus Christ as the one and only true God (Jn. 15:26, 16:14)

- Serve as a teacher and reminder of the words of Jesus Christ (Jn. 14:26)

- Demonstrate the sin of the world (and unbelief in Christ) in contrast with true righteousness (Jn. 16:8)

- Bring judgment on evil and the evil prince of the world (Jn. 16:11)

- Take from what is of Jesus (and the Father) and make it known (Jn. 16:14-15)

It is this 'Comforter' who also appears to be referred to elsewhere in scripture as the Lord's Spirit of truth who is with us in these last days. I will demonstrate this through scripture included herein and in Parts 2 and 3. Meanwhile, for starters, consider the following strong statements made by the Lord to 'Jacob' and his Judah remnant who have eyes to see and ears to hear him in last days 'Babylon':

Fear thou not; for I am with thee: be not dismayed; for I am thy God: I will strengthen thee; yea, I will help thee; yea, I will uphold thee with the right hand of my righteousness. For I the Lord thy God will hold thy right hand, saying unto thee, Fear not; I will help thee. (Is. 41:10,13)

Come ye near unto me, hear ye this; I have not spoken in secret from the beginning; from the time that it was, there am I: and now the Lord God, and his Spirit, hath sent me. Thus saith the Lord, thy Redeemer, the Holy One of Israel; I am the Lord thy God which teacheth thee to profit, which leadeth thee by the way that thou shouldest go. (Is. 48:16-17)

God here in this line of scripture through Isaiah is impressing upon 'Jacob' that he is the "first and the last" and the Sovereign God who "laid the foundations of the earth." God tells last days 'Jacob' many times in scripture that he is *with him.*

The Lord is Awakened in these End Times

I will describe in detail in *Volume 2* how God will hide his anointed and certainly will do so in these last days. 'Jacob' we know is "hidden" and I will discuss in Chapter 9 how the spiritual "birthing" of God's children happens quietly, behind-the-scenes. Even if these holy children's "births" are known (via the tracking of their bloodlines), they will not be made public due to world Babylon's anti-Christ powers that are in place. But this is God's plan.

As for the end times Holy Spirit in the person of the Spirit of truth or 'Comforter,' it appears that he is hidden. There is scripture that indicates that he is somewhat of a "sleeper" who must first be "awakened," perhaps also by spiritual "birthing." The 'Daughter of Zion,' who I will discuss in Chapter 7 as a witness herself to the Lord and as his bride as shown in scripture, remarks several times in the Song of Solomon, "stir not up, nor awake my love, till he please" (SoS. 2:7, 5:5).

Perhaps the Lord sleeps in these last days until his "hour is come," which in some ways, though not a direct application, reminds us of when Jesus told his mother at the wedding, "my hour has not yet come" (Jn. 2:4). If the Lord is kept hidden and obscure like 'Jacob,' possibly as a "root of dry ground who has no form of splendor...or beauty that we should desire him" (Is. 53:2), then the prophetic prayer and strong concern of the Prophet Amos may apply. Amos asked God a couple of times about last days 'Jacob's ability to fight a massive Chaldean enemy:

...by whom shall 'Jacob' arise? For he is small. (Am. 7:2,5)

God promised Amos that he will take care of future 'Jacob' in the last days. Interestingly, this was foreshadowed in *original* Jacob's dream in Bethel of angels on the ladder and God reminding him about his covenant promise to his fathers Isaac and Abraham. God assured Jacob that he would "keep him" and bring him into the land. Jacob *awoke* from his dream to realize God's presence. This is applicable again in these end times for the final 'Jacob.'

The Lord arises to the righteous cause of the 'Jacob'-Judah "small flock" remnant

Just like original Jacob in a figurative sense, the Lord in the end times will awaken from his sleep. First, he is called to do so primarily by those in his flock who are being persecuted at the hands of the anti-Christ Chaldeans. The following represent prophetic requests to the Lord by those in his "small flock" remnant who we know will awaken in these last days at the time of their persecution, according to scripture. In the book of Isaiah (Chapters 51 and 52), God speaks to his flock telling them several times to "awake," "arise," and "shake yourselves from the dust." They, in turn, request his presence for help:

Shall not God search this out? for he knoweth the secrets of the heart. Yea, for thy sake are we killed all the day long; we are counted as sheep for the slaughter. Awake, why sleepest thou, O Lord? arise, cast us not off forever. (Ps. 44:21-23)

O Lord God, to whom vengeance belongeth; O God, to whom vengeance belongeth, shew thyself. Lift up thyself, thou judge of the earth: render a reward to the proud. Lord, how long shall the wicked, how long shall the wicked triumph? (Ps. 94:1-3)

Awake, awake, put on strength, O arm of the Lord; awake, as in the ancient days, in the generations of old. Art thou not it that hath cut Rahab, and wounded the dragon? (Is. 51:9)

The 'Jacob army' appear to be canaries in the coal mine who are the first to experience the high-tech surveillance-combined-with-military grade-intelligence tools-version of persecution used by world Babylon in the last days. They are the victims of a large-scale psychological operation in 'Babylon'-U.S. They pray in order to awaken the Lord so that he will help them in their resistance and fight. I discuss end times Babylon in detail in *Volume 2*.

In coming Chapters (4-8), I will describe the end times kingdom war fought by the 'Jacob army' versus the anti-Christ Chaldeans as being of an unconventional variety (as just noted). It involves a struggle to shed light and truth once-and-for-all on the highly cruel and unusual iniquities in which the Chaldeans engage in, in secret, in an otherwise "unseen" world. So, this is a battle that we are told has "justice as the measuring line and righteousness as the plumb line" (Is. 28:17).

Scripture says that the Lord will "observe like a leopard" (Hos. 13:7), likely applying to these end times. He likely sees lawlessness and a lack of faith and truth, corroborating the issues the 'Jacob army' are contending with. In the same context and circumstances as these last days, we are told, "Then the Lord awaked as one out of sleep, and like a mighty man that shouteth by reason of wine. And he smote his enemies out of the hinder parts..." (Ps. 78:65-66). In his *Parable of the Woman and Judge*, a picture of God's elect including the faithful 'Jacob'-Judah remnant- asking for justice against lawlessness in the last days, Jesus promised to avenge his people and asked:

I tell you, he will see that they get justice, and quickly. However, when the Son of Man comes, will he find faith on the earth? (Lk. 18:8)

Notice Jesus referred to a time *when the Son of man comes*, implying *a future time of his presence, perhaps in the person of the Holy Spirit.* Jesus here also implied that there will be a lack of faith, which we know always goes hand-in-hand with lawlessness based on the Apostle Paul's teachings. This lawless time on earth is consistent with other scripture that says that the Son of man (end times 'Comforter') will come to live in the last days that will be like the days of Noah and Lot. Patient endurance and tolerance of this lack of faith is why Jesus is described as longsuffering (Matt. 17:17). It is these last days of time about which Jesus said that that the Son of man "must first be rejected"

(Lk. 17:25) and suffer many things. We are told that he will then hide his face in the end times until they "acknowledge their offense" (Hos. 5:15). We are told:

What if God, although choosing to show his wrath and make his power known, bore with great patience the objects of his wrath—prepared for destruction? (Rom. 9:22)

So, Jesus' Spirit becomes awakened and is present with his people in their sufferings in these last days. We are told that he "bears long" with his elect.

The Lord's Work on Earth and his Presence with the 'Jacob'-Judah Remnant

While I will discuss the Lord's own fighting in the kingdom war in more detail in Part 2, there are clear indications in scripture of the Lord's involvement and his presence on earth in this war. We are told that he "rises up" to do his "work." This behind-the-scenes work to counter the aforementioned Chaldean psychological warfare operation is referred to as his "strange work" (Is. 28:21) and the "operation of his hands" (Is. 5:12). His "work" likely sets in motion the "overflowing scourge" and his "trap" that is mentioned in scripture. It is also described as a "continuing whirlwind" (Jer. 30:23) against the wicked. Jesus in his first time on earth talked about his works alone as being his testimony and witness for him being the Lord. About the Lord's works in the *last days* we are told:

Yea, before the day was I am he; and there is none that can deliver out of my hand: I will work, and who shall let it? (Is. 43:13)

For he will finish the work, and cut it short in righteousness: because a short work will the Lord make upon the earth. (Rom. 9:28)

In fact, in the book of John Jesus spoke to his disciples about the 'Comforter' to come and in this same conversation mentioned about one, "greater works shall he do" (Jn. 14:12). It stands to reason that greater works than Jesus did will be miracles that are to be revealed in these last days.

His presence with the 'Jacob'-Judah remnant- his witnesses

So, the earlier prayers of the righteous 'Jacob'-Judah remnant for help in the last days are answered as they will see some relief in enduring a righteous battle versus the anti-Christ Chaldeans. As shown above, the Lord is fighting amongst them and we are told that he "shall be seen over them" (Zech. 9:14).

If God's persecuted elect have any questions about the Lord's presence with them in the last days all they need to do is turn to scripture. Over and over again in his word God assures of this presence. He tells 'Jacob' and his Judah-centric remnant: "I will hold your hand" (Jer. 30:10); "I am with you" (Jer. 42:11); "I am in the midst" (Jer. 14:9); etc. Through the Prophet Zechariah we are told that the 'Jacob army' will be "mighty" and fight because, "the Lord is with them" (Zech. 10:5). The following well-known verse you may recall was spoken directly by God to 'Jacob':

When thou passest through the waters, I will be with thee; and through the rivers, they shall not overflow thee: when thou walkest through the fire, thou shalt not be burned; neither shall the flame kindle upon thee. (Is. 43:2)

In fact, members of the 'Jacob army' will ultimately be witnesses themselves to the Lord's presence. God is clear in his Word that he likes to have witnesses of himself, in large part to combat the lack of faith on earth as described earlier. John the Baptist had the incredible honor of announcing Jesus' presence in his own day, "so that all men through him might believe" (Jn. 1:7). Jesus spoke of an 'Elias' who was still to come. The Lord also spoke through the ancient Prophet Malachi of a "messenger to come" (John the Baptist) with a strong indication for an *end times* messenger in our day. The following included Jesus' own words:

And he answered and told them, Elias verily cometh first, and restoreth all things; and how it is written of the Son of man, that he must suffer many things, and be set at nought. (Mk. 9:12)

Behold, I will send you Elijah the prophet before the coming of the great and dreadful day of the Lord. (Mal. 4:5)

The Lord will certainly have messengers and witnesses in the last days. Both end times 'Jacob' and the 'Daughter of Zion' will be a couple of the Lord's witnesses who will be delivered directly by the Lord from their battle against anti-Christ Chaldean persecution. At the time when the 'Daughter of Zion' gives spiritual "birth" to 'Jacob,' he appears to be delivered from his persecution. He then proclaims as a witness of God:

He is near that justifieth me; who will contend with me? let us stand together: who is mine adversary? let him come near to me. (Is. 50:8)

This is 'Jacob's deliverance; God will have been with him all along. Consider the following verses in regard to 'Jacob's witness of God's works for him in fighting against the anti-Christ Chaldeans. God speaks directly to 'Jacob' in the following verses:

Fear ye not, neither be afraid: have not I told thee from that time, and have declared it? ye are even my witnesses. Is there a God beside me? yea, there is no God; I know not any. (Is. 44:8)

I have declared, and have saved, and I have shewed, when there was no strange god among you: therefore ye are my witnesses, saith the Lord, that I am God. (Is. 43:12)

Why sayest thou, O Jacob, and speakest, O Israel, My way is hid from the Lord, and my judgment is passed over from my God? (Is. 40:27)

As for the 'Daughter of Zion,' I will describe in Chapter 7 how she is in travail in the last days from persecution at the hands of the anti-Christ Chaldean army. Because of her ultimate deliverance, she will be a witness to the Lord's direct presence as well. God asks, "Is not the Lord in Zion? Is not her king in her?" (Jer. 8:19). We know that she is told directly that the "Lord will redeem thee from the hand of thy enemies" (Mic. 4:10). She is the one who gives symbolic "birth" to the Lord himself. In the verse below, Jesus is likely referring to his own Spirit's future revealing on earth, "born" as a manchild

(Revelation, Chapter 12). Like 'Jacob' above, the 'Daughter of Zion' will be an obvious witness. She is likely the woman referred to by Jesus as follows:

A woman when she is in travail hath sorrow, because her hour is come: but as soon as she is delivered of the child, she remembereth no more the anguish, for joy that a man is born into the world. (Jn. 16:21)

Jesus spoke this to his disciples after they were wondering about a previous statement that he made about his going away and then returning. Jesus told them:

A little while, and ye shall not see me: and again, a little while, and ye shall see me: and, Because I go to the Father. (Jn. 16:17)

This appears to be another reference to his coming again to earth in the same (human) form.

His Arms are Still Outstretched to his Rejecters

Jesus' people who had previously rejected him (as shown above) and realize in their tribulation that they are not saved will get an initial glimpse of his presence. This is described as, "The people walking in darkness have seen a great light…" (Is. 9:2). While ultimately, we are told that all flesh will see the glory of the Lord at his revealing, it appears there will be some form of initial revealing of the Lord's Spirit during the dark Day of the Lord- enough to cause his people to recognize and run away from the Anti-Christ.

While the righteous, faithful 'Jacob army' will enjoy the Lord's presence in a secret, hidden way during their persecution, others who had denied him to this point will receive a wake-up call. I describe this in more detail in *Writings of Lion's Lair, Volume 2*, a time when God's people seek him at this time during their worldwide wandering. Consider the following:

They shall walk after the Lord: he shall roar like a lion: when he shall roar, then the children shall tremble from the west. (Hos. 11:10)

This will be about the time Jesus is "birthed"- a man briefly revealed who is to rule with an iron rod- but he will be caught up. A very large deception will follow with lying signs and wonders and with the Anti-Christ committing the abomination of desolation and a beast system that causes God's people to realize they have been deceived and to flee.

To both wayward houses of Judah and 'Ephraim' who are wandering and seeking in the last days we are told several times through Isaiah, "but his hand is stretched out still" (Is. 5:25, 9:12). Similarly, the Apostle Paul reminded, "But to Israel he saith, All day long I have stretched forth my hands unto a disobedient and gainsaying people" (Rom. 10:21).

Once Day of the Lord troubles come upon his people who do not initially escape and are not saved, a remnant among them will finally heed the call and will seek his presence. Verses that follow indicate this:

Come, and let us return unto the Lord: for he hath torn, and he will heal us; he hath smitten, and he will bind us up. (Hos. 6:1)

Come now, and let us reason together, saith the Lord: though your sins be as scarlet, they shall be as white as snow; though they be red like crimson, they shall be as wool. (Is. 1:18)

Then shalt thou call, and the Lord shall answer; thou shalt cry, and he shall say, Here I am. If thou take away from the midst of thee the yoke, the putting forth of the finger, and speaking vanity. (Is. 58:9)

Scripture indicates that the Lord will reach out a "second time" for his house of Israel remnant. When they seek him, he will answer.

~

Although we live in a faithless and sinful generation, the Lord remains with us, with his arms outstretched. Even those who miss an initial deliverance in the first "watch" of the night and remain after he hides his face will have a way to seek and find him.

King David always believed that God was with him. His prayer might apply to many others who will seek the Lord during coming troubles in these last days:

For this shall every one that is godly pray unto thee in a time when thou mayest be found: surely in the floods of great waters they shall not come nigh unto him. (Ps. 32:6)

I describe 'Israel's and the Gentiles' path back to the Lord's Kingdom in *Writings of Lions Lair, Volume 2,* as well as in my books, *Biblical End Times, Volumes 1 and 2.*

3.3 The Lord's Spirit with us (Part 2)

In Part 1 of this series, I showed how scripture tells us that the Lord will awaken in these end times, arise to the cause of his 'Jacob'-Judah "small flock" remnant, and do his work *on earth* on their behalf. In this passage, I will continue to demonstrate the Lord's presence on earth within the context of how he fights against his enemy and produces his righteous cause. Taken altogether, his personal battle will be a clear dividing line between what is good versus evil in the last days.

In this passage, the following two sections cover our Lord's presence with us:

- The Lord fights for himself and his servants
- The Lord is present in righteousness

I will address each of these topics in more detail herein. In my next passage, Part 3, I will continue to discuss the Lord's presence with us in terms associated with his activities of saving his people in this last days time period.

The Lord Fights Alone for Himself and his Servants

There are many scriptural references to the Lord's Spirit's presence with us here in these last days. Many are in reference to his fighting against the anti-Christ Chaldean enemy. A primary location of the Lord's war in the last days is in the Chaldean nation of 'Babylon'-U.S., though ultimately his judgment and punishment will also come upon the nation of Israel and then the entire world. I describe this judgment that will begin with these two countries in *Volume 2*.

The Lord fights for himself and his own name in the last days

Scripture shows how the Lord virtually single-handedly fights the Chaldean army. We learn that, since there is little to no true faith on earth in the last days, as discussed in Part 1, the Lord is left to fight alone. Recall through Isaiah, he says, "I have trodden the winepress alone, and of the people there was none with me..." (Is. 63:3). The Prophet Habakkuk foresaw:

Thou didst march through the land in indignation, thou didst thresh the heathen in anger. (Hab. 3:12)

The Lord observes like a leopard (Hos. 13:1) while he is here in the last days and likely finds lukewarm faith at best. Speaking of his people in his original and eternal homeland (country of Israel) and the corrupt, sinful, "bloody city" of Jerusalem, God says through the Prophet Ezekiel's vision, "I sought for a man among them that should make up the hedge and stand in the gap before me for the land...but I found none" (Ez. 22:30). Similarly, look at what the Lord says about fighting his last days battle, especially against 'Babylon' and how he finds no help:

For I beheld, and there was no man; even among them, and there was no counsellor, that, when I asked of them, could answer a word. (Is. 41:2)

And I looked, and there was none to help; and I wondered that there was none to uphold: therefore mine own arm brought salvation unto me; and my fury, it upheld me. (Is. 63:5)

Wherefore, when I came, was there no man? when I called, was there none to answer? Is my hand shortened at all, that it cannot redeem? or have I no power to deliver?... (Is. 50:2)

Therefore will I number you to the sword, and ye shall all bow down to the slaughter: because when I called, ye did not answer; when I spake, ye did not hear; but did evil before mine eyes, and did choose that wherein I delighted not. (Is. 65:12)

Because of a lack of faith on earth the Lord will be forced to perform a quiet, "strange" work (Is. 28:21) that people do not understand due to enormous Chaldean deception in the last days. It is the manifestation *on earth* of warring dark principalities, powers and authorities versus Jesus Christ and his coming Kingdom. It is only a war that the Lord can fight. Consider God's following rhetorical questions:

Who hath directed the Spirit of the Lord, or being his counsellor hath taught him? With whom took he counsel, and who instructed him, and taught him in the path of judgment, and taught him knowledge, and shewed to him the way of understanding? (Is. 40:13-14)

Herein, I will describe in detail how the spiritual war of the Lord versus the anti-Christ Chaldeans in the last days is an unconventional one. What the Chaldeans do in secret would never be approved of if it were known to the general public. This first phase of the Lord's destruction against Chaldean evil goes on quietly, behind-the-scenes. How else can verses like the following be interpreted?

For the moth shall eat them up like a garment, and the worm shall eat them like wool… (Is. 51:8)

Therefore will I be unto Ephraim as a moth, and to the house of Judah as rottenness. (Hos. 5:12)

Through his "strange work" in these last days, the Lord has to fight a massive wall of deceit that has been constructed against him. Recall that the devil is the "father of lies" and his anti-Christ system is tightly controlling the propagandized message. So, the Lord's battle while he is with us is one to shed truth and light. Again, he does this as a result of fighting alone, in a righteous battle. I will discuss the righteous component of his battle on this earth in this passage below. Meanwhile, the following verses show how the Lord fights single-handedly in these end times:

Therefore saith the Lord, the Lord of hosts, the mighty One of Israel, Ah, I will ease me of mine adversaries, and avenge me of mine enemies. (Is 1:24)

Thine hand shall be lifted up upon thine adversaries, and all thine enemies shall be cut off. (Mic 5:9)

Let God arise, let his enemies be scattered: let them also that hate him flee before him. (Ps. 68:1)

The Lord shall go forth as a mighty man, he shall stir up jealousy like a man of war: he shall cry, yea, roar; he shall prevail against his enemies. I have long time holden my peace; I have been still, and refrained myself: now will I cry like a travailing woman; I will destroy and devour at once. (Is. 42:13-14)

This is a real, tangible battle, the results of which will be seen some day by all of the world's inhabitants. This will be the revealing of the mystery of iniquity and likely the Lord himself at the same time. True justice will be known along with a very clear dividing line between what is good versus what is evil.

The Lord battles to avenge his name and his elect

The spiritual war in the last days is a very real battle with a very real, practical purpose. The Lord is returning on earth to avenge his name and his persecuted elect. Much of this takes place in this current last days time period *prior* to Jesus' culminating return to earth as described in the book of Revelation where he deals the final blow to his enemy.

So, prior to his return to set up his Millennial Kingdom, his Spirit is *with us* and fights as I have shown above and in Part 1. You are likely familiar with Jesus' *Parable of the Vineyard* in which the owner planted a vineyard, went "into a far country for a long time" (Lk. 20:9), and left husbandmen in charge. This owner (representing God) occasionally sent servants to gather the fruit of the vineyard but his servants were persecuted and sent away empty-handed. He finally sent his own son and they killed him (representing the "stone the builders rejected"- Lk. 20:17)- a reference to Jesus crucified.

This is context and background for the Lord to return to the earth to avenge himself, his servants, and to win the war and be set up as the cornerstone. The Apostle Paul refers to the Lord's return to claim his vineyard as follows:

Who goeth a warfare any time at his own charges? who planteth a vineyard, and eateth not of the fruit thereof? or who feedeth a flock, and eateth not of the milk of the flock? (1 Cor. 9:7)

Much of the Lord's righteous remnant vine are the elect and servants in these last days in 'Babylon'-U.S. where we are told the Lord is *with them*. 'Babylon'-U.S. is likely where the Lord will first shine light on iniquity and persecution and in doing so will justify his servants. The Prophet Micah, as a type of 'Jacob' says he accepted his punishment and discipline brought on him by the Lord, but he anticipated redemption in saying, "(The Lord) will bring forth the light, and I shall behold his righteousness" (Mic. 7:9). Indeed, we are told that the Lord will "lift up (his) hand" (Is. 26:11) and will "march through the wasteland" (Ps. 68:7) in these last days so that his servants' persecutors, especially in the nation of 'Babylon,' will be "ashamed." The Lord says specifically to 'Jacob' and his remnant:

Thus saith the Lord, your redeemer, the Holy One of Israel; For your sake I have sent to Babylon, and have brought down all their nobles, and the Chaldeans, whose cry is in the ships. (Is. 43:14)

Their Redeemer is strong; the Lord of hosts is his name: he shall thoroughly plead their cause, that he may give rest to the land, and disquiet the inhabitants of Babylon. (Jer. 50:34)

I will describe herein how the Lord is *with them* (i.e. with his servants). Their persecuting adversary including nobles, kings, leaders (i.e. "riders on horses") "shall be confounded" (Zech. 10:5). These are the consequences, with prior precedent, of unrighteously holding God's people hostage and mistreating them.

So, to continue with the analogous story of the *Parable of the Vineyard*, the owner (God) will return to destroy those (i.e. whose vine is the "vine of Sodom and of the fields of Gomorrah"- Deut. 32:32) who persecute his children and his servants (i.e. his righteous vine, 'portion of Jacob'). Jesus pointed to this last days time period and said, "And shall not God avenge his very elect?" (Lk. 18:7). We are also told in the prophetic *Song of Moses*:

Rejoice, O ye nations, with his people: for he will avenge the blood of his servants, and will render vengeance to his adversaries, and will be merciful unto his land, and to his people. (Deut. 32:43)

The Lord will give strength and might via his "arm" to the 'Jacob army' in their battle amidst last days persecution (see Chapter 8). Again, we are told that he is "with them" and "in the midst" in their struggles. The 'Jacob army' recognizes this along the way and they gain confidence. They say, "Through God, we shall do valiantly" (Ps. 60:12). The following verses show how the greatly outnumbered, out-powered 'Jacob army' can stand against, overcome and defeat the anti-Christ force that comes against them. Note again how these show that the Lord is in control and is *with them* as they battle:

And I (God) will beat down (David my servant's) foes before his face, and plague them that hate him. (Ps. 89:23)

The Lord of hosts shall defend them; and they shall devour, and subdue with sling stones; and they shall drink, and make a noise as through wine; and they shall be filled like bowls, and as the corners of the altar. (Zech. 9:15)

Thou ('Portion of Jacob') art my battle axe and weapons of war: for with thee will I break in pieces the nations, and with thee will I destroy kingdoms; And with thee will I break in pieces the horse and his rider; and with thee will I break in pieces the chariot and his rider. (Jer. 51:20-21)

And the remnant of Jacob shall be among the Gentiles in the midst of many people as a lion among the beasts of the forest, as a young lion among the flocks of sheep: who, if he go through, both treadeth down, and teareth in pieces, and none can deliver. (Mic. 5:8)

The Lord himself will give strength to his righteous 'Jacob'-Judah "small flock" remnant.

Leaders of the 'Babylon nation and the 'Babylon' kingdom will be defeated

I showed above how the Lord will bring down current last days kings of 'Babylon'-U.S. who reside in the U.S. and are against him and his elect. The following verses pertain to coming destruction on these kings because of the Lord's presence, his observations, and his eventual wrath against them. The following support this:

That thou shalt take up this proverb against the king of Babylon, and say, How hath the oppressor ceased! the golden city ceased! (Is. 14:4)

And it shall come to pass in that day, saith the Lord, that I will cut off thy horses out of the midst of thee, and I will destroy thy chariots: And I will cut off the cities of thy land, and throw down all thy strong holds. (Mic. 5:10-11)

Woe unto them! for they have fled from me: destruction unto them! because they have transgressed against me: though I have redeemed them, yet they have spoken lies against me. (Hos. 7:13)

The last verse above speaks to the fact that the Lord will accomplish his initial work in 'Babylon' to shed light and truth and save people through their acceptance of him but they will turn their backs. Because of their lack of faith, they will do this at their own peril. The Lord himself says to his remnant, "We would have healed Babylon, but she is not healed: forsake her, and let us go every one into his own country: for her judgment reacheth unto heaven, and is lifted up even to the skies" (Jer. 51:9).

Ultimately, beyond the nation of 'Babylon' the Lord will punish all nations and the leaders of these nations. We are told that his wrath and indignation will be against "all nations" and against a "multitude of shepherds." The following is from a prophetic Psalm of King David, a day when he says, "The Lord shall send a rod of strength out of Zion," again showing the Lord's presence:

The Lord at thy right hand shall strike through kings in the day of his wrath. He shall judge among the heathen, he shall fill the places with the dead bodies; he shall wound the heads over many countries. (Ps. 110:5-6)

The punishment of the Lord can be expected to extend beyond 'Babylon' the nation and will ultimately be against the entire world *kingdom* of 'Babylon.' I made a reference above to wicked, corrupt leaders and rulers. We will find in these end times that many, if not all, rulers and leaders of nations are complicit with anti-Christ Chaldean plans. This is a pre-requisite in these last days for those in powerful leadership roles- i.e. to be complicit in plans against the Lord and his coming Kingdom. Incidentally, this is why we are told the Lord "shall break in pieces and consume these kingdoms..." (Dan. 2:44). Similarly, scripture also says, "with the breath of his lips shall he slay the wicked" (Is. 11:4). The kings who are fortunate enough to survive and remain will serve the Lord Jesus Christ (Ps. 72:11). We are even told in King David's Psalm above that the Lord will "rule in the midst of his enemies."

The Lord is Present in Righteousness

As you would expect, the Lord will fight a last days war that is for a righteous cause versus wicked world Babylon's kingdom. In this section, I demonstrate how the Lord *is present* in this undertaking: he is with his anointed "small flock" remnant; he represents the dividing line for righteousness; he saves the poor; and he pleads for his people to come near.

The Lord is with the righteous 'Jacob army'

I have already described above (and in Part 1) the Lord's presence in fighting with his anointed 'Jacob'-Judah remnant. He is *with them* while they are the initial canaries who take a righteous stand and through whom God sets a "standard" to sound the alarm about Chaldean iniquities (organized crime). God says he is pleased for his (servant's) righteousness sake..." (Is. 42:21) in taking their stand. Meanwhile, as the righteous judge of his people's oppressive enemies, God says, "produce your cause, bring forth your strong reasons" (Is. 41:21) against (my) people. God's anointed remnant's battle is a strong indication of worldwide trouble to come in the Day of the Lord. The Lord says to 'Jacob' who will be saved out of the time of 'Jacob's trouble':

Fear thou not; for I am with thee: be not dismayed; for I am thy God: I will strengthen thee; yea, I will help thee; yea, I will uphold thee with the right hand of my righteousness. (Is. 41:10)

Can you imagine being a recipient of that incredible promise from a God who is among them? On behalf of his 'Jacob army,' God shows his presence in speaking directly to them in scripture regarding their last days righteous cause. God says about this:

- "I the Lord have called thee in righteousness" (Is. 42:6)

- "I will plead thy cause" (Jer. 51:36)

- (I will) "execute judgment (for 'Jacob')" (Mic. 7:9)

- "I the Lord speak righteousness, I declare things that are right" (Is. 45:19)

- (I will lift up my hand...) "when thy hand is lifted up, (our persecutors) will not see; but they shall see, and be ashamed..." (Is. 26:11)

The Lord himself *on earth* in the last days becomes the voice of righteousness on behalf of his 'Jacob'-Judah remnant in their spiritual battle. This is tangible, and will be felt by many, but the extent to which the Lord himself is visibly seen in this preliminary period prior to his hiding his face and then his subsequent revealing is unclear.

The Lord himself is the last days dividing line of righteousness versus evil

The true plumbline of righteousness in the last days is the Spirit of the Lord Jesus Christ- the cornerstone. He is the rock of righteousness and justice, described as: "a tried stone"; "a rock of offense"; and a "snare." He is called these things because his righteousness necessarily exposes his enemies and their dark works that are done in secret and are artificially couched behind veneers of phony "social justice" and "cancel culture" causes. The following verses speak about Jesus as the rock that becomes an "offense" and a "snare":

And whosoever shall fall on this stone shall be broken: but on whomsoever it shall fall, it will grind him to powder. (Matt. 21:44)

Wherefore? Because they sought it not by faith, but as it were by the works of the law. For they stumbled at that stumblingstone; As it is written, Behold, I lay in Sion a stumblingstone and rock of offence: and whosoever believeth on him shall not be ashamed. (Rom. 9:32-33)

And he shall be for a sanctuary; but for a stone of stumbling and for a rock of offence to both the houses of Israel, for a gin and for a snare to the inhabitants of Jerusalem. (Is. 8:14)

Jesus has already earned the designation as the cornerstone, but he does so all over again through his Spirit on earth in these last days. He is hated all over again because of his righteousness in a world that is wayward and decided upon abiding in their own lies and transgressions.

As the rock just described, Jesus is the one in the Prophet Daniel's dream interpretation who is the stone that is "cut out of the mountain with hands" (Dan. 2:45) that is shown to break in pieces the world kingdom of iron and clay in the last days.

Jesus is the clear dividing line between what is good and evil in the last days. This will be revealed in the story of how anti-Christ Chaldean iniquities persecute his 'Comforter' again for his righteous life. The Lord has to defend *himself* (see earlier in this passage) from the lies and iniquities against him. Consider the following verses:

Arise, O God, plead thine own cause: remember how the foolish man reproacheth thee daily. (Ps. 74:22)

Thus saith the Lord, Keep ye judgment, and do justice: for my salvation is near to come, and my righteousness to be revealed. (Is. 56:1)

But the Lord of hosts shall be exalted in judgment, and God that is holy shall be sanctified in righteousness. (Is. 5:16)

The Lord has to come back to defend his own name against the very same anti-Christ spirit that put him to death on the cross two thousand years ago. It has since persecuted numerous others including many of God's saints. This system is the arm of the devil- the tempter and the accuser- who will "stand condemned" (Jn. 16:11) through Jesus' righteousness.

Through the Lord's work *on earth,* he will bring out truth that reveals a very clear line between what is right and wrong, and between what is good and evil. This will reveal the ruling powers of 'Babylon' and their anti-Christ Chaldean cohorts as oppressors who employ a large secretive minion-"mob" army with a policy of "no talking" to enable their own greed, corruption and power. We are told in scripture that they "rejoice" to oppress and "devour the poor secretly" (Hab. 3:14).

I already mentioned earlier how the nation of 'Babylon's leaders will be exposed. In terms of the country of Israel's last days corrupt leaders, specifically, the Lord will "set his face against them" in his work. We are told in the Prophet Ezekiel's vision that the Lord will gather them to "execute judgment(s)," "recompense their ways," and "melt them" in the fire of his wrath.

The Lord is with us to save the poor and needy

What has been shown in ancient scripture will again be true in these last days. God has always said leaders are to look out for oppressed victims, including the poor, fatherless, widow, foreigner, etc. Jesus preached in his Sermon on the Mount about these oppressed as the ones who will eventually be blessed and will inherit the Kingdom. The following verses show how the poor will be saved and their oppressors will be judged *in the Lord's presence*:

For thou hast been a strength to the poor, a strength to the needy in his distress, a refuge from the storm, a shadow from the heat, when the blast of the terrible ones is as a storm against the wall. (Is. 25:4)

But with righteousness shall he judge the poor, and reprove with equity for the meek of the earth: and he shall smite the earth: with the rod of his mouth, and with the breath of his lips shall he slay the wicked. (Is. 11:4)

He shall judge the poor of the people, he shall save the children of the needy, and shall break in pieces the oppressor. For he shall deliver the needy when he crieth; the poor also, and him that hath no helper. He shall spare the poor and needy, and shall save the souls of the needy. He shall redeem their soul from deceit and violence: and precious shall their blood be in his sight. (Ps. 72:4,12-14)

The Lord saves. We are told that the meek shall "increase their joy" and the poor will "rejoice" in the Holy One of Israel in the last days (Is. 29:19). Of course, through Isaiah (Chapter 61), we are told that the Lord will come once again to "preach good tidings to the meek," "bind up the brokenhearted," and "proclaim liberty to the captives." This is the answer to the prophetic prayers of those such as Hannah, Elizabeth and Mary, the mother of Jesus, who prayed for the humble to be exalted and the oppressor/enemy to be brought down by the coming Messiah to be "birthed."

The Lord in his presence in the last days will plead with his own people to understand true righteousness and faith versus the tricks and trade of his evil adversary and accuser. The Lord, through his case, will ask his people to come near (i.e. "let us reason"- Is. 1:18) and plead with them because of the "controversy" (Mic. 6:2) that he has. Scripture also tells us that he will be "quick to testify to rampant sin and lawlessness." God says:

Hearken unto me, my people; and give ear unto me, O my nation: for a law shall proceed from me, and I will make my judgment to rest for a light of the people. My righteousness is near; my salvation is gone forth, and mine arms shall judge the people; the isles shall wait upon me, and on mine arm shall they trust. (Is. 51:4-5)

And I will come near to you to judgment; and I will be a swift witness against the sorcerers, and against the adulterers, and against false swearers, and against those that oppress the hireling in his wages, the widow, and the fatherless, and that turn aside the stranger from his right, and fear not me, saith the Lord of hosts. (Mal. 3:5)

In these last days there will only be so much time to recognize and love the Light and Truth before he "hides his face." Otherwise, people will be at risk of even greater deception and danger in the midst of lawlessness to come in the Day of the Lord.

Ultimately, the Lord's judgment will be according to the law and what is true righteousness when his truth is revealed once and for all. Secrets will be revealed for all; we are told "he will set iniquities and secret sins before people" (Ps. 90:8). This is why the Apostle Paul tells us:

Therefore judge nothing before the time, until the Lord come, who both will bring to light the hidden things of darkness, and will make manifest the counsels of the hearts: and then shall every man have praise of God. (1 Cor. 4:5)

This is corroborated by other scripture that tells us that all things will ultimately be revealed.

His people return once they recognize the Lord's righteous cause

It will be much better to be redeemed beforehand than to face the Lord's cause in righteousness and judgment in the period of his wrath to come when his fire will go forth to clearly separate between good and evil. This is described in some scripture as a "purging" process. His law and its implications will go forth again at this time. His unsaved people will return in their sorrow at this time as shown in the following:

And many people shall go and say, Come ye, and let us go up to the mountain of the Lord, to the house of the God of Jacob; and he will teach us of his ways, and we will walk in his paths: for out of Zion shall go forth the law, and the word of the Lord from Jerusalem. (Is. 2:3)

And many nations shall come, and say, Come, and let us go up to the mountain of the Lord, and to the house of the God of Jacob; and he will teach us of his ways, and we will walk in his paths: for the law shall go forth of Zion, and the word of the Lord from Jerusalem. (Mic. 4:2)

When the Lord does his work to demonstrate truth (versus the secret, lying, deceptive mystery of iniquity) and then reveals himself there will be no denying and no grey area as to what is good versus evil. His justice and judgment will be perfect. At this time, he will say, "They shall know that I am the Lord" (Ez. 30:19). The Lord's people will acknowledge in return:

For the Lord is our judge, the Lord is our lawgiver, the Lord is our king; he will save us. (Is. 33:22)

Yea, in the way of thy judgments, O Lord, have we waited for thee; the desire of our soul is to thy name, and to the remembrance of thee. (Is. 26:8)

...for when thy judgments are in the earth, the inhabitants of the world will learn righteousness. (Is. 26:9)

The Lord's fighting and the outcome of his fight to reveal truth and justice will be good news for all of those who desire to be with, and to serve, their one true God, Jesus Christ. In Part 3, I will provide more detail about how the Lord is present in these last days to save his people. In my books, *Biblical End Times, Volumes 1 and 2*, I show the path back to the Kingdom for all believers upon the Lord's defeat of the adversary.

3.4 The Lord's Spirit with us (Part 3)

In Parts 1 and 2, I described how the Lord's Spirit of truth, 'Comforter,' will be with us in these last days in doing his work. The Lord will arise to support his own cause as well as that of his 'Jacob army' in the ongoing spiritual kingdom war against world Babylon's Chaldeans. I demonstrated the Lord's Spirit's presence among us as he fights for his Kingdom's cause.

In this passage, I will address how the Lord's Spirit is with us in the context of saving and delivering his faithful believers. The salvation of his anointed remnant out of persecution in last days Babylon will be a powerful witness and very compelling news for remaining Gentiles or those in the house of Israel who seek their Messiah. These will come to understand the powerful opportunity for deliverance through faith in Jesus Christ. I discuss this issue more in *Writings of Lion's Lair, Volume 2.*

The Lord's presence in delivering 'Israel' in these last days can be considered in two phases based on the prophetic story that we observe in scripture. The two phases include the deliverance of both remnants of his people who are ultimately saved in these last days. These include:

- The anointed 'Jacob'-Judah ("small flock") remnant
- The larger house of Israel remnant

I will address these respective remnants in detail later, but the emphasis here is on *the Lord's presence among us* in the process of Israel's anointed remnant's last days deliverance. In *Volume 2*, I will show how the larger house of Israel and Gentile believers will see the light of the "small flock" remnant in the Day of the Lord before they ultimately return to the Kingdom at the end of the age. Meanwhile, the delivery process for each remnant of 'Israel' is addressed in its own section below.

The Lord's Presence in Delivering his 'Jacob'-Judah "Small Flock" Remnant

The Lord's presence in the last days among his anointed remnant is well-established. This is his "small flock" who I discuss in Chapters 4-8 herein. They are the few faithful grapes remaining on his otherwise corrupt and stripped vine. They are the last days Judah/house of David remnant that will ultimately raise a banner on God's holy hill. The Lord will hear their prayers and calls for help as they cry out about persecution by their anti-Christ Chaldean enemies. His faithful flock will wait on him. A couple of verses applicable to their faith are as follows:

Why shouldest thou be as a man astonied, as a mighty man that cannot save? yet thou, O Lord, art in the midst of us, and we are called by thy name; leave us not. (Jer. 14:9)

For the Lord is our judge, the Lord is our lawgiver, the Lord is our king; he will save us. (Is. 33:22)

I describe prophecy in the Psalms in a couple other passages in *Volumes 2 and 3*, many of which were written by King David, particularly applicable for Israel and God's end times "small flock." This flock's prayers in the last days are very likely represented in the ancient Psalms that recorded King David and his people asking for their Lord's help and deliverance in their time. A few of these verses include:

Deliver the poor and needy: rid them out of the hand of the wicked. (Ps. 82:4)

Deliver me in thy righteousness, and cause me to escape: incline thine ear unto me, and save me. (Ps. 71:2)

Send thine hand from above; rid me, and deliver me out of great waters, from the hand of strange children… (Ps. 144:7)

These ancient prayers reflect the very same battle of the anti-Christ Chaldean adversary versus the Lord and his anointed that is raging in our current last days time period. Wicked, corrupt Chaldean leaders who hold captive and persecute the 'Jacob'-Judah remnant's resistors in the last days are accurately represented by King David's ancient observations regarding their denial and mocking of God. In these end times, you can be assured that world rulers holding God's people captive are repeating the exact same statement below about 'Jacob' and his anointed remnant who are clinging to their faith and refusing to bow to the new world order system:

He (they) trusted on the Lord that he would deliver him: let him deliver him, seeing he delighted in him. (Ps. 22:8)

World leaders will finally look on and be ashamed when God carries out what he has already promised he will do. He will save his righteous "small flock" remnant, shield them, and give them refuge from these enemies. God will also see to it that they are delivered and rescued. They will ultimately be led back to the holy land by the Lord himself albeit with intermediate steps along the way. These steps are described in more detail below.

The Lord in the midst while saving the 'Jacob'-Judah remnant

The Lord tells his anointed remnant many times, "I am with thee." The Lord is "in the midst" in the last days to save, deliver, and "keep" them. He also tells them several times not to be afraid. He says, "there is no strange God among you" (Is. 43:12). The Lord's own "arm" of might and strength accomplishes this, along with his servant 'Jacob.' God assures 'Jacob' that his enemy will not prevail against him. The Prophet Jeremiah was a "type" of end times 'Jacob,' about whom God said he knew before he was born and whom he decided to raise up as an "iron pillar" and as a "fenced brazen wall" against his whole land. God told him:

Be not afraid of their faces: for I am with thee to deliver thee, saith the Lord. (Jer. 1:8)

And they shall fight against thee; but they shall not prevail against thee; for I am with thee, saith the Lord, to deliver thee. (Jer. 1:19)

God told Jeremiah that he was with him. Jeremiah was God's anointed as are those who are his faithful last days Judah remnant servants, including 'Jacob' himself. The following verses show how God is with his "small flock" as the "saving strength of his anointed" once again to save them from persecution and affliction in these last days:

Therefore fear thou not, O my servant Jacob, saith the Lord; neither be dismayed, O Israel: for, lo, I will save thee from afar, and thy seed from the land of their captivity; and Jacob shall return, and shall be in rest, and be quiet, and none shall make him afraid. For I am with thee, saith the Lord, to save thee… (Jer. 30:10-11)

The mountains saw thee, and they trembled: the overflowing of the water passed by: the deep uttered his voice, and lifted up his hands on high. Thou wentest forth for the salvation of thy people, even for salvation with thine anointed; thou woundedst the head out of the house of the wicked, by discovering the foundation unto the neck. Selah. (Hab. 3:10,13)

But I will have mercy upon the house of Judah, and will save them by the Lord their God, and will not save them by bow, nor by sword, nor by battle, by horses, nor by horsemen. (Hos. 1:7)

We are furthermore told that the Lord who saves this particular small 'Jacob'- Judah flock will "be seen over them" (Zech. 9:14) and will defend them. The Lord will be with them.

Note from the last verse above that it is God himself who will save this remnant in what can be inferred as some sort of supernatural escape (out of 'Babylon,' or its system). We are also told that in these last days an "angel of the Lord" will go before them. This unconventional rescue of God's flock, likely to happen quietly and unseen, is further described in the following:

Thus saith the Lord; As the shepherd taketh out of the mouth of the lion two legs, or a piece of an ear; so shall the children of Israel be taken out that dwell in Samaria in the corner of a bed, and in Damascus in a couch. (Am. 3:12)

(Note: In at least some cases, 'Samaria' and 'Damascus' can generally be thought of in prophetic terms as part of today's mingled 'northern kingdom' within Babylon, and its close anti-Christ Chaldean allies. I discuss Israel's last days 'northern kingdom' in more detail in *Volume 2*). One principle of interpretation we are given in scripture is the invading Assyrian asking through Isaiah, "is not Samaria as Damascus?" (Is. 10:9). Exactly how this escape from 'Babylon' happens and where this remnant will go first appears to be up for debate. But they will be with the Lord. We are told that this particular remnant will return directly "unto the mighty God" (Is. 10:21). We are also told:

And it shall come to pass in that day, that the remnant of Israel, and such as are escaped of the house of Jacob, shall no more again stay upon him that smote them; but shall stay upon the Lord, the Holy One of Israel, in truth. (Is. 10:20)

So, the Lord's Spirit will be among his "small flock" at the time of their deliverance and exodus/escape out of 'Babylon'-U.S.'s system. He will gather and assemble them himself. Clues about this are scriptural references at this time when the Lord addresses the 'Daughter of Zion,' 'Israel,' and the daughters of Jerusalem. The Lord is offering his flock forgiveness along with relief from fear and captivity. They are told a couple of times, "The Lord thy God is in the midst of thee." One example in scripture about this time of the Lord's salvation is as follows:

Behold, the Lord hath proclaimed unto the end of the world, Say ye to the daughter of Zion, Behold, thy salvation cometh; behold, his reward is with him, and his work before him. (Is. 62:11)

This is the Lord rescuing and saving his small remnant of people from their oppression and captivity in the nation of 'Babylon.' This is a time of extreme anti-Christ Chaldean corruption and lawlessness along with coming war. God says that he will deal with his people's oppressors (Zeph. 3:19), especially through the "sword" of war at this time. He says that he will send to 'Babylon' and bring down all of their nobles (Is. 43:12), and that he will "feed them that oppress with their own flesh" (Is. 49:26).

So, during this last days tumultuous time, God intentionally plans to save his elect. The Lord will have to save a "seed" or else his people will become as Sodom and Gomorrah (Is. 1:9); that is, they would be utterly destroyed. This is also referred to in scripture as the time when no flesh would be saved, unless it was for the sake of the Lord's elect (Matt. 24:22). Additional scripture tells us that the Lord will finish his work and will "cut it short in righteousness" at this time (Rom. 9:22).

The Lord as his small remnant's pathmaker

In his rescue, deliverance and saving of his "small flock" remnant from the nation of 'Babylon,' the Lord will then lead them in the way they should go. Perhaps the original pillar of fire by night and pillar of a cloud by day was a foretelling, symbolic sign for his people's *last days* exodus, an event that I describe in *Volume 2*. This time, the Lord, his Spirit of truth, appears to be among them himself. In speaking to his captive 'Jacob'-Judah flock in 'Babylon' about their deliverance and being with them to show them the way God says:

Depart ye, depart ye, go ye out from thence, touch no unclean thing; go ye out of the midst of her; be ye clean, that bear the vessels of the Lord. For ye shall not go out with haste, nor go by flight: for the Lord will go before you; and the God of Israel will be your reward. (Is. 52:11-12)

Thus saith the Lord, thy Redeemer, the Holy One of Israel; I am the Lord thy God which teacheth thee to profit, which leadeth thee by the way that thou shouldest go. (Is. 48:17)

Behold, I will do a new thing; now it shall spring forth; shall ye not know it? I will even make a way in the wilderness, and rivers in the desert. (Is. 43:19)

God is showing how in a last days unraveling, chaotic nation of 'Babylon' that he will lead his flock out and provide a way to navigate the treacherous times and obstacles in their way. This will include making a path for them to eventually arrive at their final destination-Jerusalem.

Their journey back to the homeland will take some time and will have stops along the way. Punishment through God's four dreadful judgments (Ez. 14:21) must first come upon and decimate the country of Israel. The Day of the Lord will obviously not be the time to go back to the homeland. Thus, his flock's intermediate stops during this time are unclear; but any supernatural option is possible.

God will provide for his "small flock" during their exodus. Again, we already have a "picture" of this in his people's original exodus out of Egypt with God providing for their needs while they were in the desert. In the meantime, prophetic verses below applying to the last days anointed remnant remind us of the house of 'Israel's initial exodus:

When the poor and needy seek water, and there is none, and their tongue faileth for thirst, I the Lord will hear them, I the God of Israel will not forsake them. I will open rivers in high places, and fountains in the midst of the valleys: I will make the wilderness a pool of water, and the dry land springs of water. (Is. 41:17-18)

The beast of the field shall honour me, the dragons and the owls: because I give waters in the wilderness, and rivers in the desert, to give drink to my people, my chosen. (Is. 43:20)

After the Lord's journey with his people and their temporary refuge, he will lead his "small flock" back to Jerusalem at the time the house of Israel returns along with Gentiles from all corners of the earth. Upon returning to their final heavenly Millennial Kingdom destination, God will be with them. The following verses show their return:

But there the glorious Lord will be unto us a place of broad rivers and streams; wherein shall go no galley with oars, neither shall gallant ship pass thereby. (Is. 33:21)

But, The Lord liveth, that brought up the children of Israel from the land of the north, and from all the lands whither he had driven them: and I will bring them again into their land that I gave unto their fathers. (Jer. 16:15)

Of course, upon reaching their final destination, this will be the time when the whole house of Israel and Gentile believers converge to meet the Lord Jesus for the beginning of his Millennial Kingdom.

The Lord's Presence in Delivering his Large Remnant

The Lord will also be with his larger, worldwide faithful house of Israel remnant in the last days, although not in the same manner as he accompanies his smaller remnant. This is the point in time that the Lord stretches out his hand a second time to recover his remnant from the "four corners of the earth" (Is. 11:11-12). Although this larger remnant's path to return to the holy land will be via a different one than the small, holy remnant, those who seek and find Jesus Christ will still be comforted along the way. God will still save and deliver them out of danger. He will bring them back home. The difference that the large remnant will experience is that while the Lord's Spirit may always be found, there will be a time when God is no longer "in the midst"; this is because he will hide his face for a time during the Day of the Lord.

God will still be directly responsible, however, for saving his faithful larger remnant of 'Israel' and seeing that they come out of world 'Babylon's system. In doing so, his large remnant will be wandering and seeking him during a time of being outcast and spiritually barren, not to mention suffering much turmoil and personal tribulation in the Day of the Lord. This is his remnant of people who will initially recognize that they are "not saved" at this point (Jer. 13:20).

So, in their wandering, they will not be given a clear path as is the small remnant who follow the Lord. They will instead have to wait for the Lord and endure the Day of the Lord. This is by God's design and will serve to make his people desperately yearn for their true God in earnest. God will ultimately come and gather his true believers to his holy land to establish his Kingdom. His delivered people will become an example of God's gracious blessings and through them others worldwide including additional Gentiles will see and will also be saved and blessed. This will be the time that God rejoins the house of Judah and the house of Joseph.

The Lord saves his faithful large remnant

Just as was the case with his small, righteous flock, the larger house of Israel's remnant will suddenly find themselves held captive, oppressed and persecuted in the Day of the Lord. This is why they will seek their Savior and we are told will be saved from "all the ends of the earth" (Is. 45:22).

Scripture says that God will rescue, deliver and become a sanctuary for his large remnant. While these are his people who have never acknowledged Jesus Christ or who have possibly even blasphemed him prior to their turmoil, those who return to seek him will still find him. God says, "I will save my flock" and he also declares that he will have mercy on them. Nevertheless, many of God's people will be fearful of the pursuing, persecuting adversary at this time and will have to rely on his following promise:

Say to them that are of a fearful heart, Be strong, fear not: behold, your God will come with vengeance, even God with a recompence; he will come and save you. (Is. 35:4)

While his people will not see him while he has hidden his face, those who are righteous and not deceived by false gods will seek his Spirit that is still among them. God's large remnant will have to wait patiently for his revealing at this time- a time when he says, "my righteousness is near" (Is. 51:5).

Meanwhile, in their oppression, turmoil and persecution God's large remnant's prayers will be similar to those of Job's in his affliction as they wait for their Messiah's return. They will have similar faith as follows:

For I know that my redeemer liveth, and that he shall stand at the latter day upon the earth... (Job 19:25)

Perhaps they will also pray like King David did at the time of his anguish from persecution. As you know, King David was always keenly aware of God's presence and acknowledged him frequently as follows, rhetorically asking:

Whither shall I go from thy spirit? or whither shall I flee from thy presence? (Ps. 139:7)

There will likely be some supernatural signs of the Lord's presence during the Day of the Lord. God will also have witnesses who give their testimony. In addition, scripture tells us that God will listen for and hear his people who seek him. Consider the following verses:

Behold, the Lord's hand is not shortened, that it cannot save; neither his ear heavy, that it cannot hear... (Is. 59:1)

...for I have mercy upon them: and they shall be as though I had not cast them off: for I am the Lord their God, and will hear them. (Zech. 10:6)

Later in this section, I will show that God's people will finally get to visibly see their Lord God. This will be the time when "he shall appear, we shall be like him; for we shall see him as he is" (1 Jn. 3:2). This also represents the time at which God tells his people, "I will be found of you" (Jer. 29:14).

The Lord frees his large remnant from oppressive 'Babylon' world kingdom rulers

The house of Israel's large remnant that God brings out of the world (i.e. "out of Egypt") will occur as a deliverance *process* rather than as a sudden, discrete event such as that which is likely for the "small flock" remnant. This process involves God's work in freeing his captive, persecuted people from world Babylon's leaders (i.e. "wild beasts"). It involves a quiet, behind-the-scenes battle that will happen even largely before God hides his face. This same continuing process (i.e. like a "moth eating a garment" or God's "trap") that benefited his small remnant and that his 'Jacob army' themselves were a part of could very well be the same one that later benefits his large remnant.

In his saving of his people in the Day of the Lord, God in his wrath will bring down all of world 'Babylon's kings and their cooperating anti-Christ Chaldean cohorts. This will ultimately include the Anti-Christ himself. The King of Babylon and the 'Assyrian' are among key rulers who will be brought down so that the Lord's captive people may be freed. As for the latter, God's people will pray just as they did in the ancient time of King Hezekiah that God will deliver them at the hands of the king of Assyria:

Now therefore, O Lord our God, save us from his hand, that all the kingdoms of the earth may know that thou art the Lord, even thou only. (Is. 37:20)

I describe in *Volume 2* how the country of Israel's rulers will also be found complicit with anti-Christ Chaldean world rulers, likely including at least some of the current day versions of kings just mentioned. God will rescue those whom they hold captive. In the following verses from the Prophet Ezekiel, God is referring to Israel's *own* Chaldean-serving shepherds/kings who have oppressed their own flock:

This is what the Sovereign Lord says: I am against the shepherds and will hold them accountable for my flock. I will remove them from tending the flock so that the shepherds can no longer feed themselves. I will rescue my flock from their mouths, and it will no longer be food for them. For this is what the Sovereign Lord says: I myself will search for my sheep and look after them. As a shepherd looks after his scattered flock when he is with them, so will I look after my sheep. I will rescue them from all the places where they were scattered on a day of clouds and darkness. (Ez. 34:10-12)

Because you (shepherds) shove with flank and shoulder, butting all the weak sheep with your horns until you have driven them away, I will save my flock, and they will no longer be plundered. I will judge between one sheep and another. (Ez. 34:21-22)

These verses confirm that God is going to rid his own land of Israel of those corrupt shepherds who have oppressed and persecuted their citizens and his flock. God says that he will, "rid the land of savage beasts" (Ez. 34:25). This time period will represent a changing of the guard from historic leaders in the country of Israel who are a bad, corrupt vine to a replacement by God's servant-children who he brings from the "land of the north" (Jer. 16:15); these are likely God's Judah-centric "small flock" remnant.

Overall, as oppressive, corrupt Chaldean leaders and their societies across the world are exposed, brought down and defeated throughout the Day of the Lord, God's people who are wandering and running from persecution, the "sword," and wartime conditions will gain at least some relief and freedom from their captivity. God is directly involved at this time and will single-handedly assure that his faithful people are delivered from their oppression. This will be in addition to that which we see in the country of Israel above.

The Lord frees his large remnant from captivity and calls for their final exodus

God promises his large remnant at this time that he will "save (his) people" and "take (them) from among the heathen" at the time that he brings them back into his land. This will be toward the end of the Day of the Lord after anti-Christ spirit corruption in the country of Israel has been purged. The following verses support God freeing his house of Israel from captivity worldwide, "from the ends of the earth":

But thus saith the Lord, Even the captives of the mighty shall be taken away, and the prey of the terrible shall be delivered: for I will contend with him that contendeth with thee, and I will save thy children. (Is. 49:25)

Therefore thus saith the Lord God; Now will I bring again the captivity of Jacob, and have mercy upon the whole house of Israel, and will be jealous for my holy name… (Ez. 39:25)

And I will be found of you, saith the Lord: and I will turn away your captivity, and I will gather you from all the nations, and from all the places whither I have driven you, saith the Lord; and I will bring you again into the place whence I caused you to be carried away captive. (Jer. 29:14)

That then the Lord thy God will turn thy captivity, and have compassion upon thee, and will return and gather thee from all the nations, whither the Lord thy God hath scattered thee. (Deut. 30:3)

Perhaps before his people who are newly freed from captivity get to see his return, they will hear him in their midst. At this time scripture says, "They shall walk after the Lord: he shall roar like a lion: when he shall roar, then the children shall tremble from the west" (Hos. 11:9-10). The following verses allude to God's people being able to hear him or at least suggest that they may be able to feel his presence as they are persuaded to return to him and eventually return back to their land. Consider the following:

I will say to the north, Give up; and to the south, Keep not back: bring my sons from far, and my daughters from the ends of the earth… (Is. 43:6)

And thine ears shall hear a word behind thee, saying, This is the way, walk ye in it, when ye turn to the right hand, and when ye turn to the left. (Is. 30:21)

The Lord also shall roar out of Zion, and utter his voice from Jerusalem; and the heavens and the earth shall shake: but the Lord will be the hope of his people, and the strength of the children of Israel. (Joel 3:16)

And I will bring the blind by a way that they knew not; I will lead them in paths that they have not known: I will make darkness light before them, and crooked things straight. These things will I do unto them, and not forsake them. (Is. 42:16)

This will be an amazing time when God's faithful people realize they are close to seeing their long-awaited Messiah and Savior. His people will ultimately get to see him when he joins them and brings them back in their return to the land. God says that, "after I have plucked them out I will return" (Jer. 12:15).

The Lord's Spirit leads his large remnant back into the holy land- their final destination

Although the presence of his Spirit will have been with his faithful large remnant, and while they were drawn to him, heard him roar, and accepted Jesus Christ as their Savior in the Day of the Lord, he will become more fully visible when he leads his people and they regather in their land at the end of the period. The following verses show how God will be in the lead in directing his people back to their land at the time of their regathering:

And it shall come to pass, after that I have plucked them out I will return, and have compassion on them, and will bring them again, every man to his heritage, and every man to his land. (Jer. 12:15)

They shall come with weeping, and with supplications will I lead them: I will cause them to walk by the rivers of waters in a straight way, wherein they shall not stumble: for I am a father to Israel, and Ephraim is my firstborn. (Jer. 31:9)

That thou ('Jacob') mayest say to the prisoners, Go forth; to them that are in darkness, Shew yourselves. They shall feed in the ways, and their pastures shall be in all high places. (Is. 49:9)

The last verse above is God working through his servant 'Jacob' at the time that he will direct the house of Israel back to their land. God's plan from the beginning of re-joining the house of Judah with the house of Israel will be accomplished at this time just prior to Jesus Christ's glorious reign.

~

Both remnants of Israel, the "ransomed of the Lord," who return to the land will rejoice in their freedom from bondage and a recognition of the one true God- Jesus Christ- as the only one who saves and sets them free. This will be an answer to their faithful, ancient prophetic prayer as follows:

And it shall be said in that day, Lo, this is our God; we have waited for him, and he will save us: this is the Lord; we have waited for him, we will be glad and rejoice in his salvation. (Is. 25:9)

In retrospect, those in God's faithful remnant will realize that their Lord has been present with them all along. See my books, *Biblical End Times, Volumes 1 and 2*, that describe the Lord's faithfulness to believers and their final deliverance.

Chapter 4.

An Anointed Remnant

Passages from Lion's Lair provided in this chapter include:

4.1 God's End Times Holy Children

4.2 Roles of God's End Times Servants

4.3 A Judah and House of David Remnant

4.1 God's End Times Holy Children

In this chapter, I will discuss attributes of God's holy children in these last days. These are his anointed children who will inherit his Millennial Kingdom under Jesus Christ's reign. As such, they will be tested, proven, faithful believers in Jesus Christ.

Attributes of these last days holy children addressed in this passage include the following; they are a people who are:

- Saved to continue God's Kingdom on earth
- Created and chosen by God
- Reserved as a "seed" for God's inheritance
- Persecuted and then glorified

I will address each of these attributes in separate sections below. Meanwhile, although I am discussing a particular last days "first fruits" holy people in this passage, it is important to remember that *all* who enter into the Millennial Kingdom as faithful Jesus Christ-believers will be considered holy. *All* of these will also experience the unbelievable joys of life under Jesus, the King, in his Kingdom. The Apostle Paul tells believers, "For ye are all children of God by faith in Christ Jesus" (Gal. 3:26).

All who live with Jesus Christ in his Millennial Kingdom will be a "holy nation" and will have his Spirit written on their hearts. This is according to scripture. *All* will also receive a "new heart" and a "new spirit" to worship him and to understand his law.

A Holy People Saved to Continue God's Kingdom on Earth

In scripture, it is clear that some of God's children will receive an initial "special helping" of holy spirit even before the Millennial Kingdom so that they may do his work in the end times in an otherwise hostile, faithless world; that is, so they can get out the truth of God's message, first and foremost the Gospel of Jesus Christ and his provision for salvation. Related to this, in his Sermon on the Mount, Jesus told us that the "peacemakers" will be called the children of God in heaven (Matt. 5:9).

In Chapter 9, I will explain how these children are associated with God accomplishing his plan. These children include the holy, royal, faithful 'Jacob'-Judah remnant who are God's children and who fight this spiritual war against the anti-Christ Chaldeans in these last days. It would certainly appear, and make sense, that the one who "restrains" (i.e. the 'Restrainer' in 2 Thess. 2) and holds back the lawlessness that is to come will be among them.

Due to the ongoing spiritual kingdom war and destruction of God's vineyard, God has planned to save and set aside a holy remnant for his inheritance to fulfill his covenant promises through Abraham (Isaac and Jacob) and King David. God calls these last days servants his own or his "chosen" ones. They will enter his Kingdom with holy and royal distinction. These are his royal inheritance and will be those whom Christ will call his brethren. Related to this we are given the following verse:

For both he that sanctifieth and they who are sanctified are all of one: for which cause he is not ashamed to call them brethren. (Heb. 2:11)

This holy people are God's children or "seed" of inheritance about whom the following verse refers:

And as Esaias said before, Except the Lord of Sabaoth had left us a seed, we had been as Sodoma, and been made like unto Gomorrha. (Rom. 9:29)

God will set aside a holy "seed" of his people to fulfill and continue his covenant promises for his Kingdom to come. It is this seed against which the anti-Christ Chaldeans will continue to fight against in the ongoing kingdom war.

A Holy People Created and Chosen by God

As just alluded to above, given the spiritual kingdom war here on earth there would ultimately be "no flesh remaining" unless God himself set aside his own "elect" people in these last days. A very good example is end times 'Jacob.' God repeatedly says in scripture that he "formed" him, foreknew him, and chose him as his own.

Similarly, the house of Jacob and last days Judah-centric "small flock" remnant are chosen and have been formed specifically for God's purpose. They will proceed into the Millennial Kingdom and will be recognized by the people of the world as righteous victors over evil. These will be the ones, who as witnesses, testify and attribute victory in the kingdom war to the work of the hands of the one true God, Jesus Christ. God says about this remnant:

This people have I formed for myself; they shall shew forth my praise. (Is. 43:21)

Though we are told in scripture that all have fallen short and that none is righteous, God will redeem this remnant for his own purpose. God has formed them "unto himself" for his own glory and testament to being the one and only God of the universe. Demonstrating that God has created these people for himself, for his purpose, and for his glory (Is. 43:7), we are given the following descriptors about these select holy servants in scripture. God calls them:

- The "branch of my planting" (Is. 60:21)

- The "work of my hands" (Is. 29:23, 45:11, 60:21)

- "Born by me from the belly" (Is. 46:24)

- "A special people unto (him)" (Deut. 7:6)

- "Carried from the womb" (Is. 46:24)

These last days holy children also fit a more stringent definition of the Apostle Paul's description of spiritual children in the book of Romans, Chapter 8. In talking about them Paul calls them God's "elect" who are called for his purpose. Paul says further:

For whom he did foreknow, he also did predestinate to be conformed to the image of his Son, that he might be the firstborn among many brethren. Moreover whom he did predestinate, them he also called: and whom he called, them he also justified: and whom he justified, them he also glorified. (Rom. 8:29-30)

(Christ) In whom also we have obtained an inheritance, being predestinated according to the purpose of him who worketh all things after the counsel of his own will. (Eph. 1:11)

In Romans, the Apostle Paul also addresses glorification through suffering and how God's children are "killed all day long" and are counted as "sheep for slaughter" (Rom. 8:36). Across all of his writings, it is clear that Paul was highly in touch with, and in the midst of, the continuing spiritual kingdom war of his own day.

A Holy People Reserved as a "Seed" for God's Inheritance

God's holy children in these perilous last days are also frequently referred to as his inheritance or his "seed." Consistent with the designation of being "chosen" as discussed above, God's holy inheritance, as expected, are those who will serve him and his son Jesus Christ. The following prophetic verses from the Psalms are written within a context for future generations:

A seed shall serve him; it shall be accounted to the Lord for a generation. They shall come, and shall declare his righteousness unto a people that shall be born, that he hath done this. (Ps. 22:30-31)

Know ye that the Lord he is God: it is he that hath made us, and not we ourselves; we are his people, and the sheep of his pasture. Enter into his gates with thanksgiving and into his courts with praise… (Ps. 100:3-4)

In scripture, the word "seed" as used by King David in the verse above many times is referring to God's holy inheritance. In Jesus' *Parable of the Wheat and Tares*, he told us that the "good seed" that are planted are the "children of the Kingdom" (Matt. 13:38).

Other vegetation-related terms such as tree, branch, stem, etc. also sometimes indicate this. As such, prophetic scripture tells us that God's vineyard, or vine, becomes stripped in these last days. God's "small flock" remnant are then the few remaining grapes on the vine or olives left on the tree. We are told that his holy seed- as represented by a tree- will remain only as a stump after the tree is cut down (Is. 6:13) as a result of his judgment administered via the Chaldeans.

The following are representative vegetation-related descriptors of God's little remaining holy seed in the midst during the last days spiritual kingdom war:

- "seed of the blessed of the Lord" (Is. 65:23)

- "(beautiful, glorious) Branch of the Lord" (Is. 4:2)

- "precious fruit of the earth" (James 5:7)

- "a stem of Jesse, a Branch will grow out of his roots" (Is. 11:1)

- "(hope that a tree) will sprout again and a tender branch thereof will not cease" (Job 14:7)

God calls his inheritance "my people," consistent with his ancient 'Israel' bloodline that is "chosen" as discussed above. To use one more descriptor, they represent 'Israel' that will "shoot forth its branches" and will "yield fruit" (Ez. 36:8) for the greater remnant of Israel and Gentiles. This is why they are saved. They will communicate a message of righteousness, faith, and salvation through Jesus Christ.

These are the people who will also inherit God's promises for a people, land and an opportunity to rule (i.e. "children of the promise"). Knowing the end from the beginning, God has declared this reward for his people from the times of ancient scripture. God obviously foretold this in his covenant promises to Abraham, Isaac and Jacob, as well as David, but also through the following:

For thou art an holy people unto the Lord thy God: the Lord thy God hath chosen thee to be a special people unto himself, above all people that are upon the face of the earth. (Deut. 7:6)

Who are Israelites; to whom pertaineth the adoption, and the glory, and the covenants, and the giving of the law, and the service of God, and the promises… (Rom. 9:4)

…but the children of the promise are counted for the seed. For this is the word of promise, At this time will I come, and Sarah shall have a son. (Rom. 9:8-9)

Referring to the final verse above- "Sarah shall have a son"- realize that while this was fulfilled at that time in Isaac, this is also a "picture" of things to come for the 'Daughter of Zion.' I will describe 'Zion's children who are to be spiritually "birthed" in Chapter 9. She also appears to be the woman whose seed will multiply into a Kingdom full of God's children. She will be another in a line of holy Israelite women who was barren but is to be subsequently blessed. A pattern and prophetic picture of God's inheritance of a royal family in scripture can be observed through her as a Millennial Kingdom Queen-Mother; this is seen in verses such as the following:

And I will bless her, and give thee a son also of her: yea, I will bless her, and she shall be a mother of nations; kings of people shall be of her. (Gen. 17:16)

Thou shalt arise, and have mercy upon Zion: for the time to favour her, yea, the set time, is come. For thy servants take pleasure in her stones, and favour the dust thereof. (Ps. 102:13-14)

Lift up thine eyes round about, and behold: all these gather themselves together, and come to thee. As I live, saith the Lord, thou shalt surely clothe thee with them all, as with an ornament, and bind them on thee, as a bride doeth. (Is. 49:18)

Instead of thy fathers shall be thy children, whom thou mayest make princes in all the earth. (Ps. 45:16)

As will be seen in the following section, God's Kingdom's children are those who are spiritually free but will then be delivered from Chaldean bondage. The 'Daughter of Zion,' their Queen-Mother, will have experienced bondage herself according to scripture but is then delivered. Once she is free, she can deliver "children of the promise" (i.e. "as Isaac was") referred to above. The 'Daughter of Zion' represents what the Apostle Paul refers to as follows:

But Jerusalem which is above is free, which is the mother of us all. (Gal. 4:26)

Abraham's wife Sarah, the freewoman, was a foreshadow of the 'Daughter of Zion.' This is in contrast with Abraham's servant Hagar who we are told at the time was a "bondwoman," born of the flesh.

A Holy People Persecuted and then Glorified

One thing is certain. If you are in the line of God's chosen or his "seed," then you will be persecuted. The anti-Christ Chaldean surveillance and spying "machine" that is in place will find Christ's faithful and his "seed," and place them in bondage. This happens as part of the ongoing spiritual kingdom war.

I will address the persecution of God's vineyard as well as that of his Judah-centric "small flock" remnant in this book as well as in *Writings of Lion's Lair, Volumes 2 and 3*. I will not repeat that content here. Meanwhile, I did allude earlier in this passage to the holy seed that is cut down to just a stump as well as to the Apostle Paul's reference to true Christ-believers as "sheep to be slaughtered." To be in Jesus Christ means, as a natural consequence, that you will personally be a sacrifice and that you will suffer in this life. The Apostle Paul teaches that holy glorification comes as a result of suffering. The following verses support this:

And if children, then heirs; heirs of God, and joint-heirs with Christ; if so be that we suffer with him, that we may be also glorified together. (Rom. 8:17)

For it became him, for whom are all things, and by whom are all things, in bringing many sons unto glory, to make the captain of their salvation perfect through sufferings. (Heb. 2:10)

God's people suffer as part of resisting the massive anti-Christ force in today's spiritual warfare in their struggle to keep their soul and allegiance to Jesus Christ. These Chaldean "children of the flesh" who the Apostle Paul speaks about, who are themselves in bondage, believe in taking others into bondage and captivity as well. Paul said:

But as then he that was born after the flesh persecuted him that was born after the Spirit, even so it is now. (Gal. 4:29)

It should be noted here, too, that earlier in this same chapter of Galatians that the Apostle Paul interrogated his audience as to why some, even after receiving the truth of the Lord, went back and voluntarily submitted to bondage. So, *not all* have to be coerced, extorted or blackmailed to join the Chaldeans. Incomprehensibly, some join this cult of destruction and demise on their own volition.

Deliverance and glory through Jesus

Jesus set the ultimate example of what it means to serve. It follows that those who God says that he "foreknew," "predestinated," and "conform to the image" of Jesus are the ones who he calls his holy children. As shown above, they suffer with him. Jesus also gave us the strategic example and lesson of submitting in the battle but in doing so winning the larger war. This is also a lesson of endurance in faith. Thus, we are told:

For whatsoever is born of God overcometh the world: and this is the victory that overcometh the world, even our faith. Who is he that overcometh the world, but he that believeth that Jesus is the Son of God? (1 Jn. 5:4-5)

Jesus was victorious and so are we through him. We also have examples in scripture of submitting to captivity, which I have explained prior can still meet with approval in God's eyes, yet is very different from *joining* or pledging some oath to the foreign god-led oppressive and persecuting force. The Prophet Jeremiah and his righteous remnant received the following promise from God in response to his lament:

The Lord said, Verily it shall be well with thy remnant; verily I will cause the enemy to entreat thee well in the time of evil and in the time of affliction. (Jer. 15:11)

In fact, captivity will be the status quo for much of God's last days anointed remnant before he finally delivers them. In Chapter 9, I will explain the spiritual "birthing" of God's children, and that bereavement is a sign of captivity. Many of Zion's spiritual children are taken captive in the last days. But God's select remnant will still ultimately be "birthed" or "brought forth" in the last days. This "birthing" of God's holy ones will signal the beginning of the process of God's entire creation being delivered from its "groaning," captivity and bondage, and instead into the "glorious liberty of the children of God" (Rom. 8:21).

God will deliver his holy people for the whole creation to witness. We see how he often tells them, "fear not." God's holy children will become conquerors through patience along with knowing and understanding his promise to his faithful servants. That is, he will redeem them as we see as follows:

And they shall call them, The holy people, The redeemed of the Lord: and thou shalt be called, Sought out, A city not forsaken. (Is. 62:12)

And they shall be mine, saith the Lord of hosts, in that day when I make up my jewels; and I will spare them, as a man spareth his own son that serveth him. (Mal. 3:17)

I will write in more detail about how end times 'Jacob' and his house are a clear example of how God will deliver those who he calls his own in the last days. In addition to telling 'Jacob' that he will save him and his seed "from the land of their captivity" (Jer. 30:10), God says:

For I am the Lord, I change not; therefore ye sons of Jacob are not consumed. (Mal. 3:6)

Hearken unto me, O house of Jacob, and all the remnant of the house of Israel, which are borne by me from the belly, which are carried from the womb: And even to your old age I am he; and even to hoar hairs will I carry you: I have made, and I will bear; even I will carry, and will deliver you. (Is. 46:3-4)

End times 'Jacob' and his sons along with the daughters of Jerusalem are the holy family who will go into the anti-Christ Chaldean fire of persecution first to be tested and refined in the last days. They are the ones akin to those God speaks about who are placed in an "iron furnace" of persecution and captivity. God says:

Behold, I have refined thee, but not with silver; I have chosen thee in the furnace of affliction. (Is. 48:10)

Of course, we are given in scripture the very similar, albeit symbolic story of Daniel being thrown into the lion's den and his Judah-tribe comrades being thrown into the fiery furnace while in captivity in Babylon. They all would not bow down to the foreign gods of Babylon. In a true test of their faith, God delivered them all. In doing so, his glory was made manifest as the one and only God who can save and deliver in the midst of Babylonian false gods.

~

In conclusion, I demonstrated in Chapter 3 that we should consider the Lord's Spirit of truth as being here with us in these last days. This current passage shows how the Lord is also keeping a holy remnant in the midst of growing darkness. After world Babylon's kingdom is defeated, God's firstborn son of the Kingdom, Jesus Christ, and those he calls his holy children will claim victory and move into the

Millennial Kingdom as part of God's inheritance. I discuss the path back to the Kingdom for all believers in my two books, *Biblical End Times, Volumes 1 and 2.*

4.2 Roles of God's End Times Biblical Servants

Jesus Christ was the ultimate servant who gave his life so that we might find our salvation through him. Jesus and his disciples also gave us many examples and inspired words about what faithful servanthood looks like. To begin, as servants of our Lord in these end times, we must be awake and watching for his return.

In the meantime, in the midst of the ongoing kingdom war, Christ followers in these last days should expect to be identified and targeted by the high-tech anti-Christ Chaldean surveillance machine. We will know that we are on track if we find ourselves hated, rejected, isolated, persecuted, in bondage, and enduring ongoing temptations.

Those who maintain strong faith and are willing to "lose their life" in order to preserve it (Lk. 9:22) will ultimately be recognized as what the Apostle Paul refers to as "more than conquerors" in God's coming Kingdom. Jesus Christ-believers who maintain their faith in the midst of a violent world that persecutes his servants should also keep in mind the following verse: "Who is he that overcometh the world, but he that believeth that Jesus is the Son of God?" (1 Jn. 5:5).

In this passage, I will address those roles specific to end times servants of the Lord who are named in scripture. There are many instances where particular servants are referred to including, but not limited to, those I will address in more detail in Chapters 4-8 such as: 'Jacob'; 'David'; and the 'Daughter of Zion.' In *Writings of Lion's Lair, Volume 3*, I will address end times personas of the Major Prophets Jeremiah, Isaiah, and Ezekiel. My passages in Chapter 3 already described the servant who comes in the person of the Holy Spirit and who appears in these last days as the 'Comforter' and/or 'Restrainer,' or end times Son of man.

Through our collective understanding of all of these and other biblical servants living among us, we can gain an idea about their roles and activities here in the last days. I address these herein within the following topic areas:

- Watchmen
- Prophetic messengers
- Bearers and recipients of God's promises
- Warriors and fighters

From among the compilation of prophetic scripture referring to end times servants, I will describe these activities in more detail in separate sections below.

Watchmen

In Chapter 1, I showed how as God's servants we are to be awake and watching for Jesus' return. Jesus instructed his disciples in his day to be watchful. Jesus also spoke both directly and through his parables about watching in these end times. As one example, he said:

For the Son of Man is as a man taking a far journey, who left his house, and gave authority to his servants, and to every man his work, and commanded the porter to watch. (Mk. 13:34)

Watching for Jesus our Master is a natural, distinguishing characteristic of a faithful and wise servant and of those who have the oil of the Holy Spirit to keep their lamps burning in these last days so that they will be able to "see" amidst the growing darkness.

End times watchmen described through the personas of Major Prophets

End times watchmen and their activities can be detected through the personas of Major Prophets that I address in *Volume 3*. The Prophet Isaiah is a picture of a servant in end times 'Babylon'-U.S.'s wilderness and is watching for the Lord who has hidden his face from his people. Applicable in an end times context, Isaiah says:

And I will wait upon the Lord, that hideth his face from the house of Jacob, and I will look for him. (Is. 8:17)

We are in the last days, close to the time when the Lord will hide his face from Israel. We are told through Isaiah's end times vision (Chapter 21) that 'Babylon' will come under attack at about this same time. God tells Isaiah to set up a watch as follows:

Prepare the table, watch in the watchtower, eat, drink: arise, ye princes, and anoint the shield. For thus hath the Lord said unto me, Go, set a watchman, let him declare what he seeth. (Is. 21:5-6)

Perhaps it is the Prophet 'Ezekiel's persona who is the answer to God's request for a watchman above. An *end times* 'Ezekiel,' repeatedly referred to as 'Son of man,' is also in the wilderness in last days 'Babylon.' We find Ezekiel giving several stark prophetic warning signs to the house of Israel for these last days according to God's instructions for him as follows:

Son of man, I have made thee a watchman unto the house of Israel: therefore hear the word at my mouth, and give them warning from me. (Ez. 3:17)

End times 'Ezekiel' is a watchman for the entire house of Israel; thus, his words are particularly applicable for those in the country of Israel as well as for those in 'Babylon'-U.S. including Israel's last days 'northern kingdom' within. He gives specific warnings about coming war, famine, etc.

We see in scripture how effective prophetic 'watching' is many times accompanied by warnings, including in these last days. Similar to Ezekiel, Jeremiah was obviously a watchman in his day with a strong warning message communicated on behalf of God. Jeremiah warned his people because they preferred foreign gods, wicked ways and would not take heed of God's warnings. Jeremiah's prophecies also carried strong and direct application for these end times. The following warning through Jeremiah was given within a clear last days context:

Also, I set watchmen over you, saying, Hearken to the sound of the trumpet. But they said, we will not hearken. (Jer. 6:17)

In terms of how watching and warning applies to end times prophet-like, biblical servants, 'Jacob' is a God-appointed messenger who operates in a similar manner, capacity and spirit as Jeremiah did in his day. In Chapter 6, I will describe end times 'David' in more detail below who raises a "banner" to the world about the anti-Christ Chaldean kingdom war and their persecution of God's people.

End times watchmen described through a few Minor Prophets

Just as is the case with the Major Prophets above, the Minor Prophets Micah, Hosea and Habakkuk in particular also foretold of end times watchmen. Micah and Hosea were both contemporaries of Isaiah with last days prophecies for the whole house of Israel despite living in the time of the kingdom that was newly divided between Judah and the northern kingdom. The timing of Habakkuk's prophecy is less certain, although it is thought by some to be around the time of Jeremiah (ref: Bible Hub). Like Jeremiah's words, his was given for the house of Judah prior to the Babylonian invasion. Regardless, most importantly, Habakkuk's prophetic vision is for an "appointed time (and) speaks of the end," which has significant importance in these end times.

We are indeed in the day of the watchman that was described by the Prophet Micah due to the disobedience of the house of Israel. Prophetic words through Micah tell us about the Lord's controversy with his people, including in a context for these last days. The Lord asked Micah to plead with them about their violence, deceit and wickedness.

If you are awake and watching in our current day, and if you can understand the signs of the last days and of the end of the age, then you will relate with God pleading with his people as well as the Prophet Micah's laments about finding "no cluster of first ripe fruits" and how "the good man is perished out of the earth" (Mic. 7:1-2). Note Micah's complaint in the following verses and how he says that he will watch and wait, similar to his contemporary Isaiah in the section above:

The best of them is as a brier: the most upright is sharper than a thorn hedge: the day of thy watchmen and thy visitation cometh; now shall be their perplexity…Therefore I will look unto the Lord; I will wait for the God of my salvation: my God will hear me. (Mic. 7:4,7)

God also addressed Micah's contemporary, the Prophet Hosea, while observing that his people had "transgressed my covenant" and "trespassed against my law." God pointed out to Hosea the same kind of sin and corruption as that which was lamented above by Micah. This is the same time about which we are told that a particular end times servant who is a watchman for the house of Israel in Ephraim walks with God but that he finds that the "prophet is a snare of a fowler in all his ways…" (Hos. 9:8). This is likely a picture of an end times servant in 'Babylon'-U.S. Through Hosea God warned that his house of Israel will be punished via an enemy invasion from outside of the country. Here, God said the following in and end times context:

Set the trumpet to thy mouth. He shall come as an eagle against the house of the Lord, because they have transgressed my covenant, and trespassed against my law. (Hos. 8:1)

While God mentions the "house of the Lord" here, this is still a prophecy that includes his last days 'northern kingdom.' I will show in *Volume 2* how the last days country of Israel and the last days 'northern kingdom' closely mirror each other in terms of prophetic events to come.

To this point, in considering the same kind of end times disobedience and coming punishment on God's house of Israel, specifically in the country of Israel, the prophecy of Habakkuk showed him as a distressed figure crying out to the Lord about strife, contention and violence. Habakkuk's complaint was as follows:

Therefore the law is slacked, and judgment doth never go forth: for the wicked doth compass about the righteous; therefore wrong judgment proceedeth. (Hab. 1:4)

God replied to Habakkuk how he will perform a work of punishment, raising up the anti-Christ Chaldeans, a "bitter and hasty" nation, who are an instrument of God's judgment against his people. In the midst of a picture of widespread destruction and persecution by them (also applying for the last days), Habakkuk pledged that he would watch:

I will stand upon my watch, and set me upon the tower, and will watch to see what he will say unto me, and what I shall answer when I am reproved. (Hab. 2:1)

Jesus Christ's last days lost sheep have among them servants like 'David' and 'Jacob' (see Chapters 5 and 6) who are last days Habakkuk-types and are also like the children of Issachar, a tribe alongside Judah on the east side of the Tabernacle about whom scripture says had an "understanding of the times" in their day. These are current day watchmen who will continue to keep an eye on how God will do his work in these end times.

Watchmen's warnings finally heeded

Once there is an awakening in today's 'northern kingdom' of Israel, not to mention war, famine, etc. there will be an exodus out of 'Babylon's "system." They will finally heed the warning that they did not hear as given in Jeremiah's words in the section above. In the midst of Day of the Lord terrors, Israel's watchmen and messengers will strongly and loudly encourage this exodus. Specifically, we read again in Jeremiah:

For there shall be a day, that the watchmen upon the mount Ephraim shall cry, Arise ye, and let us go up to Zion unto the Lord our God. (Jer. 31:6)

This represents watchmen repeating the words of God given in scripture to "flee" and to "come out of her," referring to leaving world Babylon's dark spiritual kingdom of which the U.S. is a part.

Prophetic Messengers

In addition to watchmen, Israel in these last days should listen for the Lord's prophetic messengers who are biblical servants communicating the signs of the times. In *Volume 3*, I provide a series about end times prophecy discerned from scripture from the days of Moses. Even in this ancient scripture, God foretells of a particular end times servant-prophet who will be raised up to deliver God's message to his people as follows:

For the Lord thy God hath chosen him out of all thy tribes, to stand to minister in the name of the Lord, him and his sons forever. The Lord thy God will raise up unto thee a Prophet from the midst of thee, of thy brethren, like unto me; unto him ye shall hearken; I will raise them up a Prophet from among their brethren, like unto thee, and will put my words in his mouth; and he shall speak unto them all that I shall command him. (Deut. 18:5,15,18)

In considering specific last days prophets, we have the Lord's Holy Spirit himself in the person of the 'Comforter' or 'Restrainer' about whom we are told will demonstrate the sin of the world, will bring judgment on evil, and will also perform the following duties:

- Testify of and glorify Jesus Christ as the one and only true God (Jn. 15:26, 16:14)

- Serve as a teacher and reminder of the words of Jesus Christ (Jn. 14:26)

- Take from what is of Jesus (and the Father) and make it known (Jn. 16:14-15)

You may be reminded here about the Two Witnesses who will testify of Jesus Christ as described in the book of Revelation. These will prophesy to the world during the first half of the final "week of years" at the end of the age. These will also be obvious prophetic messengers of the Lord, referred to as follows:

And I will give power unto my two witnesses, and they shall prophesy a thousand two hundred and threescore days, clothed in sackcloth. These are the two olive trees, and the two candlesticks standing before the God of the earth. (Rev. 11:3-4)

Similarly, we are told about the last days servant 'Jacob's role as a God-appointed messenger and a "light to the Gentiles." God tells 'Jacob,' "thou shalt be as my mouth." Jacob himself observes, "And he hath made my mouth like a sharp sword…" (Jer. 49:2). Recall here what God told Jeremiah, who in some ways represents end times 'Jacob':

Say not, I am a child: for thou shalt go to all that I shall send thee, and whatsoever I command thee thou shalt speak. (Jer. 1:7)

Along these same lines, Jesus spoke of a last days Elijah-type servant figure for whom 'Jacob' is also a candidate. This is a figure who is also similar to John the Baptist and who will encourage people to repent and to prepare for the return of Jesus. The following verses, the first in the words of Jesus, refer to this servant:

And Jesus answered and said unto them, Elias truly shall first come, and restore all things. (Matt. 17:11)

Behold, I will send my messenger, and he shall prepare the way before me: and the Lord, whom ye seek, shall suddenly come to his temple, even the messenger of the covenant, whom ye delight in: behold, he shall come, saith the Lord of hosts. (Mal. 3:1)

Behold, I will send you Elijah the prophet before the coming of the great and dreadful day of the Lord: And he shall turn the heart of the fathers to the children, and the heart of the children to their fathers, lest I come and smite the earth with a curse. (Mal. 4:5-6)

Notice that these verses refer to an *end times* biblical figure who will be present *before* Jesus' return and will *prepare* the way before him. Perhaps there is also a tie-in of this servant back to the two witnesses referred to above.

Bearers and Recipients of God's Promises

Many of God's end times biblical servants are recipients of his ancient promises. Some will inherit his promises for his ruling scepter, the priesthood, and his inheritance including his people and land.

It is amazing that we live in the end times during which we will see God's ancient promises begin to be fulfilled (again), even prior to the Millennial Kingdom. Last days biblical characters likely living among us today will begin to assume these positions. God will do this for his name's sake and to make a point to the world that he alone is God. He will put down those in the existing, proud, idol-worshiping house of Israel and will instead raise up his chosen inheritance. The following verse about God's chosen king who will eventually serve Jesus, the King of Kings, according to his covenant is just one example of this:

I will overturn, overturn, overturn, it: and it shall be no more, until he come whose right it is; and I will give it him. (Ez. 21:27)

It is furthermore amazing to consider that many or all of God's chosen servants among his righteous remnant inheritance will once again gather in the wilderness, this time likely in 'Babylon'-U.S. during the Day of the Lord, prior to their return to the land of Israel.

Promise to end times 'David' and the Levites

To begin, in his end times role prior to the Kingdom 'David' is "the Branch" who raises a banner or a signal to the world about anti-Christ Chaldean persecution and its evil kingdom's plans. His will be another voice that will facilitate the aforementioned exodus of God's people out of world 'Babylon's Chaldean system.

In Chapter 6, I will address end times 'David' as a 'Zerubbabel'-type figure who will build the temple and will receive the unbelievable honor of introducing Jesus for the Kingdom. We see his involvement in building the temple as follows:

And speak unto him, saying, Thus speaketh the Lord of hosts, saying, Behold the man whose name is the Branch; and he shall grow up out of his place, and he shall build the temple of the Lord. (Zech. 6:12)

He will be the Davidic Prince who will rule in service to Jesus and as a shepherd for God's people in the Millennial Kingdom. As you would expect, Prince 'David' will reign in righteousness. This will be in direct contrast to the vast corruption among world leaders that is uncovered in the last days. His reign will fulfill God's original promise given directly to King David and even signaled prior to this in Moses' prophetic vision about Judah when Moses declared, "The sceptre shall not depart from Judah, nor a lawgiver from between his feet..." (Gen. 49:10). Meanwhile, just a couple of examples in scripture of God's covenant promise for a Davidic king in the end times and continuing forever are as follows:

The Lord hath sworn in truth unto David; he will not turn from it; Of the fruit of thy body will I set upon thy throne. If thy children will keep my covenant and my testimony that I shall teach them, their children shall also sit upon thy throne for evermore. (Ps. 132:11-12)

His seed also will I make to endure forever, and his throne as the days of heaven. (Ps. 89:29)

When one thinks of King David historically and how he set up his house in Jerusalem, he also re-established the high priests and Levites to resume offerings and worship to God in advance of his son Solomon constructing the temple. Similarly, when end times 'David' builds the temple in preparation for the Millennial Kingdom, the last days Levites will again be alongside. Eternal promises to Aaron's house and the Levites include:

And thou shalt gird them with girdles, Aaron and his sons, and put the bonnets on them: and the priest's office shall be theirs for a perpetual statute: and thou shalt consecrate Aaron and his sons. (Ex. 29:9)

Neither shall the priests the Levites want (lack) a man before me to offer burnt offerings, and to kindle meat offerings, and to do sacrifice continually. (Jer. 33:18)

And he shall have it, and his seed after him, even the covenant of an everlasting priesthood; because he was zealous for his God, and made an atonement for the children of Israel. (Num. 25:13)

It is possible that those from among the end times house of Aaron and other Levites will be among the last days "small flock" remnant that gathers in the wilderness of 'Babylon'-U.S. for a time prior to returning to the land.

Promise to end times 'Jacob'

Next, the covenant promise of the inheritance of Israel is to Jacob, which of course came through his fathers Abraham and Isaac and subsequently through Joseph and Ephraim. End times 'Jacob' will raise up the tribes of Israel in their return. This family of inheritance will start in the wilderness where it is apparent that the house of Israel will begin to take root and grow again.

There are many assurances for end times 'Jacob,' but a few prophetic promises about his inheritance for a people that were given through his forefather, original Jacob, and then through Moses, respectively, in their last words to the house of Joseph (Ephraim) are as follows:

Joseph is a fruitful bough, even a fruitful bough by a well; whose branches run over the wall: Even by the God of thy father, who shall help thee; and by the Almighty, who shall bless thee with blessings of heaven above, blessings of the deep that lieth under, blessings of the breasts, and of the womb. (Gen. 49:22,25)

And of Joseph he said, Blessed of the Lord be his land, for the precious things of heaven, for the dew, and for the deep that coucheth beneath, And for the chief things of the ancient mountains, and for the precious things of the lasting hills, His glory is like the firstling of his bullock, and his horns are like the horns of unicorns: with them he shall push the people together to the ends of the earth: and they are the ten thousands of Ephraim, and they are the thousands of Manasseh. (Deut. 33:13,15,17)

End times 'Jacob' is a Patriarch who will regather the tribes and will receive God's Kingdom's blessings of a people and land on behalf of the heavenly Israel. Just as with the Davidic Prince and the house of Aaron discussed above, 'Jacob' is directly chosen and anointed by God who says, "For the Lord hath chosen Jacob unto himself, and Israel for his peculiar treasure" (Ps. 135:4).

Servants will come from among their own people

In scripture referring to end times servants, such as those discussed in this passage, God makes a special point to emphasize that Israel's leaders will come from among their own people (i.e. from "among thy brethren"). This is logical since these will include many who will be fulfilling positions according to God's original covenant promises to his people. The point about their leaders arising from among them presumably is important because they will have been a people that has been scattered, wandering, persecuted and without knowledge of their Messiah for centuries. Furthermore, they will be wearied because of Day of the Lord terrors. Scripture that reassures Israel about the future and about a leader of their own is as follows:

Then shall the children of Judah and the children of Israel be gathered together, and appoint themselves one head, and they shall come up out of the land: for great shall be the day of Jezreel. (Hos. 1:11)

And it shall come to pass in that day, that I will call my servant Eliakim the son of Hilkiah: And I will clothe him with thy robe, and strengthen him with thy girdle, and I will commit thy government into his hand: and he shall be a father to the inhabitants of Jerusalem, and to the house of Judah. (Is. 22:19-21)

And their nobles shall be of themselves, and their governor shall proceed from the midst of them; and I will cause him to draw near, and he shall approach unto me: for who is this that engaged his heart to approach unto me? saith the Lord. (Jer. 30:21)

Of course, most importantly, it will be Israel's own Messiah, Jesus Christ, who will be on his throne reigning as the King of Kings and Lord of Lords in the midst of these other servants.

End times Fighters and Warriors

In these end times, the spiritual kingdom war is raging. Those who are truly awake can see this. In Chapter 8, I address the last days 'Jacob army' and their righteous role in fighting this war. God's servants such as those named in this passage above are part of the 'Jacob'-Judah remnant. These are the "small flock" remnant who are holy, royal and anointed and who will ultimately earn the designation as overcomers and conquerors.

The following verses show the rhetorical questions God asks that point to his end times servants and their role on the righteous side of this war. These questions are prophetic and along the same lines as the question posed by the Lord that the Prophet Isaiah heard in his heavenly vision. God asked, "Whom shall I send? And who will go for us?" Additional questions by God suggesting his call for an end times servant-warrior include:

Who will rise up for me against the evildoers? Or who will stand up for me against the workers of iniquity? (Ps. 94:16)

Who raised up the righteous man from the east, called him to his foot, gave the nations before him, and made him rule over kings? He gave them as the dust to his sword, and as driven stubble to his bow. (Is. 41:2)

Shall iron break the northern iron and the steel? (Jer. 15:12)

These questions show God making a point to believers and assuring them that in the last days kingdom war, and in the midst of the ensuing darkness, that he has righteous servants who are doing his work.

The most comforting aspect for believers in today's kingdom war is that the Lord himself is on earth and in the war. (See my prior passages in Chapter 3 entitled, *The Lord's Spirit is with us*, for detail). Scripture clearly tells us that the Lord himself is fighting for his people against the anti-Christ enemy.

In addition to fighting for them, the Lord will give his last days servants power to fight for themselves in the kingdom war. They essentially have the same promise from God that he gave to Jeremiah in his day. God told Jeremiah, "And they shall fight against thee; but they shall not prevail against thee; for I am with thee, saith the Lord, to deliver thee" (Jer. 1:19).

The following are verses that show the fighting power that God will give to the 'Jacob army' so that they can defend themselves and eventually defeat the anti-Christ Chaldean kingdom enemy in the quiet, unseen, unconventional war that begins in these last days, even prior to the Day of the Lord:

I have raised up one from the north, and he shall come: from the rising of the sun shall he call upon my name: and he shall come upon princes as upon morter, and as the potter treadeth clay. (Is. 41:25)

By this therefore shall the iniquity of Jacob be purged; and this is all the fruit to take away his sin; when he maketh all the stones of the altar as chalkstones that are beaten in sunder, the groves and images shall not stand up. (Is. 27:9)

Who art thou, O great mountain? Before Zerubbabel thou shalt become a plain: and he shall bring forth the headstone thereof with shoutings, crying, Grace, grace unto it. For who hath despised the day of small things? For they shall rejoice, and shall see the plummet in the hand of Zerubbabel with those seven; they are the eyes of the Lord, which run to and fro through the whole earth. (Zech. 4:7,10)

Thou art my battle axe and weapons of war: for with thee will I break in pieces the nations, and with thee will I destroy kingdoms; And with thee will I break in pieces the horse and his rider; and with thee will I break in pieces the chariot and his rider; With thee also will I break in pieces man and woman; and with thee will I break in pieces old and young; and with thee will I break in pieces the young man and the maid. (Jer. 51:20-22)

You will notice that these end times servants are given incredible power by God, even to the point of bringing down nations and kings in the war versus the anti-Christ kingdom. Of course, it will be Jesus Christ himself who will be the rock that finally crushes the entire evil kingdom at the end of the Day of the Lord. Jesus will be the one who will have saved, redeemed, given power to, and provided victory for his righteous faithful servants in the kingdom war.

~

All faithful believers worldwide should be encouraged in these last days, despite the darkness. Jesus has his appointed faithful servants working by his side in order to defeat his evil adversary and to bring in his glorious Kingdom. I describe this war and these servants in detail in my book, *Biblical End Times, Volume 1.*

4.3 A Judah and House of David Remnant

In upcoming chapters, I will go into some detail about specific last days biblical figures. In this passage, I will examine some additional characteristics of their remnant who will eventually serve in the Millennial Kingdom in the presence of Jesus Christ. These are likely part of the "house of David" and likely others who are part of the saved "remnant" of Judah in the last days. In scripture, a remnant "vine" also appears to describe this group of God's people. In some other cases, terms like "Jerusalem" or "Zion," just like 'Israel' or 'Jacob,' represent actual individuals, in addition to or in lieu of, the broader remnants or physical locations that they represent.

The "(Judah) remnant within a (Judah) remnant" described in this current passage is a group of God's people who will ultimately find their Millennial period existence in the strip of land that stretches from sea to sea (Mediterranean to Dead Sea), just south of the strip of land that will include the main Judah tribal remnant. According to scripture in the book of Ezekiel, this strip of land will include the City of Jerusalem where God's "holy hill" is; that is, Mount Zion where God's sanctuary and temple will be. This is where Jesus Christ will reign and be worshiped.

Why discuss a Judah remnant?

Just as God established a people for himself as represented by Jacob and his 12 tribes, within his people he selected a tribe (Judah), and a remnant of that tribe, to come especially close to him. This is many times described as his own "inheritance" and a people who can be thought of as an "inheritance within an inheritance." They will be a *ruling* people in God's Kingdom, fittingly coming primarily through the 'Davidic' line, but possibly through other lines of Judah as well. They will have the incredible honor of leading a procession through the gates of God's temple itself in their worship and honor of Jesus Christ. The following selected verses refer to this selected remnant:

(After his people's captivity and oppression) *he chose the tribe of Judah, Mount Zion, which he loved. He built his sanctuary like the heights, like the earth that he established forever. He chose David his servant and took him from the sheep pens; from tending the sheep he brought him to be the shepherd of his people Jacob, of Israel his inheritance. (Ps. 78:67)*

As when juice is still found in a cluster of grapes, and men say, 'Don't destroy it, there is yet some good in it,' so will I do on behalf of my servants; I will not destroy them all. I will bring forth descendants from Jacob, and from Judah those who will possess my mountains; my chosen people will inherit them, and there will my servants live. (Is. 65:8)

What sets this remnant apart?

First and foremost, these are God's people who live in the last days that resemble the times of Noah and Lot. They will choose to serve only Jesus Christ and will *not* bow down to the current day foreign god system of Babylon's new world order. They are also similar to Judah's Daniel, Shadrach, Meshach and Abednego who refrained from worshiping these kings and their gods in ancient Babylon. The last days anointed Judah-centric remnant is set apart and distinguished by the following attributes:

- Holy
- Royal
- Righteous and faithful
- Persecuted
- Saved

Each of these attributes describing a Judah-centric remnant that God sets aside for himself in the last days is discussed below.

A Holy People

As rare, true believers with strong faith in Jesus Christ in the end times, this Judah remnant fits the definition of "God's elect." These are servants to whom the Apostle Peter addressed as: "strangers in the world"; "scattered"; "an inheritance that can never perish"; and "chosen according to the foreknowledge of God the Father, through the sanctifying work of the spirit." In speaking about this people in the context of their trust in the rejected cornerstone, Jesus Christ, Peter also said:

But you are a chosen people, a royal priesthood, a holy nation, a people belonging to God." (1 Pet. 2:9)

This Judah remnant also fits the Apostle Paul's description of a people who have the "Spirit of Christ" and who are "heirs of God and co-heirs with Christ." Paul described them as those God *"foreknew and predestined* to be conformed to the likeness of his Son." These are servants who have been "called," "justified," and "glorified," according to the Apostle Paul (Rom. 8:30).

It only stands to reason that a chosen Judah remnant who will be ruling on behalf of Jesus Christ from the temple area in the Millennial Kingdom will possess these holy qualities. In the coming day when God destroys Jerusalem's enemies he says that he will make the house of David to be, "like God, like the Angel of the Lord going before" (Zech. 12:8). This will be the day leading into the Millennial Kingdom when God will pour out a "spirit of grace and supplication" (Zech. 12:10) as well as a cleansing and sanctifying "fountain" on those in the house of David (Zech. 13:1).

The following verses address the house of David's anointing and favor in the context of God setting up Jerusalem/Zion in his heavenly Kingdom.

Pass through the gates! Prepare the way for the people…They will be called the holy people, the Redeemed of the Lord; and you will be called Sought After, the City No Longer Deserted. (Is. 62:10-12)

Additional attributes of Judah's anointed remnant discussed as follows will further support the case that they fit the apostles' descriptions of an "elect" people.

Millennial Royalty

The ruling Judah remnant in the Millennium will serve the King of Kings and Lord of Lords, Jesus Christ. They, themselves, will be given holy and royal distinction. I will discuss the Millennial 'Prince' David in passage to follow; he will preside over an extended royal family. In Jacobs's last prophetic words about his sons in the book of Genesis and about Judah in particular he said, "He (the ruler to whom the staff and scepter belong- i.e. 'David') will tether his donkey to a *vine*, his colt to be the choicest branch; he will wash his garments in wine, his robes in the blood of grapes" (Gen. 49:11).

Here, I will introduce another key end times figure, the 'Daughter of Zion.' She will embody all of the attributes discussed in this passage that describe the ruling Judah remnant for the Millennium (i.e. holy, royal, righteous, faithful, persecuted, and redeemed). That is, she will embody and directly represent the living temple of Jesus Christ. Her name 'Zion' is even used in a figurative sense to represent the royal fortified palace; the gates of the holy temple are also frequently referred to in scripture as the "Gates of the Daughter of Zion." She will be a Matriarch figure in the Kingdom who is "no longer deserted" but instead is blessed with the royal family of Judah.

The 'Daughter of Zion' will have many companions and will preside over an extended Judaic family, which will ultimately fulfill God's covenant promise to David that his descendants will be, "as countless as the stars of the sky" (Jer. 33:22). Royal companions of the 'Daughter of Zion' will include "honored women" who are "daughters of kings" and sometimes are referred to in scripture as the "daughter(s) of Jerusalem." She will also inherit holy sons who will be princes "throughout the land" (Ps. 45:16). In one of his prophetic Psalms, King David prayed for and envisioned a heavenly, prosperous family in Zion saying, "That our sons may be as plants grown up in their youth; that our daughters may be as corner stones, polished after the similitude of a palace" (Ps. 144:12).

Several verses speaking about the Millennial royal family and about an appointed time that is set for the 'Daughter of Zion' are as follows:

Who will arise and have compassion on Zion, for it is time to show favor to her; the appointed time has come. For her stones are dear to your servants... (Ps. 102:13-14)

Can a country be born in a day? Or a nation brought forth in a moment? Yet no sooner is Zion in labor than she gives birth to her children...rejoice with Jerusalem and be glad for her, all you who love her... (Is. 66:8,10)

And of Zion it will be said, 'This one and that one were born in her: and the highest himself will establish her.' The Lord will write in the register of the peoples; 'This one was born in Zion.' (Ps. 87:5-6)

We are told that the Matriarch 'Zion' will be the bride of the Lord. The Lord says to Zion, "so shall thy sons (also) marry thee."

A Righteous and Faithful People

This holy, royal Judah "remnant" that God sets aside for himself, not surprisingly, will be shown to be a particularly *righteous* remnant. As noted in the Isaiah verse (65:8) earlier in this passage they will represent a few grapes on the vine in the last days who are spared by God as a result of their faith and obedience. Our end times figures, albeit not perfect, including 'Jacob' (who comes through the "waters of Judah"), 'David', the 'Daughter of Zion,' the 'Daughter(s) of Jerusalem,' and additional sons of God will ultimately be honored and rewarded by God for their righteousness. God says, "For Zion's sake I will not keep silent, for Jerusalem's sake I will not remain quiet, till her righteousness shines out like the dawn, her salvation like a blazing torch. The nations will see your righteousness and all kings your glory" (Is. 62:1).

The following verses clearly point to a righteous, faithful remnant of God's chosen people who inherit his land and his kingdom:

Then will all your people be righteous and they will possess the land forever. They are the shoot I have planted, the work of my hands, for the display of my splendor. (Is. 60:21)

The righteous will flourish like a palm tree, they will grow like a cedar of Lebanon; planted in the house of the Lord, they will flourish in the courts of our God... (Ps. 92:12)

For the Lord loves the just and will not forsake his faithful ones. They will be protected forever...the righteous will inherit the land and dwell in it forever... (Ps. 37:28)

A People who Face Persecution in the Last Days

It is clear that this Judah remnant suffers extreme persecution for their faith in the last days due to their righteous battle versus the anti-Christ Chaldeans. As God's people who represent particular bloodlines of interest to Chaldean rulers, these people have been "sold." God prophetically observed, "And what do I have here: For my people have been taken away for nothing, and those who rule them mock" (Ps. 52:5). Due to illegal tactics used by the Chaldeans (i.e. surveillance, tracking, following, stalking, mocking, harassment, racketeering, etc.), this Judah remnant (and possibly others) will be imprisoned and held in captivity, in plain sight, likely even in 'Babylon'-U.S.

Intense persecution by the anti-Christ Chaldeans will cause God's people to fully turn back to him and to cry out for his help in the last days. Even as a righteous remnant, God's people are pushed to the point of fully seeking him for forgiveness and deliverance as part of his vine that is persecuted, stripped and decimated at the hands of the anti-Christ Chaldean army. His remnant will pray similar to:

O God, the nations have invaded your inheritance...they have devoured Jacob and destroyed his homeland...Help us, O God our savior, for the glory of your name; deliver us and forgive our sins for your names's sake. Why should the nations say, There is no God? (Ps. 79:1,7,9-10)

But now you have rejected and humbled us; you no longer go out with our armies. You made us retreat before the enemy...you gave us up to be devoured like sheep and have scattered us among the nations. (Ps. 44:9-11)

Restore us, O God; make your face shine upon us, that we may be saved...Watch over this vine, the root your right hand has planted, the son you have raised up for yourself. Your vine is cut down...let your hand rest on the man at your right hand, the son of man you have

*raised up for yourself. Then we will not turn away from you; revive us
and we will call on your name.* (Ps. 80:7,16-18)

Apostles as servant-examples

In these last days it has been prophesied and is evident that God's
people are an "object of cursing" (Zech. 8:13). True faithful believers
are the only ones standing in the gap between the ultimate coming of
Jesus Christ's Kingdom and an interim new world order led by the
Anti-Christ. Here, we cannot forget about the prophets and apostles
who suffered for the sake of serving the one true God of Israel, Jesus
Christ. They were forerunners who served as examples for the Lord's
servants in the end times, demonstrating that there can be no obtaining
God's Kingdom without facing persecution. We learn from the
Apostle Paul:

*For your sake we face death all day long; we are considered as sheep
to be slaughtered.* (Rom. 8:36)

*Wherein I suffer trouble, as an evil doer, even unto bonds; but the
word of God is not bound. Therefore I endure all things for the elect's
sakes, that they may also obtain the salvation which is in Christ Jesus
with eternal glory.* (2 Tim. 2:9-10)

A People Delivered from and Saved out of Persecution

Due to their persecution Judah's and the house of David's anointed
remnant in the last days is referred to several times as a group of
"survivors." They must fend for themselves, relying solely on God
against an anti-Christ Chaldean army onslaught. In *Volumes 2 and 3*,
I will describe the Chaldeans' tremendous power in more detail and
that they are a "law unto themselves"; this Judah-centric remnant
comes to a realization, "the help of man is worthless" (Ps. 60:11).

While this remnant is a chosen people, an inheritance through God's
covenant promise, they have to *earn* their right to the Kingdom
through demonstrating faith and righteousness, and by taking a stand
against the full weight of the anti-Christ Chaldean evil empire. I am

personally reminded of the verse, "To everyone who has been given much, much is demanded" (Lk. 12:48). They will ultimately find that the persecution they suffer will be entirely insignificant when compared to their inheritance in God's Kingdom.

Otherwise, in return for their longsuffering and perseverance God offers this Judah remnant an escape in the final days. Scripture says many times that the Lord will save Zion and that her people will escape the "sword among the nations." Judah's anointed remnant and the restraining force of the Holy Spirit will have to be physically and/or supernaturally removed from their current place in societies (mostly 'Babylon'-U.S.) in order to be saved. This *appears* to be represented in scripture as:

- And now ye know what withholdeth that he might be revealed in his time...only he who now letteth will let, until he be taken out of the way. (2 Thess. 2:6-7)

- 'Jacob' being saved out of the time of "Jacob's trouble" (Jer. 30:7)

- God's people entering their rooms, shutting their doors until his wrath has passed by (Is. 26:20)

- "Who are these that fly along like clouds, like doves to their nests?" (Is. 60:8)

When this Judah remnant is saved from their real and present physical danger they will enter into a place of God's protection. This is an answer to King David's prophetic prayer for his people, "May the Lord answer you when you are in distress, may the name of the God of Jacob protect you. May he send help from the sanctuary and grant you support from Zion" (Ps. 20:1).

God promises in his Word that 'Jacob' will no longer be afraid and in addressing Judah and 'Israel' he has foretold, "I will save you and you will be a blessing" (Zech. 8:9). He also promised a time for them through the Prophet Zephaniah when, "The Lord, the King of Israel is with you, never again will you fear any harm" (Zeph. 3:15).

Righteousness and faith will prevail against the Anti-Christ Chaldeans

In Chapter 6, I will discuss 'David's battle with the anti-Christ Chaldean army as a representation and microcosm of a broader battle of God's people versus this Satanic army that God brings to purify and refine his people in the end times. This is an "accusing" and lying army that targets and disparages God's people and relies on invoking their feelings of guilt, fear or shame so that they will surrender, join the Chaldeans and renounce their faith.

Judah's righteous remnant will be shown to have survived this severe, purifying "test" of being schemed against, judged and accused by the Chaldean army; they will be recognized for demonstrating true, strong faith in Jesus Christ as the *only* God with *true* authority to both charge and forgive. This remnant will uphold the specific Judah tribal trait of being warriors in spiritual battle and earn the Apostle Paul's designation of being "more than conquerors" in Jesus Christ (Rom. 8:36).

Scripture tells us that Judah's holy remnant will ultimately be rewarded by living in "tents of righteousness." They will be given peace in his Kingdom. This is another answer to one of King David's prophetic supplications, this time for the "peace of Jerusalem." He wrote, "Pray for the peace of Jerusalem: May those who love you be secure. May there be peace within your walls and security within your citadels" (Ps. 122:6-7). There is other refreshing scripture about borders that are drawn for God's people for which the enemy will not be able to cross.

In the meantime, King David summed up:

The Lord sits enthroned over the flood; the Lord is enthroned as King forever. The Lord gives strength to his people; the Lord blesses his people with peace. (Ps. 29:10-11)

Not surprisingly, God's city Zion/Jerusalem will be called the "City of Truth" (Zech. 8:3), the "City of Righteousness" (Is. 1:27), and the "Faithful City" (Is. 1:27). Peace for the Lord's anointed Judah-centric remnant will finally come by being present with the Lord and being in the absence of wickedness. The picture of God's people's deliverance presented through Nahum reminds us, "for the wicked shall no more pass through thee; he is utterly cut off" (Nah. 1:15).

~

In conclusion, the establishment of Judah's and house of David's remnant as a ruling party in God's Millennial Kingdom will prove God's character as a just, merciful and loving God- a sovereign, all-powerful God who always keeps his covenant promises to his people when they return to him.

While this Judah remnant will be given special blessings in his Kingdom there will be countless others who will enjoy a heavenly Millennial Kingdom existence as a result of their true faith and salvation in and through the Lord Jesus Christ. I discuss the path back to the Lord's heavenly Kingdom in my books, *Biblical End Times, Volumes 1 and 2.*

Chapter 5.

End Times 'Jacob'

Passages from Lion's Lair provided in this chapter include:

5.1 'Jacob'- An End Times Servant (Part 1)

5.2 'Jacob'- An End Times Servant (Part 2)

5.1 'Jacob'- An End Times Servant (Part 1)

As Isaiah wrote from his current day perspective of coming captivity of the nation of Judah at the hands of the Babylonians, among other things, he also provided an unmistakable end-times vision for the house of Israel that is applicable for our current last days time period. A significant amount of scripture in the book of Isaiah, including parts of Chapters 41 through 53, is dedicated to discussing God's chosen end-times servant, 'Jacob,' who comes from the "waters of Judah."

God reassures 'Jacob' not to fear in a war that is waged against him by a powerful enemy- the last days anti-Christ Chaldeans- who serve the adversary's false gods and idols, and engage in numerous occult rituals, sorceries, and wicked acts. They target the saints with wicked acts.

For reference, these minions are part of the enemy who is also referred to as the "daughter of Babylon," the queen of kingdoms (Is. 47:5). This anti-Christ Chaldean criminal mob is allowed by God to wage a silent, behind-the-scenes, spiritual war against the house of Israel (apparently worldwide), especially in the last days. According to scripture in Isaiah this is clearly a different kind of war and one that cannot be well-understood or foreseen by people in the last days.

In the big picture, God's people in the house of Israel including 'Jacob' are oppressed by these enemies and taken captive in this war. They are also plundered and looted (Is. 42:22). Through this the worldwide house of Israel is spiritually tested and refined. At least part of this remnant suffers from "hard bondage" at the time when God raises up the Chaldean enemy.

There ultimately turns out to be good news for 'Jacob' and the house of Israel *remnant* in this last days war. 'Jacob' manages to lead an end-times army of sorts who fight back in this silent, unconventional-type war.

(I'll let you, the reader, ponder how a silent, unconventional yet large-scale war might take place in the current day; as a clue, the current day Chaldeans engage in illegal, high tech surveillance activities)

The World will Witness the Victory of End Times 'Jacob' and the House of Israel

'Jacob' himself and a "small flock" *remnant* of the house of Israel will achieve a huge public victory over their dark, secret enemies- a victory that the whole world will see and rejoice in as shocking truth is revealed. Given the war will have been secret until the end this will be a sudden, "unforeseen" catastrophe and disaster that will ultimately come upon the house of 'Jacob's enemy (Is. 47:11).

At this time, likely "all things" including Israel's holy "small flock" *remnant* will be revealed worldwide. They will eventually be exiled, regathered and re-established in their restored, rebuilt land (Is. 44:26) for the beginning of their heavenly Millennial Kingdom. Israel will rejoice and acknowledge their one true God of old, whereas they had largely failed to do so prior to this last days event. They will see God's grace; he will forgive their transgressions (Is. 44:22), establish their righteousness, and give them eternal salvation (Is. 45:17, 51:6). Every knee will bow and every tongue will confess (Is. 45:23) by Christ. The Lord Jesus Christ will return to reign in Zion/Jerusalem for all eyes to see.

Descriptors of End Times 'Jacob'

Scripture from parts of several chapters in the book of Isaiah that are used for this passage (i.e. Chapters 42, 49, 50, 52 and 53) are referred to by some as "servant songs." These songs are specific to an *end-times* biblical 'Jacob' figure who wins (only by God's power and help) the war described above for himself and the house of Israel's remnant. According to these servant songs the following characteristics can be attributed to 'Jacob' in this end-times war: (Chapters of the book of Isaiah given in parentheses)

- Is persecuted, oppressed, afflicted and "crushed"; a "guilt offering" (52, 53)

- Is despised and rejected, a "man of sorrows" (49, 52, 53)

- Is chosen and delighted in by God (42, 49, 53)

- Receives instruction, knowledge, and awakening directly from the Lord (50, 53)

- Offers himself as a personal sacrifice, does not "hide his face" (50, 53)

- Walks in righteousness (42, 50, 53)

- Brings justice to the nations/earth (42, 49, 50, 53)

- Is a "light for the Gentiles" (42, 49)

- Assists in freeing captives (42)

- Restores tribes of Jacob/Israel from afar (49)

- Opens eyes that are blind (esp. unbelieving Israel) to the secret of lawlessness, iniquity (42, 49, 52)

- Is personally redeemed, restored, and vindicated (49, 50, 53)

- Is rewarded by God (49, 52, 53)

(Note: Even for those who believe Isaiah Chapter 53 might not be applicable to a figure other than Jesus Christ, or Christ's first coming in-person, the above themes from this Chapter about 'Jacob' still remain as described elsewhere in the chapters of Isaiah noted. Overall, there is good reason to believe that scripture in Isaiah 53 also speaks about an end-times non-deity servant of Jesus Christ.)

Based on what we know now about end-times 'Jacob' as described above in the book of Isaiah, and elsewhere in scripture, he appears to be a candidate for the type of "overcomer" that is mentioned several times in the book of Revelation.

To close, I will repeat how unusual it is that pastors, prophecy experts, and other bible-believing leaders of our time do not discuss such a significant figure in the scripture. Perhaps it is due to the same reason that end-times 'Jacob' appears to be hidden (Is. 49:2-3) until the final event described above. After all, those who are truly awake realize how dangerous it is in our current times to speak out about what we know is biblically true and is going to come to pass. So, believe it or not, some pastors or teachers are actually prevented from discussing this type of material. There are likely many others who have taken secret oaths, and as a result, are blinded as to the truth about coming events in the last days.

In the following passage (Part 2), I will describe end times 'Jacob's character and his activities in more detail. Note that I also discuss 'Jacob's story in detail in my books, *Biblical End Times, Volumes 1 and 2*.

5.2 'Jacob'- An End Times Servant (Part 2)

In Part 1 of *'Jacob'- An End Times Servant*, I wrote a relatively short, high-level summary of 'Jacob's persona according to prophetic scripture.

The theme of his last days story is a familiar one in scripture and one that is a picture for what will happen, or is soon to come, for the house of Israel. (Note: Thus, keep in mind that Jacob's story herein is also a picture for God's last days vineyard and remnant of the house of Israel as a whole, albeit on a slightly different timeline.)

Last days 'Jacob' is oppressed, taken captive and persecuted by the anti-Christ Chaldean "mob"-army. He is somewhat of an informal leader of a righteous Judah-centric remnant that appears to reside in current day 'Babylon'-U.S. and battles against the Chaldeans and 'Jacob' and his remnant will ultimately receive deliverance directly from God. This likely coincides with the time that they are told to "flee" Babylon. 'Jacob' will subsequently be established as a patriarch in God's Millennial Kingdom at the time of his people's regathering.

So, last days 'Jacob' who comes through the "waters of Judah" is a holy remnant member of the original patriarch, Jacob. Through last days 'Jacob,' Israel's remnant vine will be delivered, restored and set up in the land promised to Abraham, Isaac and Jacob in ancient days. While only a remnant will survive and return, 'Jacob's inheritance and seed as 12 tribes will once again grow to be as the "dust of the earth" in the Kingdom to come as was also originally promised by God.

In this passage, I will provide more in-depth detail about last days 'Jacob' according to scripture. I will do so within the following sections entitled:

- God's chosen servant
- God's battle warrior
- A leader and patriarch in God's kingdom
- Victory for 'Jacob' and Glory for God

Content within each of these sections about last days 'Jacob' is given below.

God's Chosen Servant in the End Times

God addresses last days 'Jacob,' 'Israel,' directly and personally in prophetic scripture many times as "my servant." God also refers to him as, "my called" and "my elect." Just a couple of examples in scripture are as follows:

Behold my servant, whom I uphold; mine elect, in whom my soul delighteth; I have put my spirit upon him… (Is. 42:1)

But now thus saith the Lord that created thee, O Jacob, and he that formed thee, O Israel, Fear not…I have called thee by thy name; thou art mine. (Is. 43:1)

Note in the latter verse above God says, "Fear not." God is alluding to 'Jacob's battle with the anti-Christ Chaldeans. In scripture, God tells 'Jacob' not to fear several times and directly promises, "I will help thee," more than once. God himself provides divine, sovereign protection to 'Jacob'; this is summarized in the following verses:

Yet now hear, O Jacob my servant; and Israel, whom I have chosen: Thus saith the Lord that made thee, and formed thee from the womb, which will help thee; Fear not, O Jacob, my servant; and thou, Jesurun, whom I have chosen. (Is. 44:1-2)

Remember these, O Jacob and Israel; for thou art my servant: I have formed thee; thou art my servant: O Israel, thou shalt not be forgotten of me. (Is. 44:21)

End times 'Jacob' and his remnant will "not be forgotten" by God because of his eternal covenant promises to Israel's forefathers.

God's Battle Warrior

End times 'Jacob' is God's battle warrior versus the anti-Christ Chaldeans. "Warrior" in this sense does not imply a warrior in terms of conventional warfare but rather in the sense of spiritual warfare and righteousness that is required to sustain, endure and to ultimately reveal light and truth in the midst of the mysterious sea of anti-Christ Chaldean iniquity and lawlessness that is present in our last days society.

A 'David versus Goliath'-type battle

Perhaps the best prophetic illustration of 'Jacob's last days 'David-and-Goliath'-type battle versus the Chaldeans is given through the Prophet Amos who receives end times visions from God. Amos was frightened by a couple of very troubling visions that represented the widespread destruction done by the end times Chaldeans. The first vision included locusts stripping the land of its crops- i.e. God's people. The second vision was that of a judgment by fire, which consumed "the deep," and devoured the land. Both visions, in general, represent the anti-Christ Chaldeans carrying out God's judgment on his disobedient people.

A disturbed, frightened Amos interceded for God's people and asked for his forgiveness on their behalf. Here, Amos was also especially concerned about whether God would even leave a remnant. Similar to the Prophet Ezekiel's observation and question asked more than once of God about his coming judgment (i.e. "Will you completely destroy the remnant of Israel?"), Amos asked specifically about end times 'Jacob' twice, saying:

By whom shall Jacob arise? For he is small. (Am. 7:2,5)

Amos foresaw that last days 'Jacob' would not stand a chance by himself. 'Jacob' will be very small versus the enormous, powerful Chaldeans. God responded to Amos that he would not destroy 'Jacob.'

One interesting observation in Amos' first vision of the locusts was that he said these destroying locusts will be found at the beginning of the "second crop" or "latter growth." This crop is quite possibly representative of the "fig tree generation," addressed by Jesus, which will "certainly not pass away" before all last days events take place (Mk. 13:28, Matt. 24:32). There are strong indications that the last days generation including 'Jacob' is the same as this fig tree generation.

Turning the other cheek

'Jacob' is held captive, oppressed and is persecuted in the last days. He likely endures the brunt of the full gamut of Chaldean tactics. I will describe, especially in *Writings of Lion's Lair, Volume 3*, that Chaldeans "sharpen their tongues like snakes" (Ps. 140:3), and seek to destroy people by accusation and slander. Lies they use also serve to "justify" their crimes against others and to motivate their troops. As a result of these tactics scripture says that 'Jacob' is: "despised"; "abhorred by the nation(s)"; "rejected"; and a "man of sorrows." Through Isaiah we learn about 'Jacob':

I gave my back to the smiters, and my cheeks to them that plucked off the hair: I hid not my face from shame and spitting. (Is. 50:6)

'Jacob' endures these mob attacks by "turning the other cheek," as he says through Isaiah, which we know is an instruction also originally given by Jesus. Chaldean smiting and harassing are only the beginning of their many attacks and assaults. The full gamut of their criminal tactics destroys a targeted person over time. The "desolation" of 'Jacob' described below is a result of the cumulative effects over time of anti-Christ Chaldean captivity and persecution:

For they have devoured Jacob, and laid waste his dwelling place. (Ps. 79:7)

...for they have eaten up Jacob, and devoured him, and consumed him, and have made his habitation desolate. (Jer. 10:25)

As I mentioned earlier, end times 'Jacob' can be considered to be a picture of what happens to much of the remnant of the house of Israel. So, this kind of desolation as a result of persecution will likely happen to others who are of 'Israel' and of course numerous Jesus Christ-believers in the last days.

'Jacob' – an intercessor

While end times 'Jacob' is an heir to a Millennial Kingdom inheritance and recipient of God's promise he must earn his way. His persecution is not only God's punishment for his own transgressions but it appears that 'Jacob' takes on persecution for the sins of his people/nation of Israel overall. God asks, "Is Israel a servant? Is he a homeborn slave? Why is he spoiled?" (Jer. 2:4), referring to 'Jacob's captivity at the hands of the Chaldeans. Jacob's intercession for his people's transgressions is apparent in the following verses:

He was taken from prison and from judgment: and who shall declare his generation? For he was cut off out of the land of the living: for the transgression of my people was he stricken. (Is. 53:8)

For the transgression of Jacob is all this, and for the sins of the house of Israel. What is the transgression of Jacob? is it not Samaria? And what are the high places of Judah? Are they not Jerusalem? (Mic. 1:5)

Who gave Jacob for a spoil, and Israel to the robbers? Did not the Lord, he against whom we have sinned? For they would not walk in his ways, neither were they obedient unto his law. (Is. 42:24)

'Jacob' will no doubt be familiar with and led by the example set by his Lord and Savior, Jesus Christ, who took on persecution and suffering for the sins of all people who call on his name. Last days 'Jacob' himself becomes an oppressed, persecuted slave of the Chaldeans as a result of his people serving other gods and their related transgressions. Many of 'Jacob's people in the house of Israel are even a part of the very Chaldean army that persecutes him. God finally hands most of them over to these false gods. As I will describe in detail in *Volume 2*, the original Babylon scenario repeats in the last days.

'Jacob' given strength

I mentioned at the outset of this section how Jacob must possess spiritual strength, an ability to remain righteous, and an endurance to withstand repeated attacks by the anti-Christ Chaldean "mob." God himself gives 'Jacob' strength to remain in the battle. You may recall the seer Balaam's ancient visions applicable to the last days that he relayed to Balak instead of cursing Israel as he was asked to do. In Balaam's visions (Numbers, Chapters 23-24), he foresaw 'Jacob' in the end times as being blessed with God's favor and as:

- Having the "strength of a unicorn"

- Lifting himself up as a "young lion to his prey"

- "Piercing" his enemies with his arrows

God will give 'Jacob' strength and weapons to use in his unconventional, end times, David-versus-Goliath-type battle versus the anti-Christ Chaldeans in the last days.

A foreshadow of victory

The Prophet Micah addressed the last days time period referring to, "the day God visits," and speaking from the perspective of a future end times figure, likely 'Jacob,' he said:

Rejoice not against me, O mine enemy: when I fall, I shall arise; when I sit in darkness, the Lord shall be a light unto me. I will bear the indignation of the Lord, because I have sinned against him, until he plead my cause, and execute judgment for me: he will bring me forth to the light, and I shall behold his righteousness. (Mic. 7:8-9)

'Jacob's own cause is one of righteousness, which I discuss in more detail in a section below. Not only is this verse above a warning to 'Jacob's enemies, but Balaam's oft-repeated vision (of Israel's blessing) is another warning to these enemies. Balaam observed about

'Jacob' and 'Israel, "Blessed is he that Blesseth thee, cursed is he that curseth thee" (Num. 24:9).

A Leader and Patriarch

In addition to providing a victory to 'Jacob' (and his remnant) against the anti-Christ Chaldeans, as discussed in the next section, God will work through 'Jacob' to accomplish many other powerful feats that all of the world will see and will be blessed by. These feats that earn 'Jacob' power and position in God's coming Kingdom will include freeing captives, providing truth, and regathering God's people. Most importantly, he will proclaim to be a witness to Jesus Christ as the one and only God.

'Jacob' helps to free the captives

'Jacob' will be used by God to perform duties very similar to those Jesus declared during his early ministry when he read the following from the book of Isaiah in his hometown synagogue:

The Spirit of the Lord is upon me, because he hath anointed me to preach the gospel to the poor; he hath sent me to heal the brokenhearted, to preach deliverance to the captives, and recovering of sight to the blind, to set at liberty them that are bruised… (Lk. 4:18)

'Jacob' is an end times servant of Jesus who accomplishes a similar feat for people of the world, according to scripture. You can see the striking similarities in that the Lord has called 'Jacob' to, "Open the blind eyes, to bring out the prisoners from prison, and them that sit in darkness out of the prison house" (Is. 42:8).

While some actual, literal prisoners will likely be freed due to justice that is administered the primary mode of deliverance will be bringing masses of people out of modern day oppression and captivity at the hands of the world Babylon's Chaldeans. This will take place once Chaldean police-state-type methods are exposed and the truth is known.

'Jacob'– a vessel for truth and light

It appears that truth and light will be shown to the world by God through 'Jacob' and his last days small remnant of 'Israel,' first to the Gentiles, prior to the larger house of Israel being aware. This is the light spoken of that causes the eyes of many blind to be open and that causes the "fullness of the Gentiles to come in." The Apostle Paul speaks about this as a "mystery" (Rom. 11:25), which takes place while much of the house of Israel, God's people, remain blinded.

What is this hidden truth and light that is shown? Scripture describes clearly that this is an understanding given to the world about the "mystery of iniquity," which is revealed in these last days. Many who unknowingly participated in assisting ruthless Chaldean world rulers will be "ashamed" and others will have "darkness made light" before them or their "crooked (paths) made straight." This light and truth will enable people to better understand their own personal circumstances and life events including possible violations of their fundamental rights. This is simply referring to the exposure and revealing of the anti-Christ Chaldean secret "mob," its powerful leaders, and its network and criminal system.

God glorified through 'Jacob'

Through 'Jacob' and his last days army, many Gentiles across the earth will get their own personal truth and justice in their lives. God says to 'Jacob': "I will also give thee for a light to the Gentiles, that thou mayest be my salvation unto the end of the earth" (Is. 49:6). Most importantly, God will be glorified. Gentiles will finally understand Jesus Christ as the one and only true God who can save them from a previously unseen monstrous enemy. Jesus will receive praise and glory "from the ends of the earth," and all praise among the nations. Scripture says:

Behold, I will lift up mine hand to the Gentiles, and set up my standard to the people… (Is. 49:22)

The Lord hath made bare his holy arm in the eyes of all the nations; and all the ends of the earth shall see the salvation of our God. (Is. 52:10)

Of course, when deliverance and justice happen for 'Jacob' and his remnant, then God's people including the larger remnant of the house of Israel will take notice. 'Jacob' and his cause in leading this effort for his people against their Chaldean enemy will point 'Israel' to Jesus Christ as their Savior. Prophetic scripture and prayer for this last days event occurs in several places, with the same request: "Oh that the salvation of Israel were to come out of Zion!" (Rom. 11:25, Ps. 14:7, Ps. 53:26).

God's people gathered under 'Jacob'

The final gathering of God's remnant vineyard of Israel will be established for the Millennial Kingdom under Jesus' reign. God says his servant 'Jacob' will return, "be in rest and at ease," and at this time will see his inheritance. In the Millennial Kingdom they will become as the "sand of the sea." In Balaam's first vision that he relayed to Balak, when he saw future 'Israel' being blessed he asked, "Who can count the dust of Jacob?" (Num. 23:10). God asks prophetically of 'Jacob' directly:

It is a light thing that thou shouldest be my servant to raise up the tribes of Jacob, and to restore the preserved of Israel... (Is. 49:6)

The following verses describe this final gathering in more detail under 'Jacob's leadership:

The remnant shall return, even the remnant of Jacob, unto the mighty God. For though thy people Israel be as the sand of the sea, yet a remnant of them shall return: the consumption decreed shall overflow with righteousness. (Is. 10:21-22)

And they shall spring up as among the grass, as willows by the water courses. One shall say, I am the Lord's; and another shall call himself by the name of Jacob; and another shall subscribe with his hand unto the Lord, and surname himself by the name of Israel. (Is. 44:4-5)

But fear not thou, O my servant Jacob, and be not dismayed, O Israel: for, behold, I will save thee from afar off, and thy seed from the land of their captivity; and Jacob shall return, and be in rest and at ease, and none shall make him afraid. (Jer. 46:27)

As a result of God's incredible grace 'Jacob' will be rewarded. Scripture indicates God's covenant promise for restoration will be fulfilled for 'Jacob' and his people in the holy land. 'Jacob' will remain a chosen leader in the Millennial Kingdom. The following verses describe 'Jacob's inheritance, belonging to God and representing his glory:

Thus saith the Lord, In an acceptable time have I heard thee, and in a day of salvation have I helped thee: and I will preserve thee, and give thee for a covenant of the people, to establish the earth, to cause to inherit the desolate heritages... (Is. 49:8)

But when he seeth his children, the work of mine hands, in the midst of him, they shall sanctify my name, and sanctify the Holy One of Jacob, and shall fear the God of Israel. (Is. 29:23)

Victory for 'Jacob' and Glory for God

While God shows himself to be sovereign and all-powerful by re-establishing 'Jacob' and his people in their land for the Millennial Kingdom, he shows himself to be *just* by giving 'Jacob' victory in *righteousness* versus Babylon's wicked Chaldeans.

The anti-Christ Chaldeans fight with a multitude of weapons, many of which are non-conventional since they target single individuals for the most part. The non-sanctioned use of many of these military-grade intelligence weapons is illegal to begin with. As I have mentioned, Chaldeans then motivate their massive army against individuals by baseless slander, accusations and lies. Since they are by nature, *anti-Christ*, many of these slander and through symbolism blaspheme God, Jesus Christ himself.

This is the reason that God gives victory to his people through 'Jacob' so that his *own name will be glorified*, for his sake. We are told:

For mine own sake, even for mine own sake, will I do it: for how should my name be polluted? and I will not give my glory unto another. Hearken unto me, O Jacob and Israel, my called; I am he; I am the first, I also am the last. (Is. 48:11-12)

Redemption

A large part of the victory for 'Jacob' and his army in the last days is redemption for the sake of justice and righteousness. Through all of his personal travails against his attackers, 'Jacob' will be proven as righteous (imputed through faith) and the anti-Christ Chaldeans as criminals and liars. This will be an answer to many ancient prophetic prayers anticipating this battle.

King David and other Psalmists interceded for last days 'Jacob' or the 'Davidic Prince' in their prophetic prayers, anticipating this end times battle against the anti-Christ Chaldean adversary. They understood, even in their time, that this battle would represent 'Jacob's and his remnant's righteousness versus their wicked enemy. They prayed:

Let integrity and uprightness preserve me; for I wait on thee. Redeem Israel, O God, out of all his troubles. (Ps. 25:21-22)

The king's strength also loveth judgment; thou dost establish equity, thou executest judgment and righteousness in Jacob. (Ps. 99:4)

Just as ancient prophets foresaw last days 'Jacob' is despised and abhorred by the nations, 'Jacob' will undertake a battle in faith and "turn his back to the smiters" (Is. 50:6). He will possess faith and a belief that the Lord will redeem him and further that, "I will not be confounded (disgraced)." In the midst of his battle God reassures his chosen servant:

Fear thou not; for I am with thee: be not dismayed; for I am thy God: I will strengthen thee; yea, I will help thee; yea, I will uphold thee with the right hand of my righteousness. (Is. 41:10)

I the Lord have called thee in righteousness, and will hold thine hand, and will keep thee, and give thee for a covenant of the people... (Is. 42:6)

Those living in these last days will see how God answers Jacob's faith and prayers and delivers victory for him. The victory that God gives 'Jacob' in the last days will be astonishing. It will be a victory that only God himself can deliver. We are told several places in scripture that as a result of 'Jacob's righteous cause and truth that is delivered, "Kings shall arise, princes shall also worship" (Is. 49:7).

This will be the case because the anti-Christ Chaldean "mystery of iniquity" will finally be exposed and defeated and a light of justice will be turned on for the world. God foretold about his servant 'Jacob':

He shall not fail nor be discouraged, till he have set judgment in the earth: and the isles shall wait for his law. (Is. 42:4)

I have not spoken in secret, in a dark place of the earth: I said not unto the seed of Jacob, Seek ye me in vain: I the Lord speak righteousness, I declare things that are right. (Is. 45:19)

'Jacob' saved

Scripture is clear in several places that God delivers last days 'Jacob' from his enemy out of the land "afar off" (i.e. 'Babylon'- "far off" from the land of Israel). Thus, his final delivery will include an exodus back to the holy land along with his remnant people.

In effect, God will save 'Jacob' from the enemy that otherwise decimates his vineyard of people. Last days 'Jacob' is saved from the Chaldean enemy that is much stronger than he, only through the power of his faith in Jesus Christ. Verses below demonstrate God's saving grace:

But fear not thou, O my servant Jacob, and be not dismayed, O Israel: for, behold, I will save thee from afar off, and thy seed from the land of their captivity; and Jacob shall return, and be in rest and at ease, and none shall make him afraid. (Jer. 46:27)

For thus saith the Lord; Sing with gladness for Jacob, and shout among the chief of the nations: publish ye, praise ye, and say, O Lord, save thy people, the remnant of Israel. (Jer. 31:7)

For the Lord hath redeemed Jacob, and ransomed him from the hand of him that was stronger than he. (Jer. 31:11)

As we are told in scripture, Jesus Christ saves. He saves souls most importantly but he also saves believers in their physical state of existence from destruction, physical harm, all types of calamities and even from his wrath that is still to come.

Weapons for defeating the anti-Christ Chaldeans

The culmination of last days 'Jacob's battle is the final defeat of his adversary. While God will ultimately save 'Jacob,' as discussed above, he will give him and his remnant the ability to fight back against his adversary. In fact, by God's grace and provision he will bless 'Jacob' with unusual, fierce strength. This is a fulfillment of scripture where God promises that 'Jacob' and his remnant will mount up with "wings like eagles" (Is. 40:29). Other verses demonstrate the power for battle that God will provide for 'Jacob':

Behold, I will make thee a new sharp threshing instrument having teeth: thou shalt thresh the mountains, and beat them small, and shalt make the hills as chaff. (Is. 41:15)

By this therefore shall the iniquity of Jacob be purged; and this is all the fruit to take away his sin; when he maketh all the stones of the altar as chalkstones that are beaten in sunder, the groves and images shall not stand up. (Is. 27:9)

And the remnant of Jacob shall be among the Gentiles in the midst of many people as a lion among the beasts of the forest, as a young lion among the flocks of sheep: who, if he go through, both treadeth down, and teareth in pieces, and none can deliver. (Mic. 5:8)

Additional insight from Balaam's prophetic visions that I have been referring to in this passage also foretells of last days 'Jacob's unusual strength. Balaam saw 'Jacob' as having the "strength of a unicorn" and as: "eating up the nations as his enemies"; "breaking their bones and piercing them through with his arrows"; and "destroying him that remaineth in the city" (Numbers, Chapter 24), likely referring to a significant Chaldean foe.

Chaldean hidden iniquity exposed

The defeat of the anti-Christ Chaldeans will be the shedding of light and truth on what they do in secret. So 'Jacob's "strength" described above will not readily be visible in an otherwise quiet, secretive worldwide war which at its root is spiritual in nature. The surprise final outcome will be enormous, however.

The Chaldeans' power is gained through using a secret system of targeting along with false accusations and "sharp" tongues as the basis and faulty reasoning for destroying one's character and motivating their vast army to deploy to persecute and destroy others. This happens via their continuous, well-disguised perfect crimes, psychological operations, "death by a thousand cuts," and even physical harm along the way.

So, the key element of God's saving grace and provision of victory for 'Jacob' is his power to reveal and uncover the Chaldeans' evil nature for all to see. Scripture says that 'Jacob' will be able to ask: "…Who will contend with me?... Who is mine adversary?" (Is. 50:8). In essence, the Chaldeans will fall into their own pit that they have dug. King David prayed for this same deliverance against the anti-Christ spirit adversary of his day. Scripture below shows how this enemy will be defeated:

Happy art thou, O Israel: who is like unto thee, O people saved by the Lord, the shield of thy help, and who is the sword of thy excellency! And thine enemies shall be found liars unto thee; and thou shalt tread upon their high places. (Deut. 33:29)

Behold, all ye that kindle a fire, that compass yourselves about with sparks: walk in the light of your fire, and in the sparks that ye have kindled. This shall ye have of mine hand; ye shall lie down in sorrow. (Is. 50:11)

Behold, all they that were incensed against thee shall be ashamed and confounded: they shall be as nothing; and they that strive with thee shall perish. (Is. 41:11)

'Jacob's final victory for the whole world to see will come only by the power of Jesus Christ. Jesus Christ will return and once-and-for-all shatter world Babylon's system. We know that Jesus is the cornerstone about whom scripture says: "And whosoever shall fall on this stone shall be broken: but on whomsoever it shall fall, it will grind him to powder" (Matt. 21:44).

~

In summary, as a result of 'Jacob's last days battle and victory on behalf of God, God's Word to *original* Jacob after he struggled with God's angel will be fulfilled all over again for the heavenly kingdom:

Thy name shall no more be called Jacob, but Israel: for as a prince hast thou power with God and with men, and hast prevailed. (Gen. 32:28)

It *may be* that, once again, last days 'Jacob' is the one for whom a "new name" will be given by God (Is. 62:2, Rev. 3:12). I describe 'Jacob's end times journey back to the Kingdom in detail in my book, *Biblical End Times, Volume 1*.

Chapter 6.

End Times 'David'

Passages from Lion's Lair provided in this chapter include:

6.1 A Davidic-line Prince and the Picture of Zerubbabel

6.2 End Times 'David'- The Warrior, the "Branch," and the "Banner" for Babylon

6.1 A Davidic-line Prince and the Picture of Zerubbabel

In *Writings of Lion's Lair, Volume 2*, I will discuss the end times oppression and captivity of God's people. I will refer to Ezekiel, Chapter 34, which describes how God will ultimately bring his people and his servant 'David' back into their land, set up his Kingdom, and will be their Lord. This will be Jesus Christ, King of Kings and Lord of Lords, who will reign here on earth during the heavenly Millennial Kingdom. That is real big news and no-doubt the greatest news we could ever hope for as believers- "Thy Kingdom come!"

A Millennial Kingdom Prince, 'David'

There will be an interesting, lesser-known, seldom-discussed addition to the temple area during the Millennial Kingdom. In addition to Levite priests, ministers, and others, such as our beloved Apostles who we are told will reign over the 12 tribes, Jesus will have a servant, 'David,' who will be a "prince among them" (Ez. 34:24). In fact, he will be their prince forever (Ez. 37:25). 'David's name here comes from the fact that he will be from the Jewish bloodline of the tribe of Judah, and specifically, from King David's line. The Millennial King 'David' will function as an earthly prince while directly serving and worshiping Jesus Christ; and thus, he will be the shepherd who will tend to the flock of regathered 'Israel.' We are told:

He will stand and shepherd his flock in the strength of the Lord, in the majesty of the name of the Lord his God. (Mic. 5:4)

But they shall serve the Lord their God, and David their king, whom I will raise up unto them. (Jer. 30:9)

A Millennial Kingdom Davidic Prince is a fulfillment of God's covenant to "establish David's line forever" on the throne. This King David-figure who scripture refers to raises questions about who he is, where he comes from, etc. And if we agree that we are living in the last days we might rightly ask the question as to whether he could be living among us today just as we wonder whether any other last days biblical characters could be. You will note that I have/will show(n) that many or all of these biblical characters will live in our last days but then progress into the Millennial Kingdom albeit with a possible supernatural escape provided by God in the interim.

King David's Own Writing- Prophetic Psalms

In this passage I examine some of King David's prophetic Psalms for some clues about an *end times* 'David.' King David's ancient war with the same anti-Christ spirit foretells of 'David's similar war in the last days. In these, it is *extraordinary* that he writes as if he expects an *end times* servant of his own inheritance to face a similar battle and to suffer distress and anguish on the same scale that he did. *Could it be that David's personal war against the anti-Christ spirit army repeats with an end times 'David' figure?*

(Note: Overall, some prophetic scripture in King David's Psalms may apply only to Jesus' first coming on earth. Other writings of his describes an end-times servant like the 'David' who I am addressing in this passage. Additional scripture could be a "picture" or represent a double fulfillment of prophetic events as experienced by King David himself. Taken altogether, many of David's Psalms are at least in part prophetic and apply to our current last days time period.)

The following verses with prophetic implication set the stage for 'David's battle here in the *end times*:

Why do the nations conspire and the peoples plot in vain? The kings of the earth take their stand and the rulers gather together against the Lord and against his Anointed One. (Ps. 2:1)

O Lord, where is your former great love, which in your faithfulness you swore to David? Remember, Lord, how your servant has been mocked, how I bear in my heart the taunts of all the nations...the taunts with which they have mocked every step of your anointed one. (Ps. 89:49-51)

Can a corrupt throne be allied with you- one that brings on misery by its decrees? They band together against the righteous and condemn the innocent to death. (Ps. 94:21-22)

Additional verses below record how King David remarkably appeared to pray for the Lord's deliverance of and the eventual victory of his *end times* 'David' servant:

For in the day of trouble he will keep me safe in his dwelling; he will hide me in the shelter of his tabernacle and set me high upon a rock...then my head will be exalted above the enemies around me; at the tabernacle will I sacrifice with shouts of joy... (Ps. 27:5-6)

Your hand will lay hold on all your enemies; your right hand will seize your foes. At the time of your appearing you will make them like a fiery furnace. In his wrath the Lord will swallow them up, and his fire will consume them. (Ps. 21:8)

May the Lord answer you when you are in distress; may the name of the God of Jacob protect you. May he send you help from the sanctuary and grant you support from Zion...We will shout for joy when you are victorious and will lift up our banners in the name of our God... (Ps. 20:1-2, 5)

In the day of my trouble I will call to you and you will answer me...no deeds can compare to yours...All the nations you have made will come and worship before you, O Lord; they will bring glory to your name. (Ps. 86:7-9)

In these verses there is a clear message of end times deliverance. You will also likely notice how some attributes or aspects of an end times "servant," 'David,' appear to be consistent with end times 'Jacob.' I will address the overcomer attribute, in particular, below.

Meanwhile, of course, it is worth re-emphasizing that this end times servant's ability to overcome and win the war waged against him by the anti-Christ spirit is owed *entirely* to the Lord's sovereignty and grace. To conclude this section, the following prophetic verses give praise to the Lord about the last days victory that an end times 'David' figure achieves:

All the nations surrounded me, but in the name of the Lord I cut them off. They surrounded me on every side, but in the name of the Lord I cut them off. They swarmed around me like bees, but they died out as quickly as burning thorns…I was pushed back and about to fall, but the Lord helped me. The Lord is my strength and my song; he has become my salvation. (Ps. 118:10-14)

Zerubbabel and a Picture of an End Times 'David' Figure who Overcomes

Zerubbabel, a descendent of King David, served as the Governor of Israel after he was highly instrumental in leading Israel's exodus back to Judah/Jerusalem from Babylonian captivity. He was then joined by a "remnant of the people" when he led the temple and altar re-building effort with Nehemiah, which God ordered through Haggai the prophet and Joshua the high priest.

We learn from the Prophet Haggai that the second temple was built during a time of a drought and unproductive harvest among the newly exiled people. At this time, God described his people as a stripped and unproductive vine, fig tree, olive tree, and pomegranate. Through Haggai, we also learn that there was a hostile environment towards the temple-building process among surrounding nations and peoples. So, in his orders, God encouraged Haggai and his contemporaries Zerubbabel and Zechariah to "be strong" in rebuilding the temple and told them, "do not fear."

In thinking about this scenario as a potential end times "picture" keep in mind that the temple that the Anti-Christ will defile in the Day of the Lord will be destroyed. And then at a later time it will be the temple of Jesus Christ that will need to be instilled, both spiritually and literally. First, Jewish people will be persecuted, on the run, and will be a spiritually barren vine. It will be evident to them that the 'Messiah' whom they chose is not who they were hoping for; then they will seek their *true* Messiah.

It will be a last days Davidic-line, 'Zerubbabel' figure who eventually, again, "lays the foundation." In then being blessed with an unimaginable honor he will introduce the true Messiah, Jesus Christ, in effect completing the "spiritual temple" along with the physical Millennial temple. Through Zechariah the prophetic word of the angel of the Lord was:

The hands of Zerubbabel have laid the foundation of this temple: his hands will also complete it... (Zech. 4:9). (Of course, the second temple was completed not too long thereafter in Zerubbabel's day, but this prophecy likely has a double fulfillment for our end times 'David' figure).

...(Zerubbabel) will bring out the capstone to shouts of 'God bless it! God bless it!' (Zech. 4:7)

In return for our end-times 'Zerubbabel's (i.e. 'David's) work in faith and righteousness in bringing his people back to their homeplace and to Jesus Christ, their Messiah, God prophetically instructed Haggai to tell his "servant" 'Zerubbabel,' "*On that day*, I will make you like my signet ring, for I have chosen you." (A signet ring is equivalent to a signature for a king). This is very likely a picture of our end-times Davidic Prince figure receiving his seat in the Kingdom.

This culminating event will be an answer to God's people's and vineyard's prayers for restoration in the last days who will request, "Let your hand rest on the man at your right hand, the son of man you have raised up for yourself" (Ps. 80:17).

The Zerubbabel picture of a Davidic-line figure overcomer

I will discuss end times 'Babylon' as a *nation* in detail in *Volume 2*. It is a land from which many of God's people and remnant will exodus. In addition, we have some clues that there will be an end times servant who will be somewhat of an overcomer and redeemer, especially for the lost sheep remnant, as well as a light for the Gentiles. Could our end times Davidic-line, servant-leader ('Zerubbabel') be one who *again* leads an exodus from 'Babylon' in the last days? A couple possible clues in the book of Zechariah would indicate that 'Zerubbabel' (i.e. 'David') at least fits the overcomer attribute as demonstrated by what the angel of the Lord says to Zechariah:

What are you, O mighty mountain? Before Zerubbabel you will become level ground." (Zech. 4:7)

Who despises the day of small things? Men will rejoice when they see the plumb line in the hand of Zerubbabel. (Zech. 4:10)

In the first verse above, the term "mountain" may refer to last days Chaldean powers, also referred to by God as a "destroying mountain" (Jer. 51:25) that are eventually defeated.

Jesus' words about an overcomer

It appears entirely plausible that the last days Davidic figure could be the overcomer that Jesus is referring to in the book of Revelation. To be fair, I also rhetorically asked in a prior passage whether end times 'Jacob' could be an "overcomer."

When speaking of "he who overcomes" to the various churches in the book of Revelation Jesus offered the following insights. In just a few selected examples below of the Millennial Kingdom duties of "he who overcomes" it certainly appears that *end times* King 'David' is a highly likely candidate. Jesus Christ himself said:

I will give (him) authority to rule over the nations. (to the Church in Thyatira, Rev. 2:26)

I will make (him) a pillar in the temple of my God. Never again will he leave it. (to the Church in Philadelphia, Rev. 3:11)

I will give (him) the right to sit with me on my throne. (to the Church in Laodicea, Rev. 3:21)

I describe end times 'David' in more detail in my next passage. I also discuss his story in-depth in my book, *Biblical End Times, Volume 1.*

~

Assuming that we are at or very near the end of the age, I believe end times 'David' and other figures who are mentioned in God's Word could live among us.

6.2 End Times 'David'- The Warrior, the "Branch," and the "Banner" for Babylon

In my last passage, I established that Prince 'David' will reign in the Millennial Kingdom in direct service to Jesus Christ- the King of Kings and Lord of Lords. I also established the likelihood that 'David' is an end times figure for whom it is prophesied to overcome, conquer and lead an exodus of his people out of end times 'Babylon.' Jesus' lost sheep will be taken and regathered back in their homeland, the holy land where 'Israel' will rejoin the (house of) Judah for a final time. Perhaps not coincidentally, this will be the first time that they are reunited since they split apart during King David's reign.

In this passage, I will discuss a little more about end times 'David,' and in particular, I will provide more detail about his possible role as a "banner" for end times 'Babylon' and the exodus of his people.

'David'- A Righteous Servant-Warrior in a Corrupt World

It is clear that end times 'David' stands as a righteous man in an otherwise corrupt world- a world full of corrupt leaders and kings. 'David' is referred to as a "righteous branch" and one who has the "Spirit of wisdom and of understanding" (Is. 11:2). It is also clear that end times 'David' has to fight his own righteous war against these corrupt, oppressive powers. The following verse that I use in my book, *Biblical End Times, Volume 1*, sets the background for the war that 'David' is involved in:

Why do the nations conspire and the peoples plot in vain? The kings of the earth take their stand and the rulers gather together against the Lord and against his Anointed One. (Ps. 2:1-2)

As a prophetic verse, this sets up what is essentially an end times war between Satan's evil earthly kingdom and God's servants who represent his Kingdom to come. In Chapter 5, I established end times 'Jacob's battles against the timeless enemy on behalf of God's Kingdom and people. Is it any wonder that the prayers of both Jacob and Moses in ancient days that pertained specifically to Judah (Jacob's son and the tribe of the Davidic line) are prophetic in reference to fighting a battle? These are given as follows:

(Jacob) *Judah, your brothers will praise you, your hand will be on the neck of your enemies; your father's sons will bow down to you. You are a lion's cub, O Judah; you return from the prey, my son. Like a lion he crouches down, like a lioness- who dares to rouse him? The scepter will not depart from Judah, nor the ruler's staff from between his feet, until he comes to whom it belongs and the obedience of nations is his.* (Gen. 49:9-10)

(Moses) *Hear O Lord, the cry of Judah; bring him to his people. With his own hands he defends his cause. Oh, be his help against his foes!* (Deut. 33:7)

The tribe of Judah and its Davidic-line appear to be pre-destined for righteous battle. As discussed above, end times 'David's battle is not only one for his own soul and life; it is a battle that represents, and is on behalf of, God's people, 'Israel.'

Israel's barren vine precedes judgment on their enemies and deliverance through 'David'

In my last passage, I established that 'David' arises in a time when Israel's vine has been laid to waste and laid barren. They are spiritually starved and are heavily oppressed at the hands of the worldwide anti-Christ Chaldean army, which is led by the nations' evil rulers, elected and unelected, who have systematically targeted and persecuted God's people. We read:

...the rulers of the nations have trampled down the choicest vines....joy and gladness are taken away from the orchards; no one sings or shouts in the vineyards... (Is. 16:8-10)

Woe to the shepherds who are destroying and scattering the sheep of my pasture!, declares the Lord...Because you have scattered my flock, driven them away and have not bestowed care on them, I will bestow punishment on you for the evil you have done, declares the Lord. (Jer. 23:1-2)

Many shepherds will ruin my vineyard and trample down my field: they will turn my pleasant field into a desolate wasteland. (Jer. 12:10)

In response to the persecution against his vineyard God's worldwide punishment and judgment will come. It will eventually be understood that this punishment is a culmination of the Judah remnant's and 'David's behind-the-scenes, unconventional war versus the anti-Christ Chaldeans. The truth about 'David's righteous struggle, which in the bigger picture represents God's vine against their evil oppressors and destroyers, will be revealed. We know that at the end of this worldwide battle that the Lord will destroy his enemies. The Lord says:

O profane and wicked prince of Israel, whose time of punishment has reached its climax...Take off the turban, remove the crown. It will not be as it was: The lowly will be exalted and the exalted will be brought low. A ruin! A ruin! I will make it a ruin! (Ez. 21:25-27)

Ultimately, Jesus will set up his own Kingdom here on earth. As a result of 'David's faithfulness, he will inherit his ancestors' throne in an incredible honor to serve the Lord and the people. (Note here how this is directly analogous to and consistent with the picture of 'Zerubbabel' presented in my prior passage). We read:

In mercy a throne will be established; in faithfulness a man will sit on it- one from the house of David- one who in judging seeks justice and speeds the cause of righteousness. (Is. 16:5)

(The throne) will not be restored until he comes to whom it rightfully belongs; to him will I (God) give it. (Ez. 21:27)

I will make an everlasting covenant with you, my faithful love promised to David. See, I have made him a witness to the peoples, a leader and commander of the peoples. Surely you will summon nations you know not and nations that do not know you will hasten to you, because of the Lord your God, the Holy One of Israel, for he has endowed you with splendor. (Is. 55:3)

Scripture tells us that Israel will serve the Lord their God (Jesus) and David their King.

'David'- The "Branch"

On the heels of God's and Jesus Christ's final deliverance and restoration for Israel and Judah, and in establishing the Millennial Kingdom and David's throne, God refers to 'David' as his "righteous branch." At the time God frees his people and restores them in their land God says through Jeremiah that, "their leader will be one of their own" and "their ruler will arise from among them." This is highly likely to be our Millennial 'David' Prince figure who is referred to several times in scripture as the "Branch." His title is likely due to his Davidic roots and in demonstrating God's sovereignty in keeping the Davidic-line inheritance on the throne. This is the case according to verses below:

In those days and at that time, I will make a righteous Branch sprout from David's line; he will do what is just and right in the land. In those days Judah will be saved and Jerusalem will live in safety... (Jer. 33:15-16)

The Lord says, "*Here is the man whose name is The Branch, and he will branch out from his place and build the temple of the Lord. It is he who will build the temple of the Lord, and he will be clothed with majesty and will sit and rule on his throne. And he will be a priest on his throne...* (Zech. 6:12)

A shoot will come up from the stump of Jesse; from his roots a Branch will bear fruit. The Spirit of the Lord will rest on him- the Spirit of wisdom and of understanding, the Spirit of counsel and power, The Spirit of knowledge and of the fear of the Lord- and he will delight in the fear of the Lord. (Is. 11:1)

God will assign 'David,' the Branch, glory and majesty, and describes him as one who will reign with an eye towards justice and doing what is right. The Prophet Isaiah discussed how this "branch" of the Lord will be "beautiful and glorious," and that the fruit of the land will be "the pride and glory" in Israel (Is. 4:2). Within the entire remnant of God's people who are established in Millennial 'Israel,' there appears to be a holy branch or small remnant of survivors who are associated with 'David,' 'Zion,' or the "house of David."

'David' - A "Banner" for his People's Deliverance and Exile from Babylon

One clue that 'David' leads a fight against 'Babylon' in the last days is the apparent scriptural references to him as a "banner," with the term banner (or "standard") generally meaning a *sign* or a *signal for battle*. While much focus is about his battle against 'Babylon' it is clear that the banner that he raises will reach a worldwide audience. Through the Prophet Isaiah we are told, "the root of Jesse will stand as a *banner* for the peoples; the nations will rally to him" (Is. 11:10). Isaiah also prophetically foretold, "He whistles to those at the ends of the earth" (Is. 5:26).

This "banner" that will be raised has special significance and importance to end times 'Babylon,' suggesting that this is the land where 'David's battle originates. As a result of 'David's and his people's resistance against the anti-Christ Chaldean army, God says, "I will chase Babylon from its land in an instant" (Jer. 50:44), meaning that Babylon will be quickly broken and become divided. Let's take a look at several verses about a "banner" that is raised in end times 'Babylon.'

Announce and proclaim among the nations, lift up a banner and proclaim it; keep nothing back, but say, Babylon will be captured...Her images will be put to shame and her idols filled with terror. (Jer. 50:2)

Lift up a banner against the walls of Babylon! Reinforce the guard, station the watchmen, prepare an ambush! The Lord will carry out his purpose, his decree against the people of Babylon. (Jer. 51:12)

See I will beckon to the Gentiles, I will lift up my banner to the peoples; they will bring your sons in their arms and carry your daughters on their shoulders...Captives will be taken from warriors and plunder retrieved from the fierce. (Is. 49:22)

Lift up a banner in the land! Blow the trumpet among the nations! Prepare the nations for battle against her; summon against her these kingdoms... (Jer. 51:27)

An end times 'David' apparently lights a very large fire in the land as a result of his war against 'Babylon's anti-Christ Chaldean army.

End times 'David's warrior attributes in the 'Babylon' war

It should be mentioned that in scripture describing an end times battle and subsequent exodus from 'Babylon' more detail is given about end times 'David.' Perhaps some more clues about him are provided in the book of Jeremiah (Chapters 50-51) where his "banner" (or "standard") is lifted up for the nations to see. 'David' here is likely among those referred to as:

- Of a tribe and inheritance ("Portion of Jacob"- i.e. and "waters of Judah") who is "not like these" (Chaldean oppressors) (Jer. 51:19)

- (God's) "war club" and "weapon for battle (Jer. 51:20)

It follows that end times 'David' is also the answer to God's rhetorical question below about an anointed servant in last days 'Babylon':

Who is the chosen one I will appoint for this (Babylon judgment)? And what shepherd can stand against me?" (Jer. 50:44)

Millennial Prince 'David' as I have described in the last couple of passages does not carry out his war alone. It is likely that a broader Judah remnant is especially targeted and faces some of the same persecution that 'David' does. In Chapter 4, I addressed the holy remnant of Judah as a group that will most likely accompany or surround an end times 'David' figure in the Millennium. I also address their spiritual kingdom battle and path through the Day of the Lord in my books, *Biblical End Times, Volumes 1 and 2*.

~

In conclusion, as a result of Israel's holy remnant's war in last days Babylon they will exodus this land described as (from the perspective of Israel at the time of the prophets): a "distant place"; "the land of the north"; and a "land you (Judah) do not know." It is possible that this last days exodus from captivity will be led by an end times biblical figure. End times 'David' is a leading candidate.

Chapter 7.

End Times 'Daughter of Zion'

Passages from Lion's Lair provided in this chapter include:

7.1 The Daughter of Zion- An End Times Figure, Millennial Kingdom Queen (Part 1)

7.2 The Daughter of Zion- An End Times Figure, Millennial Kingdom Queen (Part 2)

7.3 The Daughter of Zion- An End Times Figure, Millennial Kingdom Queen (Part 3)

7.1 The Daughter of Zion- An End Times Figure, Millennial Kingdom Queen (Part 1)

The 'Daughter of Zion' is another end times figure who has many similarities to the other figures who I have examined in some detail to this point- i.e. 'Jacob' and 'David.' She is chosen by God for a special end times role and is promised a position of royalty in his heavenly Kingdom. Like 'Jacob' and 'David,' she finds herself disciplined by God and persecuted at the hands of the anti-Christ Chaldeans. Also like 'Jacob' and 'David,' she is ultimately redeemed and delivered. In fact, it is clear in scripture (e.g. Jeremiah, Chapters 30-31) that she is freed for exile (from 'Babylon') at the same time that the anointed 'Jacob-Judah' remnant are freed.

What is interesting in scripture about the 'Daughter of Zion' is that her name, 'Zion,' is used with different connotations and can be used in current day or prophetic context. Depending on context, terms like, "Zion," "Mount Zion," and "Daughter of Zion" can be used to represent: the city of Jerusalem; the people of Jerusalem; the temple area (i.e. "holy hill"); the temple itself; heavenly Zion; an origin for (or mother of) God's holy people/royal family; etc.

In this passage, I focus on the 'Daughter of Zion' who I believe is an actual person living in these end times and proceeds into the Millennial Kingdom. In her story, however, there is also a "picture" and a very strong representation of what Jerusalem and the country of Israel will experience in the end times. Pieces of this same picture are prophesied and corroborated in many other parts of scripture as well.

Holy and Royal

The themes about the 'Daughter of Zion' in prophetic scripture are strong and clear. In a quick summary, these themes nearly exactly mirror those that I outlined in Chapter 4 about the Judah remnant- that is, the Daughter of Zion is: holy; royal; righteous; persecuted; and delivered.

This woman is chosen by God and given *very* special blessings. In describing the restoration of his holy Kingdom God says to her, "See, I have engraved you on the palms of my hands..." (Is. 49:16). God himself further says:

*Sing, O barren woman...enlarge the place of your tent, stretch your tent curtains wide...your descendants will spread out to the right and to the left...**For your Maker is your husband- The Lord Almighty is his name**- the Holy One of Israel is your Redeemer; he is called the God of the earth.* (Is. 54:1,3,5)

The 'Daughter of Zion' will be a *holy and royal* Queen in the Kingdom of God that is soon to be established. She will ultimately receive much praise and glory.

Faces Persecution

Various parts of scripture show that the 'Daughter of Zion' will be persecuted at the hands of the anti-Christ Chaldeans, similar to other last days Judah remnant biblical figures. (This is somewhat analogous to the country of Israel as a whole that will be invaded by world Babylon's Chaldeans and will be highly perplexed as a result). I have discussed several times God's creation and deployment of the anti-Christ Chaldean army as a tool of discipline against his people.

It is clear that the Lord will become angry with the 'Daughter of Zion.' Jeremiah prophetically laments that the Lord has, "covered the Daughter of Zion with a cloud of his anger!" (Lam. 2:1). The 'Daughter of Zion's "breach" is further described as being, "great like the sea" (Lam. 2:13), and we learn that she has been misled by "false prophets" and "false oracles" (Lam. 2:14).

It is possible, given what we learn in the book of Lamentations and elsewhere in scripture that she has been strongly misguided and deceived by the anti-Christ Chaldeans and has even likely been a member of their very 'army' that subsequently turns against her.

A victim of the larger war against the royal Judah bloodline

The 'Daughter of Zion' will find out that the anti-Christ Chaldeans are not even loyal to their own members; instead, they follow an occult-based, ritualistic agenda and schedule. The attack against her is likely a planned ambush and assault, most likely as a result of a larger war against members of her bloodline (i.e. royal, Judah). In scripture that also has meaning for end times Jerusalem the 'Daughter of Zion's enemies say:

We have swallowed her up. This is the day we have waited for; we have lived to see it. (Lam. 2:16)

Although a pre-planned attack, there is some indication that the 'Daughter of Zion' may also be persecuted for taking a righteous stand. The anti-Christ Chaldeans aim to intentionally mix bloodlines and "mingle seed" among God's people via arranged marriages, unions, etc., and the children that are produced. And at the very least, they engage in numerous other immoral and detestable behaviors that are likely a requirement for continuing membership; *or else*!

Does the 'Daughter of Zion' take a courageous, moral stand that leaves her as one of the very few remaining "clean" children on God's grapevine which has otherwise been decimated by the oath-taking Chaldeans according to scripture? If so, this would fit with the pattern we see with a few of the other righteous Judah tribe remnant figures in the end times.

Oppressed and Taken Captive

Scripture is clear that the 'Daughter of Zion' is sold into slavery, captivity and oppression. In addressing her, the Lord says, "You were sold for nothing," yet he promises, "without money you will be redeemed" (Is. 52:3). While the anti-Christ Chaldeans tactically plan for this oppression it is merely part of the master plan and strategy of our sovereign God. In regard to the 'Daughter of Zion,' we read:

The Lord has done what he planned: he has fulfilled his word, which he decreed long ago. (Lam. 2:17)

In the meantime, typical anti-Christ Chaldean army tactics of oppression and imprisonment against her are readily apparent in scripture:

All who pass your way clap their hands at you, they scoff and shake their heads. (Lam. 2:15)

Shepherds with their flocks will come against her, they will pitch their tents around her, each tending his own portion. (Jer. 6:3)

But now many nations are gathered against you. They say, let her be defiled, let our eyes gloat on Zion. (Mic. 4:11)

Those familiar with this criminal gang's tactics understand that they continuously track, stalk and harass their targets. Illegal surveillance and the weaponization thereof is a part of their methodology.

Made desolate

Likely as a result of numerous Chaldean tactics and their psychological weapons turned against her the 'Daughter of Zion' will find herself alone and deserted. If she is targeted by this gang, as just described, she will face powerful, organized, coordinated criminal gang tactics that are designed to isolate a targeted individual.

Accordingly, we learn in scripture that the 'Daughter of Zion' becomes "barren," "deserted," an "outcast," and without comfort. Scripture also says, "among all her lovers there is none to comfort her" (Lam. 1:2). Furthermore, her friends have become her enemies. Her abandonment is described as: "The Daughter of Zion is left like a shelter in a vineyard, like a hut in a field of melons. Unless the Lord had left us some survivors, we would have become like Gomorrah" (Is. 1:7).

In just another fascinating parallel to the *people* of Zion/Jerusalem, and prophecy for the country of Israel in the last days she finds that she has no friends to call upon. 'Zion' observes:

I called to my allies, but they betrayed me. My priests and my elders perished in the city while they searched for food to keep themselves alive. (Lam. 1:19)

This has a double-meaning including for a barren, isolated country of Israel in the last days of God's judgment. This abandoned condition is caused by Chaldean traitor, "locust" infiltration in the land over time.

A Queen without a royal family in the end times

The 'Daughter of Zion' is several times referred to in God's Word as a mother without children or as a Queen without princes. She refers to herself as one who "never bore a child," which may be the case, but this is also symbolic of a lack of family (royal, Judah) around her including a lack of the "sons of Zion."

Scripture is clear that (Judah) princes will go into captivity and be persecuted in the last days, showing they are victims of the larger, all-out assault on God's people by the Chaldeans. 'Zion' herself says, "My young men and maidens have gone into exile" (Lam. 1:18). Her princes are referred to as, "deer that find no pasture, in weakness they have fled before the pursuer" (Lam. 1:6). The Prophet Jeremiah prophetically lamented:

Her gates have sunk into the ground; he has destroyed and shattered their bars. Her kings and princes are exiled among the nations, the law is no more, and even her prophets find no vision from the Lord. (Lam. 2:9)

The verse above is another example of some of the symbolism used in scripture that is associated with 'Zion,' but that also has application to conditions in God's holy land itself.

~

At this juncture, I have established the importance of the 'Daughter of Zion' in God's Kingdom. I have also established the significance of her travails, which include a "picture" of what the people of Zion/Israel will face in these last days. Specifically, this will be a tremendous attack, internal and external, by anti-Christ spirit forces prior to Jesus Christ being revealed (again) as their true Messiah and prior to their return to the land at the time he assumes his throne.

In my next passages (Parts 2 and 3), I will address in more detail the 'Daughter of Zion's battle against the Chaldeans and her ultimate deliverance and glory as orchestrated by God himself. I also describe her complete story according to scripture in my books, *Biblical End Times, Volumes 1 and 2*.

7.2 The Daughter of Zion- An End Times Figure, Millennial Kingdom Queen (Part 2)

So many prophetic insights can be gleaned from the biblical 'Daughter of Zion' figure. Through her eyes and story, we can get a good overall picture for end time events and the significance behind them.

The 'Daughter of Zion,' who I described in Part 1 will be a Millennial Kingdom Matriarch for God's people, is commonly associated with "birth pangs," or with a woman who is "in labor" or "in travail." This signals a coming "birth(s)," which is a key sign frequently associated with significant end time event(s) to come.

But first, it causes us to recall the first time that God addressed childbirth (through Eve) in the Garden. Because of Eve's transgression God promised to make childbirth a very painful process from that time on. And because of the serpent's deception God promised to put enmity between the serpent and Eve, and between the serpent's seed and her seed.

Last days worldwide events that are playing out are a culmination of this ongoing spiritual war between the serpent's seed and the woman's seed- a war that has existed since God created man. The woman's seed is that which continued through the Abraham-Isaac-Jacob line as well as through others who have been "grafted in." True committed believers in Jesus Christ, as a whole, will find themselves in a larger and more intense spiritual battle as we approach the end of the age. This battle and resistance is against the serpent's "seed," which is Satan's army here on earth- the anti-Christ Chaldeans.

When birth pangs or "*birth pangs like those of a woman in labor*" are mentioned in scripture we can usually relate these terms to the spiritual battle between the woman's seed and the serpent's seed and the practical manifestation(s) thereof. In the case of the 'Daughter of Zion,' (representing a last days 'type' of Eve), her "birth pangs" are highly indicative of upcoming "birthing"-related events that I describe in detail in Chapter 9.

This ties back to our 'Daughter of Zion' figure's life being a good "picture" of end times events. What does the 'Daughter of Zion's birthing process symbolize? I will address some of her birth pains as they are described in scripture; these prophetically and symbolically represent:

1) Coming Chaldean-caused social unrest;
2) Coming Chaldean-caused war;
3) The "birth" of God's people or a "nation"; or
4) The birth of a significant specific person in God's kingdom.

The first two above are larger mobilizations by the adversary when they realize that their time is short; the latter two represent God's deliverance of his people and his restoration of his Kingdom.

In this passage, I will examine social unrest and war (#'s 1 and 2 above) signaled through the person who is the 'Daughter of Zion' and the related prophetic signs via her birth pains in these last days. (In my next passage, Part 3, I will address the deliverance and restoration of God's people- (#'s 3 and 4 above) - through the lens of the 'Daughter of Zion's life story).

Birth Pains and Chaldean-caused Social Unrest

In *Writings of Lion's Lair, Volume 3*, I will describe the anti-Christ Chaldean adversary as a very powerful, worldwide criminal cabal. In aggregate, they are able to oppress and hold captive entire societies around the world because they "own" and control societies' most important people (in positions of power) and institutions. They work through their dedicated army of likely hundreds of millions of people who have taken secret blood oaths and pledges of loyalty.

Scripture makes it clear that Chaldean criminal activities, tactics and false idol worship will ultimately be uncovered. In a prophecy against 'Babylon' the Prophet Isaiah described a "dire vision," one he said caused his body to be, "racked with pain, pangs seized me *like those of a woman in labor.*" Isaiah observed, "The traitor betrays, the looter takes loot" (Is. 21:2). He is describing large-scale pillaging and plundering of societies in the last days. These are the days Jesus himself described as being the "beginning of sorrows (travails)" that will involve many other warning signs including the persecution of his sheep. In the 'Daughter of Zion's country ('Babylon') these travails are described further as follows through the Prophet Isaiah:

Therefore are my loins filled with pain: pangs have taken hold upon me, as the pangs of a woman that travaileth: I was bowed down at the hearing of it; I was dismayed at the seeing of it. (Is. 21:3)

This Chaldean criminal activity is further described by the Prophet Joel who prophetically warned a couple of times, "The day of the Lord is near." Joel expounded on Isaiah's vision:

At the sight of them, nations are in anguish; every face turns pale. (Joel 2:6)

Here, Joel observed that this "army of locusts":

- Charge like warriors

- March in line, and march straight ahead

- Plunge through defenses

- Rush upon the city and run along the wall

- Climb into houses and enter through windows (like thieves)

Scripture describes the anti-Christ Chaldeans as being a "law unto themselves." Their activity is the root of end times "lawlessness," even in the western "civilized" world. Lawlessness and corruption of this magnitude in any society naturally leads to social unrest and upheaval once it is discovered or reaches a tipping point of oppression of the particular nation's citizens.

Furthermore, given lying, deceptive and corrupt Chaldean leadership in any country, that particular country cannot keep its obligations and promises to other countries. Its deceptive, underhanded deeds and dealings will be discovered, and this will lead to conflict and war. This will be the case in the end times, especially for 'Babylon'-U.S. and the country of Israel.

Birth Pains and Chaldean-caused War

In this and future *Volumes*, I will address in more detail how God created the Chaldeans as a tool of judgment against his people. While they have been responsible for scattering his sheep worldwide and exist as a worldwide organization themselves, two primary countries should be in focus in the last days- Israel and the United States. While the upcoming war will be worldwide, these countries should be a focus because they hold significant populations of Christ-believers and God's people, Israel. It is for this reason that they will experience high levels of anti-Christ spirit persecution and war-provoking activity within. This is the manifestation of a spiritual kingdom war that targets these people first, but also ravages societies at-large. It is also activity that serves to oppress other nations. Our bellwether signs learned from the 'Daughter of Zion' are consistent with the view that these two countries should be kept in focus.

Anti-Christ Chaldean-initiated invasion- Israel

In speaking through the Prophet Jeremiah, God warned his people Judah of upcoming judgment and captivity at the hands of the Babylonians. In describing a great army "who are coming from the north" God asked the following questions:

Where is the flock that was entrusted to you, the sheep of which you boasted? What will you say when the Lord sets over you those you cultivated as your special allies? Will not pain grip you like that of a woman in labor? (Jer. 13:21)

Does the above scenario sound familiar? Recall from Part 1 of this series that the 'Daughter of Zion' is betrayed and abandoned. Labor pains in this scenario signal a coming attack as a result of God's judgment for the house of Israel's sinful ways. At the same time, a spiritual "birthing" and deliverance of an anointed remnant will also instigate the battle from the enemy's side.

In this ongoing spiritual war (i.e. 'Daughter of Zion's "seed" versus the serpent's seed- the Chaldeans) nation-against-nation war will manifest. In Part 1 of the 'Daughter of Zion's story, I provided scripture about a spiritually empty, barren country of Israel and how the 'Daughter of Zion's allies betrayed her, and furthermore that priests and elders will perish in the city while they search for food to stay alive. Accordingly, we learn that the condition of the country of Israel's so-called "holy" leaders (i.e. kings, prophets and priests) is utterly decrepit and misguided in the last days. (See *Volume 2* for more detail about the Last Days Country of Israel as well as God's judgment that will come upon it). We find the following in the book Jeremiah:

So put on sackcloth, lament and wail, for the fierce anger of the Lord has not turned away from us. In that day, declares the Lord, the king and the officials will lose heart, the priests will be horrified, and the prophets will be appalled. (Jer. 4:8-9)

Similarly, the Prophet Isaiah described his nation's spiritual condition as it applied in his day as well as prophetically for the last days. Isaiah continued the "birthing" analogy and lamented as follows:

We were pregnant, we writhed in pain, we gave birth to wind. We have brought no salvation to the earth, nor brought any life into the world. (Is. 26:18)

Unfortunately, God's people have not been a light for themselves or for the Gentiles. They do not recognize or know their true Savior Jesus Christ and therefore have been unable to preach about him to the rest of the world. The anointed remnant of Christ-believers referred to above that will be "birthed" will be an event that happens in a land to the north (i.e. Babylon).

As a result of the country of Israel's starved and ignorant spiritual condition in the last days God will turn them over to their own anti-Christ-spirit dialectic, imprisoning system. This controlling system will demonstrate to those in Israel the consequences of their immoral ways. These collective ways, as a country, when uncovered by others including both (former) "allies" and enemies, will bring an invasion described by God through the Prophet Jeremiah.

Here, the 'Daughter of Zion's life is once again a highly important, symbolic sign that foretells of this coming attack. God observed her blindly dressing up for her lovers (also symbolic for Judah-Israel's lovers) and reminded her, "Your lovers despise you; they seek your life" (Jer. 4:30). Then, through the Prophet Isaiah God prophetically observed the following scenario:

At the sound of horsemen and archers, every town takes to flight...I hear a cry of a woman in labor, a groan of one bearing her first child-the cry of the Daughter of Zion gasping for breath... (Jer. 4:29,31)

The people of Israel will be forced to flee upon attack.

And so, God's promise to/through Eve in the Garden about painful childbirth will indeed carry through, including symbolically. Here,

'Zion' must prepare to be attacked by her enemies. The child to be "birthed" has significance but I will address this in Chapter 9.

Anti-Christ Chaldean-initiated invasion- 'Babylon'

Like the war that will come against the country of Israel, so will war against the nation of 'Babylon' take place. (I address both of these invasions in detail in *Volume 2*). Within our scope for this current passage, I will view the war against 'Babylon' through the eyes of the 'Daughter of Zion' and in terms of birth pains that can be attributed to her.

I will also describe how destructive anti-Christ Chaldean tactics (via Isaiah's vision) in a society like 'Babylon' bring on war. In 'Babylon,' it is 'Jacob's anointed remnant who will "raise a banner on a hilltop" as a battle cry against the oppressive Chaldeans with the effect of the rest of the world seeing. God foretold:

I have commanded my holy ones; I have summoned my warriors to carry out my wrath- those who rejoice in my triumph. (Is. 13:3)

This is the manifestation of the "woman's seed" at enmity versus the serpent's seed. Members of the holy 'Jacob'-Judah remnant and "branch" will raise a "banner" as a sign of injustice, persecution and the hypocritical ways of a nation that falsely claims to uphold individual rights and liberties. This will cause an "uproar among the kingdoms, like nations massing together," and it will ultimately lead to an attack on the nation of 'Babylon' by "faraway lands" (ref. Isaiah, Chapter 13).

In fact, God foretells the nation of 'Babylon's destruction at the hands of these nations that he uses as a vehicle for his vengeance. God encourages them as follows:

Take up your positions around Babylon, all you who draw the bow. Shoot at her. Spare no arrows; for she has sinned against the Lord. (Is. 50:14)

God's punishment will be in part due to the Babylonian-Chaldean's pride, frolicking and rejoicing as part of their actions in, "pillaging (his) inheritance." (Jer. 50:11)

So, God will eventually turn over the Babylon-U.S.'s Chaldeans to their enemies to be invaded and plundered themselves. This time, as a result of God's sovereign plan, he first uses his own anointed remnant in 'Babylon' and then summons compliant nations. This means that the foremost 'capital' country of world Babylon's *kingdom* will be invaded. It will then be the Chaldean leaders and their people- living in a land of luxuries- who are gripped by terror and, "writhe in *pain like that of a woman in labor*" (Is. 13:8). Leaders in the nation of 'Babylon'-U.S. will react as follows:

The king of Babylon has heard reports about them, and his hands hang limp. Anguish has gripped him, pain like that of a woman in labor. (Jer. 50:43)

Note again the significance of birth pains to the last days situation in the nation of 'Babylon.' There is a strong link between the 'Daughter of Zion' and 'Babylon' just as there is with our other end times figures. I will discuss Zion's direct link in more detail in my next passage. I discuss the breakdown of societies in the last days due to the lawless Chaldeans in my book, *Biblical End Times, Volume 2*.

~

God will take vengeance for himself and on behalf of his faithful anointed remnant in these last days (see *Writings of Lion's Lair, Volume 2*). Watch the U.S. and the country of Israel closely as these societies continue to unravel and become increasingly perplexed as a result of being caught in their own "trap" and "web" of crime, oppression and imprisonment that they, themselves, have long participated in and supported. Their own "system" will come back to haunt them.

With this relatively ominous news now out of the way, my next passage (Part 3) will provide some good news; that is, God's deliverance of his anointed remnant and the restoration of his Kingdom.

7.3 The Daughter of Zion- An End Times Figure, Millennial Kingdom Queen (Part 3)

In Part 1 of this series about the 'Daughter of Zion,' I showed how she fits the profile of the previously discussed anointed Judah remnant of the last days. She is holy, royal, and righteous; yet, she faces God-ordained persecution at the hands of the anti-Christ Chaldeans.

In Part 1, I described her persecution in some detail. In the midst of her story of persecution and travails, we find a prophetic picture of God's discipline that will also come upon both the country of Israel and the nation of 'Babylon.'

In Part 2 of this series, the 'Daughter of Zion's "birthing" and labor pains symbolic of an expectant mother were shown to be key signs of significant last days events that are presented in scripture. These travails foreshadow social unrest and war, worldwide, but with special importance for Israel and the nation of 'Babylon'-U.S. that includes 'Israel's 'northern kingdom' within. I surmised that this will be a result of anti-Christ Chaldean control and influence in these countries, not to mention their persecution of true Christ-believing citizens.

In this current passage, I will revisit the 'Daughter of Zion's battle against the Chaldeans. I will show how she benefits and is ultimately victorious as a result of prayer and supplication for her, and most importantly, as a result of God's sovereign plan for her deliverance and restoration. Her deliverance coincides with an exodus from 'Babylon,' and then ultimately leads to her honor and glory as a Matriarch and Queen in God's restored heavenly Kingdom.

Keep in mind, as I mentioned before, that her story is a picture of events still to come for the country of Israel and for a larger remnant of God's people.

Prayer and Supplication

The Prophet Jeremiah heard directly from God about the coming destruction and "grievous wound" that his people would suffer. God referred to his people here as his "daughter," and foretold of coming drought, famine and war on Judah-Jerusalem. This represented God's punishment against his rebellious nation and people. Jeremiah then interceded with God:

Have you rejected Judah completely? Do you despise Zion? Why have you afflicted us so that we cannot be healed? (Jer. 14:19)

This is foretelling of the 'Daughter of Zion's and her fellow Judah partners' troubles in the last days. King David, in his prophetic Psalms, also prayed for the deliverance of Zion. In two of his Psalms, both lamenting a future time when all have "turned aside" and have become corrupt, King David foresaw a time of oppression and attack against God's people and pleaded:

Oh, that salvation for Israel will come out of Zion; When the Lord restores the fortunes of his people, let Jacob rejoice and Israel be glad. (Ps. 14:7,53:6)

This Psalm can be seen as referring to *end times* 'Jacob' and 'Daughter of Zion' figures. In another of his prophetic Psalms intended for the last days, one in which King David acknowledged that, "The Lord's renown endures through all generations," and remarked that he was writing for a "future generation- a people not yet created," King David prophesied:

You will arise and have compassion on Zion, for it is time to show her favor; the appointed time has come. (Ps. 102:13)

King David wrote this Psalm during his own extreme persecution and hardship at the hands of the anti-Christ spirit of his day.

Zion's Protection and Power to Fight Back Against the Chaldeans

Through Isaiah, the Lord himself reminded the 'Daughter of Zion' of his sovereignty and the fact that she has his divine protection. As one who is a key member of his Kingdom she enjoys the, "heritage of the servants of the Lord." God promised her:

No weapon forged against thee shall prosper, and you will refute every tongue that accuses you. (Is. 54:17)

Not only is the 'Daughter of Zion' protected but scripture tells us that she is given power by the Lord to fight back against her anti-Christ Chaldean enemy. Through the Prophet Micah, the Lord instructs:

Rise and thresh, O Daughter of Zion, for I will give you horns of iron; I will give you hoofs of bronze and you will break into pieces many nations. (Mic. 4:13)

This may get you (the reader) wondering as to how a single woman can fight entire "nations" in the last days. Here, you might consider how anti-Christ Chaldean criminal and rights-violating tactics including massive amounts of "underground" conspiring, illegal surveillance and spying might be uncovered and backfire on the perpetrators.

The 'Daughter of Zion' likely also has her own army or allies of sorts. While her traitor "friends-allies" will disappear, she will likely find some allies and support as a result of her righteousness and for the larger sake and cause of justice. At the very least, we know that she will be a part of the 'Jacob'-Judah anointed remnant's army in the last days. (I will address how this "army" resists in Chapter 8). The following couple of verses point to this army's ability to fight a battle, Judah warrior-style, in the last days:

My anger burns against the shepherds, and I will punish the leaders; for the Lord will care for his flock, the house of Judah and make them like a proud horse in battle. (Zech. 10:3)

The remnant of Jacob will be among the nations, in the midst of many peoples, like a lion among the beasts of the forest, like a young lion among flocks of sheep, which mauls and mangles as it goes, and no one can rescue. (Mic. 5:8)

In this latter line of scripture through the Prophet Micah God ensures, "Your hand will be lifted up in triumph over your enemies."

Deliverance and Exodus

Indeed. The Lord will answer prayers from his 'Jacob army'-Judah anointed remnant and he will deliver on his promise to save his people and inheritance. This includes the 'Daughter of Zion.' In discussing the last days deliverance of the people of Zion-Jerusalem the Lord describes how he will defeat evil and deliver justice for the righteous. Here, God says, "Zion will be redeemed with justice, her repentant ones with righteousness" (Is. 1:27).

The anti-Christ Chaldeans will be defeated and punished as a result of their war against the 'Daughter of Zion' and her 'Jacob'-Judah remnant family. God promised that he will devour those who devour, plunder those who plunder, and spoil those who spoil (Jer. 30:16). God is no-doubt referring to the anti-Christ Chaldean criminal mob here. God says directly to 'Zion,' with broader meaning for 'Jacob,' the anointed remnant and the country of Israel as well:

But I will restore you to health and heal your wounds, because you are called an outcast, Zion for whom no one cares. (Jer. 30:17)

The healing of 'Zion's and 'Jacob's "wounds" here is another example of the Lord's coming vindication for his heritage and inherited people who will be unfairly accused and persecuted in the last days. I will discuss in a later passage as well as in *Writings of Lion's Lair, Volume 2,* about the deliverance of Israel. There will still be an element of forgiveness required, even alongside his vindication. God's grace toward the 'Daughter of Zion' is illustrated here:

Sing, O Daughter of Zion, shout aloud O Israel! Be glad and rejoice, with all your heart, O Daughter of Jerusalem. The Lord has taken away your punishment, he has turned back your enemy... (Zeph. 3:14-15)

Similarly, speaking to a last days country and people of Israel that is under judgment and chased out of their land, the Prophet Jeremiah prophetically addressed the 'Daughter of Zion' and said, *"Your punishment will end; he will not prolong your exile"* (Lam. 4:22).

Exodus from Babylon

Speaking of exile, we are given a pretty strong indication that the 'Daughter of Zion' will escape from 'Babylon's matrix-system in the last days along with her 'Jacob'-Judah remnant counterparts. She is part of the same remnant that God instructs, "flee 'Babylon,'" and who God instructs "Go ye out of the midst of her" (Jer. 51:45). God is going to punish 'Babylon,' which he says must fall, primarily because of "Israel's slain." The 'Daughter of Zion' is addressed specifically regarding this escape as follows:

Come O Zion. Escape you who live in the Daughter of Babylon. (Zech. 2:7)

Writhe in agony O Daughter of Zion, like a woman in labor. For now leave the city and camp in the open field. You will go to Babylon; there you will be rescued; the Lord will redeem you from the hands of your enemies. (Mic. 4:10)

Note the reference again here in the verse above to a "woman in labor," a symbol that I addressed in Part 2 of this series. Here, 'Zion's labor is a signal for coming war- possibly the beginning of the period of "Jacob's trouble," which scripture says 'Jacob' (and likely his remnant) will be "saved out of." A latter exodus event for this remnant- a people referred to as God's "ransomed" and a "band of survivors" is explained further through Jeremiah as follows:

Sing with joy for Jacob; shout for the foremost of nations...and say, O Lord save your people, the remnant of Israel. See, I will bring them from the land of the north, and gather them from the ends of the earth. (Jer. 31:8)

Where will God's small remnant from a country in the north go? God answers in Jeremiah, *"They will come and shout for joy- on the heights of Zion..."* (Jer. 31:12). God's holy hill will be their final destination although given coming events in the Day of the Lord there will very likely be intermediate stops along the way.

Daughter of Zion- the Honor of a Heavenly Kingdom Queen

There is much that can be said about God's coming Millennial Kingdom. Within this Kingdom, the 'Daughter of Zion' will be extremely blessed and is personally fully restored with all power, honor and beauty.

In Part 1, I established her as the wife of the Lord Almighty. The King comes to her, as is shown in the following verses:

And thou, O tower of the flock, the stronghold of the daughter of Zion, unto thee shall it come, even the first dominion; the kingdom shall come to the daughter of Jerusalem. (Mic. 4:8)

Rejoice greatly, O daughter of Zion; shout, O daughter of Jerusalem: behold, thy King cometh unto thee: he is just, and having salvation; lowly, and riding upon an ass, and upon a colt the foal of an ass. (Zech. 9:9)

This union will signal the beginning of the heavenly Millennial Kingdom in which Jesus' will reign- the Kingdom that the Lord is referring to when he said, "The house of Israel will possess the nations" (Is. 14:2). We also learn that the "captors" of this current world will become captives and that the Lord and his servant 'David' will rule over the oppressors.

The birth of the new Kingdom of God

The 'Daughter of Zion' will have a role as a Kingdom Queen and mother figure. The former barren, desolate and "outcast" 'Daughter of Zion' will become the Matriarch for God's Kingdom of holy, royal children. These blessings are described in the following verses addressed to the 'Daughter of Zion':

Lift up your eyes and look around; all your sons gather and come to you. As surely as I live, declares the Lord, you will wear them all as ornaments; you will put them on like a bride. (Is. 49:18)

Sing, O barren woman, you who never bore a child; burst into song, shout for joy, you who were never in labor; because more are the children of the desolate woman than those who has a husband, says the Lord. (Is. 54:1)

The 'Daughter of Zion's royal family on Mount Zion in Jerusalem, will fulfill the "zeal" of the Lord Almighty in accomplishing a holy inheritance in his name. This will be the anointed Judah remnant that will become God's holy vineyard, similar to ancient Judah that remained in King Hezekiah's day about whom God said, "will take root below and bear fruit above" (Is. 37:31).

~

In a happy conclusion, the 'Daughter of Zion' is promised lasting peace "like a river" from the Lord himself. It is clear from scripture that the 'Daughter of Zion' will draw close to the Lord and the Lord will honor his covenant commitment to her. To Zion, the Lord says:

And the Gentiles shall see thy righteousness, and all kings thy glory: and thou shalt be called by a new name, which the mouth of the Lord shall name. (Is. 62:2)

This is an incredibly powerful and glorious ending (and new heavenly beginning) for the 'Daughter of Zion.' I describe the Millennial heavenly Kingdom in more detail in my books, *Biblical End Times, Volumes 1 and 2.*

Chapter 8.

Prophecy of the Anointed Remnant's Battle and Resistance

Passages from Lion's Lair provided in this chapter include:

8.1 Prophetic Questions (and Answers) Given in the Bible (Part 1)

8.2 Prophetic Questions (and Answers) Given in the Bible (Part 2)

8.3 The Last Days 'Jacob army'

8.1 Prophetic Questions (and Answers) Given in the Bible (Part 1)

There are many questions asked in scripture, including different *types* (i.e. direct, rhetorical, etc.). For the purposes of this passage, I examined questions asked in the books of the Major and Minor Prophets, as well as those that are found in the "books of Wisdom" (i.e. Psalms, Proverbs, Ecclesiastes). Overall, these questions appear to fall into the following categories: demonstrating God's sovereignty; lamenting; warning of pending judgment; and demonstrating God's deliverance of his people.

I then selected specific questions that are asked in a prophetic context and yield answers and content that is useful for our purposes in understanding prophetic events to come. These questions, along with their answers, generally support, and in some cases, add new understanding to prophetic themes. In this current passage scriptural question-answer content is organized into the following categories:

- Kingdom-related
- "Called for service"- Battling against the Chaldeans
- "Called for service"- Messenger duty
- God's deliverance

Selected questions in each of these areas and their associated prophetic insights are discussed below. Many of these questions are asked directly by God to or through the particular prophet who is writing according to God's Word.

(Note: many answers to these questions point to just a few servants in the last days, including 'Jacob' and 'David' who I addressed earlier. I attempt to provide the named servant according to scripture, but the reader should consider in their own minds the possibility of some of these solely or jointly applying to Jesus Christ himself. Of course, we are told that all scripture ultimately speaks of him).

Kingdom-related

For our purposes, kingdom-related questions are those that are prophetically related to God's Kingdom, especially the coming Millennial Kingdom people and its structure, including Jerusalem and God's "holy hill." I address these as follows.

Question: *Lord- who may dwell in your sanctuary? Who may live on your holy hill?* (Ps. 15:1, King David)

Answer in context: King David was one who often pondered God's Kingdom and eternal royal throne. We know King David's deep faith, righteousness and resistance to corruption as a king. Here, he was not only alluding to himself but also in prophetic terms (possibly to Millennial Prince 'David'). David answered his own question as follows:

He whose walk is blameless and does what is righteous, who speaks truth from his heart and has no slander on his tongue, who does his neighbor no wrong and casts no slur on his fellowman, who despises a vile man but honors those who fear the Lord, who keeps his oath even when it hurts... (Ps. 15:2-4)

Question: *Who may ascend the hill of the Lord? Who may stand in his holy place?* (Ps. 24:3, King David)

<u>Answer in context</u>: This is a question similar to the one above. In prophetic terms, David foresaw vindication for a future generation of those who seek the Lord. His answer was similar to that given for the first question above, yet more concise; that is, one who is righteous. He answered specifically:

He who has clean hands and a pure heart, who does not lift up his soul to an idol or swear by what is false. (Ps. 24:4)

<u>Question</u>: *...and I will cause him to draw near, and he shall approach unto me: for who is this that engaged his heart to approach unto me? saith the Lord?* (Jer. 30:21, God)

<u>Answer in context</u>: This question was posed in the last days context of an Israel that finds itself lost in corruption, abandoned by its allies, and in the absence of God. In the coming time of "Jacob's Trouble" and an "incurable wound" as a result of the anti-Christ Chaldean adversary ("foreigners"). Modern day Israel will find itself accused, enslaved, and plundered. God addressed his own question through Jeremiah as follows:

Their leader will be one of their own; their ruler will rise from among them. I will bring him near and he will come close to me. (Jer. 30:21)

This "leader" is likely again referring to Millennial Prince 'David' who is mentioned earlier in this same chapter in the book of Jeremiah.

"Called for service"- Battling against the Chaldeans

Prophetic questions in this category, asked mostly by God himself, point directly to his end times servants who battle directly against the anti-Christ Chaldeans. Thus, you will recognize that the short answer, or main figure addressed, for each of these questions is very likely end times 'Jacob' or 'David.'

<u>Question</u>: *Can a man break iron- iron from the north- or bronze?* (Jer. 15:12, God)

<u>Answer in context</u>: This is prophetically referring to a man who has been "born" (Jer. 15:10), and with whom the "whole land strives and contends." He is a righteous servant, albeit one who must still call to God for repentance. He will be heavily persecuted at the hands of the anti-Christ Chaldeans. Jeremiah's words describe how this man sits alone, enslaved, in "unending pain," and filled with indignation. God responded:

Surely I will deliver you for a good purpose; surely I will make your enemies plead with you in times of disaster and distress. (Jer. 15:11)

Many times in his Word, God promised victory and deliverance for last days 'Jacob' over his enemy.

<u>Question:</u> The sinners in Zion are terrified; trembling grips the godless: '*Who of us can dwell with the consuming fire? Who of us can dwell with everlasting burning?*' (Is. 33:14, God)

<u>Answer in context</u>: This is a vision of last days Judah (country of Israel) amidst destruction as a result of anti-Christ Chaldean "traitors" and "betrayers" within who plunder like "locusts" and destroy God's land and people-at large. The quick answer to this question as to who can stand is simply:

This is the man who will dwell on the heights, whose refuge will be the mountain fortress... (Is. 33:16)

This again sounds like 'Jacob' who is directly referred to as a "fire" in his battle or else Millennial Prince 'David.' This servant is additionally described in this same line of scripture as:

He who walks righteously and speaks what is right, who rejects gain from extortion and keeps his hand from accepting bribes, who stops his ears against plots of murder and shuts his eyes against contemplating evil. (Is. 33:15)

<u>Question(s):</u> *Who has stirred up one from the east, calling him in righteousness to his service?* (Is. 41:2, God); *Which of you will listen*

to this or pay close attention in the time to come? ... Who handed Jacob over to become loot, and Israel to the plunderers? (Is. 42:23, God)

<u>Answer in context</u>: Our sovereign God himself will place 'Jacob' into service. I showed in Chapter 5 that end times 'Jacob' is a redeemer and an instrument to convey Jesus' Truth and Light in the last days in the midst of a massive amount of sin, darkness and corruption. God promised 'Jacob':

...You are my servant; I have chosen you and have not rejected you. So do not fear, for I am with you... (Is. 41:9-10)

In the last days God gives 'Jacob' power to "turn kings to dust" and to "thresh the mountains and crush them." This is referring to 'Jacob's battle against the anti-Christ Chaldeans.

"Called for service"- Messenger Duty

Here, we will see that God's servants like 'Jacob' and 'David' are also called to communicate like prophets or messengers to God's people. They will speak truth and give serious warnings. The Prophet Isaiah, in his own commission and prophetic vision as given by God, offered to be a messenger for his corrupt, evil-minded people. High priests, chosen by God, such as the prophetic figure "Joshua" (described through Zechariah) in the old scripture are also natural candidates.

<u>Question</u>: *Whom shall I send? And who will go for us?* (Is. 6:8, God)

<u>Answer in context</u>: God's people in Isaiah's day had hearts that were sinful and were far from him. God was preparing their land for destruction and for them to be taken into captivity. After Isaiah's own sins were atoned for by the angels as an answer to his prayer, when he was called he answered God, "Here am I, send me!" God instructed Isaiah to make the people's hearts "calloused," to make their "ears dull," and to "close their eyes."

This is very likely a picture for a repeating end times scenario given what we know about all end times prophetic scripture. There will be Isaiah-like end times watchmen and messenger(s) during these last days when people's hearts are hardened (i.e. "heartless") or are "without natural affection." In this time, due to God's discipline and worldwide destruction only a stump of holy seed will be left, just as it was in the land of Judah in Isaiah's day.

Question(s): *What man is wise enough to understand this? Who has been instructed by the Lord and can explain it? Why has the land been ruined and laid waste like a desert that no one can cross?* (Jer. 9:12, God)

Answer in context: God asks this question through the Prophet Jeremiah in the midst of a people who were deep in corruption and sin, particularly lying, deception and adultery. They deceived others and were deceived themselves. This is a clear picture of both the end times country of Israel and the larger worldwide "house of Israel" given their allegiance to world Babylon's Chaldeans. God observed:

You live in the midst of deception; in their deceit they refuse to acknowledge me. (Jer. 9:6)

Given the context, the only man who can be the one to answer these questions is someone who identifies, understands and battles with the anti-Christ Chaldeans, and who has discernment to understand their tactics and the "mystery of iniquity." Again, end times 'Jacob' and 'David' both fit these qualifications.

Question: See, I will send my messenger, who will prepare the way for me…*But who can endure the day of his coming? Who can stand when he appears?* (Mal. 3:1-2, God)

Answer in context: Here, God is explaining coming judgment in the last days and that his messenger will be like a "refiner's fire" or as a "launderer's soap" who will refine the Levites and then will pave the way for God's judgment. In this case, God is speaking to Judah (country of Israel) and its corrupt priests who are desecrating the sanctuary. He forewarns of a messenger who will purify and refine them.

Several last days watchmen will warn of Jesus' soon-coming judgment and return. According to scripture (Mk. 1:1-9), John the Baptist fulfilled a similar role when he came but there is also likely to be another "type" of John the Baptist in the end times. "Joshua," the high priest discussed through the Prophet Zechariah, is a good candidate as a result of his role in purifying the Levites. Of course, Jesus (Yeshua) is the highest of all priests and King of Kings and will administer final, decisive judgment in the Day of the Lord.

God's Deliverance

God offers deliverance for his people in the midst of their last days troubles. He maintains his position of acceptance and forgiveness of his people in the midst of their transgressions, calling for them to turn back to him. He continuously reminds them of his sovereignty and his presence so that they will have faith. This is represented by the following question: Who are you that you fear mortal men…that you forget the Lord your maker? (Is. 51:12).

The following questions-and-answers are related to God's (offers for) deliverance of his people.

<u>Question</u>: *Where is your mother's certificate for divorce, with which I sent her away? Or to which of my creditors did I sell you?* (Is. 50:1, God)

<u>Answer in context</u>: God was asking this question to a sinful, rebellious Israel. He was making the point that because of their sinful behavior they were taken captive and as a result they have turned away from him. In making his point again, he further asked, "When I came, why was there no one? When I called, why was there no one to answer? Was my arm too short to ransom you?…" (Is. 50:2). His people lacked knowledge, understanding, and were devoid of faith. God did not turn away- his people did.

<u>Question</u>: *Woe to shepherds of Israel who only take care of themselves. Should not shepherds take care of the flock?* (Ez. 34:2)

<u>Answer in context</u>: This is part of Ezekiel's last days vision and has implications for (the country of) Israel's leaders as well as those in other nations. God says that he will judge "between one sheep and another" and "between rams and goats," with the latter implying that he will look at those of power and influence and detect who are oppressive leaders. At the hands of these leaders who rule "harshly and brutally" it is clear that God's sheep will be plundered, enslaved and oppressed in the last days. As a result, God foretells us that his sheep will end up "wandering" and scattered.

Jesus came for Israel's lost sheep. God's solution to the question at hand is deliverance for Jesus Christ-believers, and as we know God foretold, "I will place over them one shepherd, my servant David, and he will tend them; he will tend them and be their shepherd" (Ez. 34:23). This is the Millennial Kingdom Prince 'David' who will serve the King, Jesus Christ.

<u>Question</u>: *Who is wise? He will realize these things. Who is discerning? He will understand them.* (Hos. 14:9, God)

<u>Answer in context</u>: The worldwide house of Israel in the last days will realize that they cannot be saved by human hands and human-created gods. In particular, they cannot be saved by "Assyria" nor "Egypt," which are merely arms of world Babylon's Kingdom that appear to provide a solution to the problems that they have created themselves.

The house of Israel here is too weighed down and is trapped by its own sin. God says that he will answer both 'Israel' and 'Ephraim' in the time of their need and will restore them.

God answers the question above himself, implying that it is one who is righteous and turns away from the imprisoning adversary who can discern. He responded:

The ways of the Lord are right; the righteous walk in them, but the rebellious stumble in them. (Hos. 14:9)

This contrasts God's Kingdom's remnant with the last days worldly kingdom population who bow down and are controlled by the oppressive, enslaving anti-Christ Chaldeans who hold them hostage in their transgressions.

~

Many of God's prophetic questions and their respective answers given through his prophets in scripture serve to highlight God's absolute sovereignty. In an end times scenario where anti-Christ Chaldean attempts at establishing Babylon's new world order will fail, God will still establish his servants, his message and ultimately his Kingdom. This will happen exactly according to his plan that was set from before man's creation. I discuss the path back to the Lord's Kingdom in the end times in my books, *Biblical End Times, Volumes 1 and 2*.

8.2 Prophetic Questions (and Answers) Given in the Bible (Part 2)

In Part 1, I chose prophecy-related questions that appear in the books of the Major and Minor Prophets as well as in the Psalms; I then provided answers in context based on supporting scripture. In this passage, I will repeat the same process, albeit with new content. This content still supports, and in some cases augments, the major prophetic themes that I have been regularly addressing to this point. Scriptural question-answer content in this passage is organized into the following categories:

- "Called for Service"- Battling against the Chaldeans
- God's protection and deliverance
- God's judgment and coming destruction

Selected questions in each of these areas and their prophetic insights are discussed below. Many of these questions are asked directly by God, either to or through the particular prophets noted.

Called for Service- Battling against the Chaldeans

Just as was the case when I addressed questions in this same category in Part 1, the answers to these questions in context are end times 'Jacob' and 'David' figures who we know resist the anti-Christ

Chaldeans. They will be servants of Jesus Christ, about whom all scripture ultimately speaks about. Their last days battle and ultimate victory is shown in the following question-and-answer content.

<u>Question:</u> *Who will rise up for me against the wicked? Who will take a stand for me against evildoer*s? (Ps. 94:16, God, likely through King David)

<u>Answer in context</u>: This verse is within a Psalm about righteous servants of the Lord battling the anti-Christ army who are described as wicked, arrogant, boastful, and who "crush" and oppress God's inheritance.

The answer to this question is the author himself, King David, who describes this 'man' practically from a third person standpoint, perhaps referring to the end times 'Davidic Prince.' This man who "stands up" is one who the Lord disciplines and who learns his law. He is one who is "upright in heart" and counts on the Lord as his refuge and fortress.

King David often prayed for and meditated upon God's inheritance and here acknowledged how the Lord will never forsake his inheritance and that this 'man' who rises up and takes a stand will be granted "relief from days of trouble."

<u>Question</u>: He who vindicates me is near. *Who then will bring charges against me? Let us face each other! Who is my accuser? Let him confront me!* (Is. 50:8, 'Jacob')

<u>Answer in context</u>: This question is asked by end times servant 'Jacob' who I have described is accused and persecuted by the anti-Christ Chaldeans. In this line of scripture 'Jacob' admits that he is weary, but that he has maintained God's Word and righteousness and otherwise not hidden his face from "mocking and spitting."

The answer here, then, is already implied. For one who has followed God's Word and law and rests in the grace and vindication of Jesus Christ there is no condemnation. It will be the ones who are the accusers whom 'Jacob' says in this part of scripture will "lie down in torment."

Question: Like a lion coming up from Jordan's thickets to a rich pastureland, I will chase Babylon from its land in an instant. *Who is the chosen one I will appoint for this? Who is like me and who can challenge me? And what shepherd can stand against me?* (Jer. 50:44, God)

Answer in context: This line of questions is asked in the last days context of God declaring judgment and punishment (i.e. "a sword") on 'Babylon' and its officials. He instructs his people to "flee" and to, "Run for your lives!"

God says here that he will chase end times 'Babylon' from its land in an instant, with the Hebrew meaning indicating an initial dividing and fragmenting within the land. The one he "appoints" for this is directly associated with lifting up a "banner" against 'Babylon.' This "banner" for judgment is mentioned twice through the Prophet Jeremiah in this line of text.

The one "appointed" is end times 'David,' the 'Davidic Prince' figure, who I have described in Chapter 6 as the "Branch" and raises an initial "banner" as a signal for battle.

Question: *Who is a God like you, who pardons sin and forgives the transgression of the remnant of his inheritance?* You do not stay angry forever but delight to show mercy. (Mic. 7:18, through Micah)

Answer in context: This servant of God lives in a last days society full of corruption and sin that includes the house of Israel within; it is decimated by the anti-Christ Chaldeans. This servant suffers persecution.

This grateful servant of God's inheritance understands the principle of God's grace, mercy and forgiveness. While he currently "sits in darkness" and remarks that he has "fallen," he has great faith and confidence that God will deliver him with justice. This servant foresees the day when his enemy will be "covered with shame," and will be, "trampled underfoot like mire in the streets."

The servant who is the rhetorical beneficiary of this prophetic question asked through the Prophet Micah is very likely or very similar to either end times 'Jacob' or 'David.' These are the ones, as we know, who are at the forefront in the battle against the anti-Christ Chaldeans in the last days on behalf of God's inheritance and remnant.

God's Protection and Deliverance

Prophetic questions and answers in this section show how in the last days battle of God's servants versus their Chaldean persecutors that God divinely protects them during this time and ultimately delivers them. His wrath then turns toward Babylon's Chaldeans.

Question: *Has the Lord struck her as he struck down those who struck her? Has she been killed as those were killed who killed her?* (Is. 27:7, God)

Answer in context: These questions are asked in the context of the coming prophetic time of the Lord's vengeance and worldwide punishment right as he is about to restore his heavenly Kingdom.

God is asking whether her who was struck (i.e. his "fruitful vineyard," which was struck by the anti-Christ Chaldeans), was struck like he struck the adversary. Of course, the Lord is the rock who will strike, punish and destroy the anti-Christ kingdom once and for all before he sets up his reign.

In this verse, it is again clear that the Lord has set-aside a remnant vine of his people for himself. He says, "I watch over it; I guard it day and night so that no one may harm it" (Is. 27:3). God says all of the world is filled with the fruit of this vine in these last days when 'Jacob' "takes root" and 'Israel' buds and blossoms.

The simple answer to this question is that God essentially protects his chosen remnant/vineyard that is faithful to him in the last days and destroys their enemies.

Question: *See, I am doing a new thing! Now it springs up; do you not perceive it? I am making a way in the wilderness and streams in the wasteland.* (Is 43:19, God)

<u>Answer in context</u>: This question asked by God invokes deep thought and mystery. God says here and elsewhere through Isaiah, "I am doing a new thing" (Is. 48:10). This is presented within the background and context of an unfaithful, sinful Israel, albeit with an Israel remnant that God is going to deliver out of Babylon. It is no wonder that right before this question, God reminded of his deliverance of his people out of Egypt- when he gave them a "path through the mighty waters." And right *after* he asks this question he refers to "wild animals" who honor him, people whom he says, "I formed for myself," and for whom he will also "make a way" in the desert in the last days.

In a nutshell, this is a prophecy for God's remnant (vineyard) about whom I showed above God watches out for and guards. The prophetic answer here is that this remnant will be protected, delivered, saved and given the opportunity for an escape out of last days 'Babylon.'

<u>Question</u>: *Can plunder be taken from warriors, or captives be rescued from the fierce?* (Is. 49:24, God)

<u>Answer in context</u>: This is another question, asked by God, in the *last days* of his people's deliverance from their oppression at the hands of their powerful enemies. In this stanza of text God mentions again he will lift up his "banner" and interestingly says that he will "beckon to the Gentiles." (Recall that last days 'Jacob' as a redeemer and a "light" to the Gentiles).

God will actually employ the help of the Gentiles and answers his own question in the following verse:

Yes, captives will be taken from warriors and plunder retrieved from the fierce. I will contend with those who contend with you, and your children I will save. (Is. 49:25)

We are told in scripture that the Gentiles will carry Israel's children back to them in their arms once they are restored and truth is revealed in the last days.

<u>Question</u>: *These double calamities have come upon you—who can comfort you?—ruin and destruction, famine and sword—who can console you?* (Is. 51:19, God)

<u>Answer in context</u>: This question is asked by our sovereign God who is addressing his people Zion and is making a point to them. It also has meaning for the 'Daughter of Zion' as well.

His people are oppressed and held captive; the 'Daughter of Zion's sons have fainted and are "like antelope caught in a net." 'Jerusalem' and her people have had to drink from the cup of God's wrath for their disobedience. They are suffering from severe distress and destruction.

God makes a very strong point about these last days so that his people will finally learn. He will take his cup of wrath against them and then hand it over to their oppressors and tormentors. God's people 'Israel' will see this happen and will finally be comforted; and more importantly, *they will finally learn that Jesus Christ is their only God.*

God's Judgment and Coming Destruction

One clear prophetic link in God's Word about the times of coming destruction is that there will be great spiritual deception that is promulgated and fueled by false prophets, some of whom do not know any better; i.e. these are deceived themselves. Others, however, have fully subscribed to the evil Chaldean agenda and proudly carry out the adversary's orders.

When his disciples asked him about signs of the last days when they were on the Mount of Olives there is a good reason that Jesus remarked first about deception. He said, "Take heed that no one deceives you" (Matt. 24:4). Deception, including that which is led by false prophets, is highly correlated with scripture about coming destruction in the last days.

<u>Question</u>: *But which of them has stood in the council of the Lord to see or to hear his word? Who has listened and heard his word?* (Jer. 23:18)

<u>Answer in context</u>: There are many questions asked in the book of Jeremiah that draw out one particular theme in the face of coming judgment. That is, Israel, God's own people, especially its prophets and priests, have gone apostate and worship false gods. They do not

know their own God. This is a clear prophetic teaching for our current last days; it is happening now.

Double-talking, two-faced anti-Christ spirit prophets and priests in Israel today are forecasting that there will be peace, on the one hand, while on the other hand they live in a society that is full of wickedness, evildoers and false (Chaldean) gods. And worse yet, some of these spiritual "leaders" very likely participate in this activity themselves.

God makes a point here that prophets who tell lies in his name will not be able to hide. The answer to the question above is that *virtually no one* hears his Word, both then and now.

<u>Question</u>: *The lion has roared—who will not fear? The Sovereign Lord has spoken—who can but prophesy?* (Am. 3:8, God)

<u>Answer in context</u>: Through the Prophet Amos, God is addressing his "whole family" he brought out of Egypt- the "house of Jacob." Last days implications of prophecy in Amos include the coming destruction of Israel and its neighbors at the hands of their enemies. And since this is an attack against the whole "house of Israel" it includes 'Babylon' where its 'northern kingdom' resides.

God has somewhat already answered his own question in scripture above but he also says, "Surely the Sovereign Lord does nothing without revealing his plan to his servants the prophets" (Am. 3:7). When a last days servant or watchman like 'Jacob' or 'David' begins warning in the midst of a sea of "false peace"-Chaldean prophets God's people had better take notice.

<u>Question</u>: *Who is it he is trying to teach? To whom is he explaining his message? To children weaned from their milk, to those just taken from the breast?* (Is. 28:9, Isaiah)

<u>Answer in context</u>: God is primarily speaking here to the pride of Ephraim's false priests and prophets who he says are, "befuddled with wine" and "reel from beer." These are likely clergy who are controlled or influenced by the anti-Christ spirit, and are therefore predisposed to believe and promulgate a lie, rather than to seek and promote truth.

These will help usher in Babylon's new world order "covenant with death," as God refers to it, without even realizing it.

God's insinuation in this question is that he is speaking to those who are like children just weaned from their milk which reminds of the Apostle Paul in the book of Hebrews who distinguishes between milk and solid food, with the latter representing the ability to *discern* between good and evil (Heb. 5:14). Those "just weaned" lack this kind of discernment.

Justice and righteousness will ultimately prevail, but those who are deceived will be "beaten down" by the "overwhelming scourge." The scourge is the Chaldean dialectic process and false god matrix that is full of lies and causes mass social unrest, confusion and confoundment. We are seeing this take hold in our current day.

Question: You descendants of Jacob, should it be said, '*Does the Lord become impatient? Does he do such things?' 'Do not my words do good to the one whose ways are upright?'* (Mic. 2:7, Micah, God)

Answer in context: Through the Prophet Micah we learn that the anti-Christ Chaldean-caused "incurable wound" has come to Judah-Jerusalem in the last days. This describes the people of 'Israel' in his land who have followed the Chaldean's false god system and then defrauded their own people- taking their land, seizing their homes, breaking up their families, etc.

Not surprisingly, due to their selling out to global Babylon's system, these false prophets reject the Prophet Micah's words of pending disaster and exile and say, "Do not prophesy about these things; disgrace will not overtake us" (Mic. 2:6). Micah's prophetic words apply to Israel's people and their prophets and priests in today's society.

The questions above are a rebuttal to the false prophets. The simple distinction is that God *does* get angry and disciplines his servants but he still looks for his people who are upright. In the midst of his coming punishment he will save a remnant.

~

Prophetic questions and answers in the books of Major and Minor prophets demonstrate some essential biblical truths. There is a major last days battle between God's servants and the anti-Christ Chaldeans. There is a remnant of Israel who stand up and battle; God will ultimately deliver and reward them. In the meantime, much destruction we see in the last days will be a result of God's wrath that is finally turned against the adversary so that they are punished for their wicked ways and destruction of his vineyard. They will no longer be remembered.

8.3 The Last Days 'Jacob army'

In the context of the last days kingdom war versus the anti-Christ Chaldean adversary, I will now turn to address in more detail God's holy warrior army of servants who will directly confront this adversary. I have already referred to these servant-warriors collectively as the 'Jacob army.'

Intro and background

World Babylon's Chaldeans are the adversary that destroys God's creation. The Chaldeans are massive in scale, encompassing leaders and multitudes of oath-takers across the world. They include Israel's own wayward people and Gentiles alike, along with their rulers, leaders and their respective Gentile armies (sometimes termed "riders on horses"). Among numerous "nations" involved are those ancient peoples and people groups who are Israel's perennial enemies, including Edom, Moab, the Philistines, the Ammonites, etc. These same groups assist in perpetuating the worldwide kingdom war against the Lord and his faithful servants to this day.

While using the ancient war narrative, Satan has accumulated multitudes of minions across the earth as part of his massive army who are pledged to secrecy and silence. They are organized crime, united and bound by a secret oath and operating via backdoor communications. Collectively, they wield enormous power. They use their unfair advantage to hide ugly truths about their oppressive, criminal activities and also perpetuate a false, occult-based, social engineering narrative in entire societies that has caused great deception of people worldwide.

God promises the "portion of Jacob" and his 'Jacob army,' whom he directs, that they will prevail in their end times, unconventional spiritual war against the Chaldeans. In doing so, the massive scale of the Chaldean "mob" will be made clear along with the scope of this war. In scripture, God reminds us that his small, select army will defeat and "break in pieces" the following:

…kingdoms; nations; the horse and its rider; chariots and charioteers (representing conventional armies); men and women; old men and youth; and the young man and the maid; the shepherd and his flock; the husbandman and his yoke of oxen; and the captains and rulers. (Jer. 51:20-23)

Clearly, this will be a comprehensive, worldwide war. And although Israel and the Middle East region has been the primary geographic focal point, for obvious reasons, it is 'Babylon'-U.S., also called the "land of the Chaldeans" (Jer. 50:25), that is a key initial staging ground for this kingdom war. In *Writings of Lion's Lair, Volume 2,* I will address in detail that 'Babylon'-U.S. includes Israel's last days 'northern kingdom' within. It is also where God's holy, "small flock" remnant army largely resides and where the kingdom adversary and its two primary leaders, the 'Assyrian' and an oppressive king of (last days) 'Babylon,' have particularly strong ties.

We are told that through his 'Jacob army' that God "sets a standard upon the wall of Babylon" (Jer. 51:17). This is a standard or signal to the world about Chaldean oppression and lawlessness that essentially communicates God's message, "Consider yourself warned!"

In the countries of Israel and 'Babylon'-U.S., especially, God allows the Chaldean "mob" and their leaders in the last days to punish his rebellious, disobedient people and to prune his vineyard. However, it is clear in scripture that there is a point at which God is satisfied that his people have endured sufficient discipline and then he turns his wrath back to the wicked kingdom adversary that has been none-too-happy and prideful to decimate the Lord's servants.

God's vengeance is shown many times in scripture during this last days time period in which we are told that he is accomplishing his "purpose," particularly against 'Babylon' and its Chaldeans. His purpose will serve to shame and put down the Chaldean's oppressive leaders and bring darkness into light so that Christ's humble, faithful believers may be redeemed, saved and exalted.

The 'Jacob army' – God's holy warriors

In scripture, we learn that the Lord's 'Jacob army'-Judah "small flock" remnant are early recipients of God's wrath against his people as a refining process; they are the initial ones who are "chosen in the furnace of affliction" (Is. 48:10). They are taken captive and heavily persecuted by the anti-Christ Chaldeans. But these are his holy, faithful, royal, and righteous remnant who remain "left of the sword." God then gives them supernatural power to fight back and become a significant part of defeating the Chaldean enemy to accomplish his purpose above.

In the midst of their battle God will give them supernatural power to fight back and become a significant part of defeating the anti-Christ spirit kingdom enemy. They are the ones about whom we are told in scripture will possess faith to "move a mountain" and to: "trample on scorpions" (Lk. 10:19); "tread down the wicked" (Mal. 4:3); and "tread upon the lion and the cobra" (Ps. 91:13). Along these lines the following is God's strong promise to them:

Therefore all they that devour thee shall be devoured; and all thine adversaries, every one of them, shall go into captivity; and they that spoil thee shall be a spoil, and all that prey upon thee will I give for a prey. (Jer. 30:16)

I have shown how the Lord will arise on behalf of 'Jacob's "small flock" remnant and fight for them. We are told that, "The hand of the Lord shall be known toward his servants, and his indignation toward his enemies" (Is. 66:14). In other prophetic scripture this remnant itself is directly associated with the Lord's fighting army when they are referred to in verses such as the Lord's "troop on earth" (Am. 9:6) and his "camp (that) is great."

For this remnant's battles the Lord answers their prayers when they are in trouble and gives them tremendous power to fight back. 'Jacob' and his unconventional "army" are described as weapons of God's "armory" and "indignation" in relation to their resistance against Chaldean-infested and controlled 'Babylon'-U.S. in the last days. This remnant's might is further described as follows:

And the remnant of Jacob shall be among the Gentiles in the midst of many people as a lion among the beasts of the forest, as a young lion among the flocks of sheep: who, if he go through, both treadeth down, and teareth in pieces, and none can deliver. (Mic. 5:8)

The nations shall see and be confounded at all their might: they shall lay their hand upon their mouth, their ears shall be deaf. (Mic. 7:16)

God will clearly give this remnant army supernatural power to fight back in their individual battles as well as collectively for his Kingdom. The following verse from Israel's ancient days is a good example of and clear precedent for the effects of this power that God will give to this very small last days holy army who will be able to chase away their enemy's minions:

One thousand shall flee at the rebuke of one; at the rebuke of five shall ye flee: till ye be left as a beacon upon the top of a mountain, and as an ensign on a hill. (Is. 30:17)

Only by God's supernatural power and rescue on their behalf will the 'Jacob'-Judah "small flock" army emerge as victors in the last days. They will be beneficiaries of the Apostle Paul's words, "For the weapons of our warfare are not carnal, but mighty through God to the pulling down of strong holds" (2 Cor. 10:4). The Psalmist observed about the adversary's coming supernatural defeat, "How are they brought into desolation, as in a moment! they are utterly consumed with terrors" (Ps. 73:19). You might recall here the example of Jesus casting out devils that then went into the nearby swine causing all of them to run off of a cliff.

God conquers through his last days servants to show the world that it is he only who is God. He will do this at the hands of his anointed remnant for his own glory. Their victory and subsequent deliverance from the lion's mouth of 'Babylon'-U.S. in the last days spiritual kingdom war will be evident.

Contents of this passage

In the remainder of this passage, I will address the 'Jacob army' in more detail according to the following components:

- Interrelation of members
- Jacob
- Judah
- Ephraim

After discussing the interrelatedness of the 'Jacob army's members, I will look at each individually. In doing so, I will consider the historical precedent of their predecessors' battles on behalf of Israel and then will show what prophetic scripture tells us about their involvement and roles as part of the last days unconventional army.

Interrelation of Members

Prior to discussing each of the major components and peoples of the 'Jacob army,' it makes sense to establish them through scripture along with their interrelatedness. Although the following verse likely refers to individual members, collectively they represent this army's major components; namely, 'Jacob,' 'Judah' and 'Ephraim,' which are discussed herein. We read:

And Ephraim is as an heifer that is taught, and loveth to tread out the corn; but I passed over upon her fair neck: I will make Ephraim to ride; Judah shall plow, and Jacob shall break his clods. Sow to yourselves in righteousness, reap in mercy; break up your fallow ground: for it is time to seek the Lord, till he come and rain righteousness upon you. (Hos. 10:11-12)

In terms of interrelatedness, we might consider original Jacob who was a Patriarch and father of the 12 tribes. Similarly, end times 'Jacob' becomes a sort of father to the 12 tribes including "sons of Jacob." In fact, end times 'Jacob' is a compilation of many biblical characters. Not surprisingly, he has the broadest role in God's last days fighting army, a role that naturally overlaps with Judah and 'Ephraim,' discussed herein, which carry the scepter and birthright promises, respectively. End times 'Jacob' may possess several bloodlines to complement his role. I have shown that he comes from the "waters of Judah" for at least part of his heritage.

Next, while 'Ephraim' has a small representation in the 'Jacob army,' Ephraim as a whole only comes to its spiritual birthing later in the Day of the Lord. You may recall from earlier that it is the holy, righteous 'Jacob'-Judah remnant versus the world anti-Christ Chaldeans at the beginning of this end times kingdom war. Unfortunately, just like the country of Israel's own leaders and people, 'Ephraim' in 'Babylon'-U.S. is largely on the wrong side of this war versus their anointed remnant's brethren. The following describes the end times state of 'Ephraim' as a proxy for Israel's last days 'northern kingdom' prior to their awakening:

Manasseh, Ephraim; and Ephraim, Manasseh: and they together shall be against Judah. For all this his anger is not turned away, but his hand is stretched out still. (Is. 9:21)

Once 'Ephraim' awakens, likely in the Day of the Lord, they will begin to seek the Lord in more significant fashion. Meanwhile, the following verses show the righteous component of 'Ephraim' (and 'house of Joseph') who are in the 'Jacob army' that join with their 'Jacob'-Judah remnant brethren after they become aware that they are also targets of Chaldean powers in the time of "Jacob's trouble":

When I have bent Judah for me, filled the bow with Ephraim, and raised up thy sons, O Zion, against thy sons, O Greece, and made thee as the sword of a mighty man. (Zech. 9:13)

…And I will strengthen the house of Judah, and I will save the house of Joseph, and I will bring them again to place them…And they of Ephraim shall be like a mighty man, and their heart shall rejoice as through wine… (Zech. 10:6-7)

And the house of Jacob shall be a fire, and the house of Joseph a flame… (Ob. 18)

In the last verse, which points to the rejoining of Joseph (Ephraim) and Jacob, you might recall here another verse about this time period which says, "And the light of Israel shall be for a fire, and his Holy

One for a flame" (Is. 10:17). It appears that end times 'Jacob' and his house is the fire and that Joseph/Ephraim is the flame in this kingdom war. Original Jacob and Ephraim were, in a way, both "spiritual" firstborns; this points to their spiritual awakening during the last days kingdom war, and perhaps their membership and partnership in the core of God's holy 'Jacob army.'

Finally, interestingly, consider that it was Joshua and Caleb of the tribes of Ephraim and Judah, respectively, in Moses' day, who had spied out the land of inheritance and were the only faithful ones retained and chosen by God in their generation to enter the land with the next generation of tribes. They were rewarded for their faith and courage. Modern day versions of Joshua and Caleb representing Ephraim and Judah are likely again among God's faithful 'Jacob army' remnant. It is a remnant that will not bow down to Babylon and will have a role in defeating the Chaldeans.

'Jacob'

In considering the house of 'Jacob's role as part of the Lord's last days fighting army that engages in the unconventional spiritual kingdom war we might first consider original Jacob from ancient days. His battle then was for his soul, a battle that was spiritual in nature. His battle was one to retain his birthright and keep his life versus his brother-turned-adversary. He showed tremendous faith, won God's love and won power by wrestling with an angel of God. Upon prevailing God gave him the new name, 'Israel.'

You may also recall Balaam the seer's ancient visions that he relayed to Moab's King Balak instead of cursing Israel as he had been asked to do. In Balaam's visions he prophetically foresaw an *end times* 'Jacob' being blessed by God. Insight from Balaam's prophetic visions (Numbers, Chapters 23 and 24) included seeing last days 'Jacob's unusual strength in battle as:

- (Having the) strength of a unicorn

- Eating up the nations as his enemies

- Breaking (his enemies') bones and piercing them through with his arrows

- Destroying him that remains in the city (likely referring to a significant Chaldean foe)

- (Lifting himself up as a) young lion to his prey

Additional prophetic scripture that I offer below corroborates that God will give 'Jacob' strength and weapons to use in his personal, unconventional 'David-versus-Goliath'-type battle versus the anti-Christ Chaldeans in the last days. Those in his remnant will likely benefit from these same weapons of supernatural origin.

Last days 'Jacob' in the 'Jacob army'

End times 'Jacob' is the captain of the 'Jacob army,' house of Jacob, "sons of Jacob," etc., and eventually the larger house of Israel that is regathered and returns to the holy land. As I alluded to above, he has the broadest role in the 'Jacob army' as the name of this army would suggest. His own fighting and the outcome of their battle will serve as a light to the Gentiles of the world and as a personal sacrifice and atonement for his people, Israel.

As an individual member, but as a symbol for all of those in the 'Jacob army,' end times 'Jacob' we know from scripture is given the strength of a unicorn in his fight. This allows him to "pierce" his enemies and rise as a "young lion" to his prey. Referring to 'Jacob's own war in 'Babylon'-U.S., one that develops into a worldwide kingdom war, God prophetically describes the outcome of his battle as a result of the power that he gives 'Jacob':

…when he maketh all the stones of the altar as chalkstones that are beaten in sunder, the groves and images shall not stand up. (Is. 27:9)

Behold, I will make thee a new sharp threshing instrument having teeth: thou shalt thresh the mountains, and beat them small, and shalt make the hills as chaff. Thou shalt fan them, and the wind shall carry them away, and the whirlwind shall scatter them: and thou shalt rejoice in the Lord, and shalt glory in the Holy One of Israel. (Is. 41:15-16)

If you were wondering more specifically about a modern day culmination of and an outcome to 'Jacob's battle from ancient times versus his brother Esau, prophetic verses from Obadiah in addition to other scripture inform us about the final fate of one of Israel's primary adversaries and rivals, 'Esau,' in these last days:

And the house of Jacob shall be a fire, and the house of Joseph a flame, and the house of Esau for stubble, and they shall kindle in them, and devour them; and there shall not be any remaining of the house of Esau; for the Lord hath spoken it. (Ob. 18)

Of course, end times 'Jacob' has plenty of help including the Lord himself in the battle in these last days. In summary, altogether, the original Jacob's blessing from God in ancient days can be seen as carrying all the way through to end times 'Jacob' and his 'Jacob army' in their last days battle.

Judah

It is not surprising that we find a Judah remnant among the last days 'Jacob army,' even as its primary component. Today's Judah remnant carries its warrior traits forward from the days of old.

At the time when the original Patriarch Jacob gathered his sons and told them about what would befall them *in the last days*, he referred to Judah as a lion's whelp rising from the prey and also told him, "Thy hand shall be in the neck of thine enemies…" (Gen. 49:8). Years later, when Moses offered his final blessings to the tribes, he asked the Lord to help Judah from his enemies.

Judah historically is among the first in battle. As a tribe on the east side of the Tabernacle, it is in first position. After Joshua died, the Israelites in the land asked the Lord who should go up and fight against the Canaanites first. The Lord simply responded, 'Judah,' and said furthermore that he had already delivered the land into Judah's hand. Judah then went and conquered Jerusalem and slew Canaanites throughout the land.

Of course, we know of King David's exploits a short time later, and how as a righteous God-led warrior, his armies conquered many peoples so that Judah/Israel in his time took back much of their God-given territory.

Last days Judah in the Jacob army- 'David'

The tribe of Judah and its Davidic line in particular appear to be pre-destined for righteous battle. It is apparent that a Judah remnant is again the first in battle in these end times in the unconventional war of righteousness versus the iniquity and wickedness of the anti-Christ Chaldeans. As shown in the earlier verse, God's 'Portion of Jacob'-remnant are referred to as his "battle axe" and weapons for war. Jesus, of course, is the Lion of the tribe of Judah. It could be that the end times Son of man or Spirit of truth who I discuss herein has Judah tribal roots, but this is unclear. It is possible that he is the last days "lion" who "leaves his thicket," "forsakes his covert," and about whom we are told catches enough prey for his whelps.

'David' and 'Jacob's last days Judah-centric "small flock" remnant are comprised of "conquerors" and redeemers on behalf of 'Israel's remnant who will serve as Jesus' Light for the Gentiles. They will arise to battle at a time when persecution of God's vineyard is underway and being stripped, suffering famine, etc. as was the case for Israel in King David's descendent Zerubbabel's day of constructing the second temple. Last days Israel will again be both spiritually and literally starved as well as heavily oppressed at the hands of the worldwide anti-Christ Chaldeans led by nations' evil rulers, elected and unelected. I described earlier that the Chaldeans have systematically targeted, persecuted and deceived Israel over the course of generations. They have "trampled" God's vineyard and "pleasant field."

End times 'David's own battle is not only one for his soul and his life; it is a battle that represents and is on behalf of God's people, 'Israel.' About this battle, in the prophetic example of Zerubbabel we find a couple of clues about 'David' who will fit the role of a warrior in the last days spiritual kingdom war versus the adversary. This is demonstrated by what an angel of the Lord said through the Prophet Zechariah:

Who art thou, O great mountain? before Zerubbabel thou shalt become a plain. (Zech. 4:7)

For who hath despised the day of small things? for they shall rejoice, and shall see the plummet in the hand of Zerubbabel with those seven... (Zech. 4:10)

In the first verse above the term "mountain" may refer to last days anti-Christ Chaldean rulers and powers also referred to by God as a "destroying mountain" (Jer. 51:25) that are eventually defeated in the last days spiritual kingdom war in which God sets righteousness as the "plummet." 'David' and 'Jacob's remnant are the ones who demonstrate "faith as a mustard seed" as Jesus described would be necessary to move such a mountain. The second verse refers to their very small remnant versus this massive, highly organized spiritual kingdom adversary.

Consistent with the strength given to 'Jacob' we are told in the book of Zechariah that this small Judah-centric remnant will eventually come to be "like God." God assures them to "fear not" and proclaims, "So again have I thought in these days to do well unto Jerusalem and to the house of Judah" (Zech. 8:15). The following verse shows the immense power given by God to Judah in their role as his "goodly horse" in the midst of their involvement in the end times spiritual kingdom war:

...for the Lord of hosts hath visited his flock the house of Judah, and hath made them as his goodly horse in the battle. Out of him came forth the corner, out of him the nail, out of him the battle bow, out of him every oppressor together. And they shall be as mighty men, which tread down their enemies in the mire of the streets in the battle: and they shall fight, because the Lord is with them, and the riders on horses shall be confounded... (Zech. 10:3-5)

It will be 'Jacob's Judah-centric remnant including some from the house of David who are first out of the gate once again in battling the anti-Christ Chaldeans in the last days unconventional, behind-the-scenes spiritual kingdom war. The "banner" that they will raise has special significance and importance. The following verses are given in an end times context referring to this "banner" or "standard." These warn of coming war against the *nation* of 'Babylon'-U.S.:

Declare ye among the nations, and publish, and set up a standard; publish, and conceal not...her idols are confounded, her images are broken in pieces. (Jer. 50:2)

Set up the standard upon the walls of Babylon, make the watch strong, set up the watchmen, prepare the ambushes: for the Lord hath both devised and done that which he spake against the inhabitants of Babylon. (Jer. 51:12)

Set ye up a standard in the land, blow the trumpet among the nations, prepare the nations against her, call together against her the kingdoms of Ararat, Minni, and Ashchenaz; appoint a captain against her; cause the horses to come up as the rough caterpillers... (Jer. 51:27)

End times 'David' will apparently light a very large fire in the land of 'Babylon'-U.S. The resulting chaos and unrest will signal weakness and bring on conventional-style war against the land. In their deliverance out of the theater of this war 'David' and the "small flock" remnant will be rewarded by God for their faith and walking with him during the last days period of anti-Christ Chaldean-caused "idolatrous commotion" and its associated chaos and strife.

Last days Judah in the Jacob army- the 'Daughter of Zion'

Given all of the associations of the 'Daughter of Zion' with Jerusalem, the Lord's holy hill, the temple, the royal remnant, etc. we might rightly assume that she is affiliated with the tribe of Judah. For these reasons along with the fact that both King David and she are referred to in scripture as the "apple of God's eye" she may even be a member of the last days house of David.

In the book of Isaiah, the Lord himself reminds the 'Daughter of Zion' of his sovereignty and the fact that she has his divine protection in the midst of her own personal battle. As one who is a key member of his coming heavenly Kingdom we are told that the 'Daughter of Zion enjoys the "heritage of the servants of the Lord." God says to her:

No weapon that is formed against thee shall prosper; and every tongue that shall rise against thee in judgment thou shalt condemn. (Is. 54:17)

Not only will the 'Daughter of Zion' be protected in the last days spiritual kingdom war but God's Word tells us that she will be given power by the Lord to fight back against her anti-Christ Chaldean foe. Through the Prophet Micah the Lord says:

Arise and thresh, O daughter of Zion: for I will make thine horn iron, and I will make thy hoofs brass: and thou shalt beat in pieces many people. (Mic. 4:13)

You may rightly wonder how a single woman will be part of an army that destroys entire "nations" in the last days. But I explained earlier in this chapter and on several other occasions to this point about God's supernatural assistance that this remnant receives in their unconventional battle.

Ephraim

In this section, as I did with 'Jacob' and Judah above, I will first look at Ephraim in historical context as it relates to fighting in battle. When considering original Jacob's words to his sons as to what would befall them *in the last days* and then Moses' last words to the tribes, we can see what they pledged for Joseph as a possible prophetic clue for 'Ephraim.' Tremendous kingdom blessings and inheritance were promised to Joseph. Otherwise, as these relate specifically to warfare we see the following in scripture:

The archers have sorely grieved him, and shot at him, and hated him: But his bow abode in strength, and the arms of his hands were made strong by the hands of the mighty God of Jacob; (from thence is the shepherd, the stone of Israel). (Gen. 49:23-24)

His glory is like the firstling of his bullock, and his horns are like the horns of unicorns: with them he shall push the people together to the ends of the earth... (Deut. 33:17)

You can see that both of these promises prophetically point to a loose association and overlap with fellow end times remnant member, 'Jacob,' who represents a compilation of biblical characters. 'Jacob' is given the strength of a unicorn (Num. 24:8). Also, it is 'Jacob' who atones for and "raises up" the tribes of Israel similar to Joseph "pushing" them together as shown above. In his Word God refers to both 'Israel' (Jacob) and 'Ephraim' as (spiritual) "firstborns" who were in a sense "greater" younger brothers. Of course, Jesus became the firstborn holy son of God's entire heavenly Kingdom.

Meanwhile, Joseph's own personal life was in many ways a 'picture' of the 'Jacob'-Judah "small flock" remnant's story in the last days spiritual kingdom war in that he was: rejected by his own; persecuted; taken captive; and then finally given strength by God to prevail and be delivered in his personal battle. This led to the saving and redemption of many others in a time of worldwide famine including those in his own father's (Jacob's) house. His initial rejection by his own family combined with ultimately contributing to the wide scale saving of lives also made him an early foreshadowing 'type' of Jesus.

In further considering the historical house of Joseph as it relates to battle recall that centuries after the original patriarchs that it was Joshua of Ephraim, the courageous spy mentioned above, who then led Israel and its fighting men into the land to successfully defeat many enemies and their armies. After Joshua died, however, Ephraim as a tribe had a pattern of frequently being left out of battles fought on behalf of Israel. In the time of the Judges they were left out of the battle that Gideon fought. They were again left out when Jephthah went to war against the Ammonites because they did not respond when Jephthah initially approached them. Also recall that when the original house of David split from Saul due to a longstanding adversarial relationship and war Ephraim followed Saul. Then, shortly thereafter, Jeroboam of Ephraim continued this split when he departed from Solomon's son Rehoboam. This act perpetuated this ongoing war against Judah that existed "all of their days."

Last days Ephraim in the 'Jacob army'

I already mentioned above that Ephraim as a whole comes to the battle late and only rejoins the remnant after its awakening in the Day of the Lord when they come to a realization that their anti-Christ Chaldean associations are actually their enemy. Up until this point, 'Ephraim's people will have had strong ties with and will have been strongly influenced by their alliances with the anti-Christ Chaldeans. (Note: This is explained in detail in the book of Hosea and as I describe in

Volume 2). Meanwhile, due to being misled and misinformed, 'Ephraim' remains blinded for a time and develops a jealousy and envy of its brethren, especially of last days royal Judah. This is a replay of the historical Ephraim-versus-Judah conflict that I address in *Volume 3*.

Even with that precedent, we must keep in mind the following things about 'Ephraim,' overall: 1) 'Ephraim' ('Joseph') inherits tremendous kingdom blessings (described above); 2) A faithful 'Ephraim' remnant eventually comes around, largely returns and reunites with Judah in the last days; 3) 'Ephraim' *does* have a small component that is among the initial righteous 'Jacob army,' who I have explained are God's firstfruits holy children in the last days.

As for 'Ephraim's part among the righteous 'Jacob army' we are not given a lot of detail in scripture but we know the following about the last days house of Joseph, some of which I have alluded to earlier in this passage. As part of the 'Jacob army,' this tribe:

- (House of Joseph) is a "burning flame" (Ob. 18)

- is an "arrow in the bow of Judah" (Zech. 9:13)

- "is as a heifer that is taught, and loveth to tread out the corn" (Hos. 10:11)

- shall become like a "mighty man" (Zech. 10:7)

- shall subdue with sling stones (Zech. 9:14)

- is the strength and covering (helmet) of (God's) head (Ps. 60:7, Ps. 140:7)

So, as you can see a small, select portion of 'Ephraim' will be a very important and significant segment of the last days fighting "small flock" army prior to the larger tribe's eventual spiritual awakening, regathering and return to the land along with the greater house of Israel. Recall that it will be the two sticks of Ephraim and Judah that are in the hand of the Son of man that will be joined thereby symbolizing the remnant of Israel becoming one again under one king, a Davidic Prince who will serve Jesus Christ, the King of Kings, in his Millennial Kingdom's reign. I describe the return to the Kingdom of

Israel's remnant and believing Gentiles in my books, *Biblical End Times, Volumes 1 and 2*.

~

In summary, it is clear that the last days 'Jacob army' and their unconventional battle and spiritual warfare against the anti-Christ Chaldeans is a big step prior to Jesus returning to defeat and destroy the beast kingdom at the end of the age. All of the glory goes to Jesus Christ.

Chapter 9.

Anointed Remnant "Birthings"

Passages from Lion's Lair provided in this chapter include:

9.1 Children of Israel "Birthed" in the End Times (Part 1)

9.2 Children of Israel "Birthed" in the End Times (Part 2)

9.3 Children of Israel "Birthed" in the End Times (Part 3)

9.1 Children of Israel "Birthed" in the End Times (Part 1)

Many times, God's Word refers to the importance and significance of (symbolic) childbirth events. When looking at prophetic scripture, "travailing" and child birthing events commonly take on particular meaning for the purpose of understanding the end times. God's children who are "birthed" (or delivered out of Babylon's "matrix" or "womb") in the last days become those who are products of the ongoing kingdom war.

In fact, childbirth- or "seed"-related events are bookends to the timeless spiritual kingdom war. To begin, as a result of sin in the Garden God told the serpent, "I will put enmity between thee and the woman; and between thy seed and her seed; it shall bruise thy head and thou shalt bruise his heel" (Gen. 3:15). This is the beginning of the kingdom war; simply put, God's servants versus Satan's minions.

In events leading up to and including the Day of the Lord, in the book of Revelation revealing Jesus Christ, the woman gives birth to the manchild, Jesus (Chapter 12). The birth triggers a response by the dragon to come after the manchild, the woman and her remnant. The Lord is caught up to his throne before he eventually returns to claim victory in the kingdom war. The woman is taken to a safe place in hiding until then.

Just as his original physical birth to Mary, might Jesus' *"re*-birth" in the book of Revelation also be considered the answer to prophetic prayers of those recorded in ancient times scripture by the likes of Hannah (mother of the Prophet Samuel), and in Jesus' time by Elisabeth and Zacharias (mother and father of John the Baptist, respectively), all of whom endured assaults by the enemy in the kingdom war?

Both of these holy mothers, Hannah and Elisabeth, were formerly barren and had prayed for children. Meanwhile, Mary and Zacharias during this time both prayed for God to exalt the humble and to put down the rich, their oppressive enemies, in another reference to the ongoing kingdom war and their anticipation of a coming savior. Mary prophetically prayed during her pregnancy, "My spirit has rejoiced in God my savior…he has shown strength with his arm…he has scattered the proud…he has put down the mighty" (Lk. 1:41,51-52). During pregnancy events, Hannah and Zacharias also, respectively, prayed for the coming future king of Israel (i.e. the "horn") to effectively save them from their enemies. We see this as follows:

The adversaries of the Lord shall be broken to pieces; out of heaven shall he thunder upon them: the Lord shall judge the ends of the earth; and he shall give strength unto his king, and exalt the horn of his anointed. (1 Sam. 2:10)

Blessed be the Lord God of Israel; for he hath visited and redeemed his people, And hath raised up an horn of salvation for us in the house of his servant David. (Lk. 1:68-69)

Jesus Christ will ultimately return again to destroy Satan, the dragon-serpent, and his entire worldwide anti-Christ system. In doing so, he will save his sheep- those who repent and call upon his name- in effect answering the ancient prophetic prayers of Hannah and Zacharias above.

Contents of this Passage

In this passage I will discuss more about the prophetic implications of "childbirthings" in the last days, particularly the birthing of God's anointed, royal remnant of Israel including those figures I have already addressed to this point in this book. The overriding background and context for this topic has been alluded to above; that is, *there are evil, anti-Christ forces working overtime in these last days to prevent God's holy family from being "birthed" and established.* So, the kingdom war continues.

Important personas pertaining to the prophetic, last days "childbirthing" of Israel's holy children will be addressed in my next couple passages. Meanwhile, the following are the most significant player-segments that emerge as part of this process:

- The 'Daughter of Zion'
- Holy, royal seed remnant (incl. Jesus himself)

In this passage, I will discuss each of these player-segments. In Parts 2 and 3 to follow, I will further address the significance of travails and pains in the "birthing" process of Israel's children, especially as they relate to the timing and sequence of major prophetic events in these last days.

The Daughter of Zion

The last, who will then be first, in the line of biblical holy mothers in 'Israel' is the 'Daughter of Zion.' She will be the mother of the re-born nation of Israel. It is logical to deduce (see Chapter 7) that the 'Daughter of Zion,' an actual biblical figure living in these last days, is the woman in Revelation 12 who gives birth to Jesus. The 'Daughter of Zion' will give "birth" to several individual children in the last days while in tremendous travail. (Her travails and birth pains are linked to significant world events). Recall that the 'Daughter of Zion' herself is part of the end times anointed Judah-centric remnant who are taken captive and heavily persecuted in 'Babylon'-U.S.

So, this is an amazing, real-life event of the 'Daughter of Zion' eventually giving "birth" in revealing, in some form, Jesus the man-child Messiah. Similar to Mary, Hannah and John the Baptist's parents above, the 'Daughter of Zion' does this in the midst of the last days spiritual war and storm that abounds. Just as with all of the aforementioned holy parents, the 'Daughter of Zion' will find herself holding out in the midst of persecution for a Savior and a King. Verses that show just the beginning of several spiritual, holy "birthings" and her extreme travail include:

For I have heard a voice as of a woman in travail, and the anguish as of her that bringeth forth her first child, the voice of the daughter of Zion, that bewaileth herself, that spreadeth her hands, saying, Woe is me now! for my soul is wearied because of murderers. (Jer. 4:31)

Now why dost thou cry out aloud? is there no king in thee? is thy counsellor perished? for pangs have taken thee as a woman in travail. (Mic. 4:9)

Ultimately, the 'Daughter of Zion' has to be taken to safety after travailing to give a final "birth" to Jesus in Revelation, Chapter 12. The same pains and grief that grips her will likely also be experienced by her other spiritual family sons and daughters (i.e. "daughters of Jerusalem") who will be spiritually "birthed" in last days perilous times.

So, the 'Daughter of Zion' is a 'type' of Eve who will experience firsthand the fulfillment of God's plan from the beginning. As a result of Eve's transgression God said to her, "I will greatly multiply thy sorrow and thy conception; in sorrow thou shalt bring forth children..." (Gen. 3:16).

Barren and desolate, then blessed

The 'Daughter of Zion' represents and fulfills the pattern of many mothers of the nation of Israel who have gone before her. We are told in scripture that she is barren and it is possible that she could be advanced in years. Recall that Sarah, the wife of Abraham, and the wives of Isaac, Leah and Rebekah, were *also* all barren prior to God himself intervening.

The lesson and pattern in the case of Israel's chosen mothers is that they may begin barren but they are ultimately blessed. In Jesus' day, Elisabeth, mother of John the Baptist, had been barren but then once she conceived she acknowledged in her prayer, "Thus hath the Lord dealt with me in the days wherein he looked on me, to take away my reproach among men." (Lk. 1:25). Then Mary, the virgin who supernaturally conceived Jesus, recognized, "For he hath regarded the low estate of his handmaiden: for, behold, from henceforth all generations shall call me blessed" (Lk. 1:48).

The last days 'Daughter of Zion' appears to be a fascinating compilation of many former mothers of the nation of Israel. On cue, she will find that her barren-ness eventually turns into incredible joy in bringing forth the last days Millennial Kingdom's children of Israel. She will even bring forth nations of Gentiles according to scripture in the book of Isaiah. Notice the similarities in the following verses of what God promised to the first mother of his people, Sarah, wife of Abraham, and then subsequently to the 'Daughter of Zion,' respectively:

And I will bless her, and give thee a son also of her: yea, I will bless her, and she shall be a mother of nations; kings of people shall be of her. (Gen. 17:16)

Sing, O barren, thou that didst not bear; break forth into singing, and cry aloud, thou that didst not travail with child: for more are the children of the desolate than the children of the married wife, saith the Lord. (Is. 54:1)

The 'Daughter of Zion' will be "highly favored" by God and eventually become a Queen-Mother to an entire heavenly Millennial Kingdom of children.

The Birth of Holy, Royal Seed- Jesus Christ, the Firstborn of the *Kingdom*

Before I address events surrounding the last days "birthings" of the children of Israel further in Parts 2 and 3 of this series, the greatest and most significant news by far is that the 'Daughter of Zion' gives re-"birth" to Jesus Christ himself. She is the mother of Jesus, who is born as a man-child (Revelation, Chapter 12) and is then caught up to his throne. The following verse in Isaiah, while certainly referring to Jesus' first physical birth, *also has meaning for his end times re-birth*:

For unto us a child is born, unto us a son is given: and the government shall be upon his shoulder: and his name shall be called Wonderful,

Counsellor, The mighty God, The everlasting Father, The Prince of Peace. (Is. 9:6)

You can see how this prophetic scripture was not entirely fulfilled at the time of Jesus' first in-person birth, life and death on earth. There is clear indication in this line of scripture that Jesus must still return to set up his Kingdom for this to be fulfilled, as well as to fulfill that which we are told in the very next verse in Isaiah:

Of the increase of His government and peace there shall be no end, upon the throne of David, and upon his kingdom, to order it, and to establish it with judgment and with justice from henceforth even forever. The zeal of the Lord of hosts will perform this. (Is. 9:7)

This is consistent with the Revelation, Chapter 12 story, mentioned at the beginning of this passage, and the interpretation that bible prophecy experts give, which is that it is Jesus who is the manchild born with an iron rod to rule the nations. And Jesus is "caught up," appearing to represent the day he spoke of himself in when he foretold of a day when he, the "bridegroom," would be taken away (Lk. 5:32). Of course, the good news is that he returns with the same rod in coming to establish his Millennial Kingdom reign on earth (Rev. 19:15).

Jesus certainly *appears* to be the *last* individual, holy child born (in sequence) to the 'Daughter of Zion' in the last days. Recall that his birth is in the middle of the final seven-year period of the Day of the Lord with a "time, times and half a time" (i.e. three and one-half years) remaining. Upon his birth, the 'Daughter of Zion' and her remnant are immediately pursued by Satan and forced to scatter.

Here, it is helpful to remember the principle of "the last shall be first" (again, here, in sequence) in interpretation, not only for the 'Daughter of Zion's holy remnant as a whole, which is likely the reigning house of David in the coming Kingdom, but also as it applies to Jesus. In Jesus' own words he refers to himself several times as the Alpha and Omega. He reminds us about this in the book of Revelation:

I am Alpha and Omega, the beginning and the ending, saith the Lord, which is, and which was, and which is to come, the Almighty. (Rev. 1:8)

I am Alpha and Omega, the beginning and the end, the first and the last. (Rev. 22:13)

So, Jesus is the last (in sequence) of the holy remnant of individuals who are born. But we know that Jesus was the firstborn when he came to the earth the first time. He was firstborn among his own brothers, in his own family, and he is also declared as the firstborn of the *Kingdom*. The following verses spoken by the Apostle Paul establish Jesus Christ as the firstborn of the *Kingdom*:

And again, when he bringeth in the firstbegotten into the world, he saith, And let all the angels of God worship him. (Heb. 1:6)

For whom he did foreknow, he also did predestinate to be conformed to the image of his Son, that he might be the firstborn among many brethren. (Rom. 8:29)

(Jesus) is the image of the invisible God, the firstborn of every creature: For by him were all things created, that are in heaven, and that are in earth, visible and invisible, whether they be thrones, or dominions, or principalities, or powers: all things were created by him, and for him: And he is before all things, and by him all things consist. (Col. 1:15-17)

Jesus is considered first of the brethren, before all things, and by him all things consist (Col. 1:17). Christ is God. In his physical death on earth we are told that he then "brought many sons to glory" (Heb. 2:10). In fact, Jesus referred to his disciples as "friends." The Apostle Paul says that among those who Jesus sanctifies he is not ashamed to call them brethren. The implication, along with scripture elsewhere in God's Word, tells us that Jesus will have siblings in his heavenly Kingdom. Speaking of brothers, the last ones to be "birthed," just prior to his own *re*-birth described above, are likely the "sons" (stars) surrounding the 'Daughter of Zion' (Revelation, Chapter 12).

To circle back around to the 'Daughter of Zion' who gives the manchild Jesus his final "birth," we recall that God is her creator who tells her, "You are engraved on the palms of my hands" (Is. 49:16). And the one who she gives spiritual birth to- Jesus- is her husband. She is told, "Your maker is your husband" (Is. 54:5). You can see here that the 'Daughter of Zion' is a 'type' of Eve in the end times. She is both created by God and then in turn she gives "birth" to God's children, including Jesus.

Together, Jesus, the 'Daughter of Zion,' and the anointed remnant are Millennial Kingdom King, Queen, and royal family, respectively. The holy, royal children in the family are a large part of that which I will address in Part 2.

Birth of a Holy, Royal Seed Remnant- End Times 'Jacob' – The Firstborn of the Nation of Israel

Just as the 'Daughter of Zion' is a mother-type to Jesus, end times 'Jacob' is an earthly father-type to him. 'Jacob' is a Patriarch-leader of the Judah remnant who goes on to be a prince in the Millennial Kingdom. The following verses *appear to* prophetically apply to end-times 'Jacob' as a father-figure to the Messiah:

I shall see him, but not now: I shall behold him, but not nigh: there shall come a Star out of Jacob, and a Sceptre shall rise out of Israel, and shall smite the corners of Moab, and destroy all the children of Sheth. (Num. 24:17)

Ask ye now, and see whether a man doth travail with child? wherefore do I see every man with his hands on his loins, as a woman in travail, and all faces are turned into paleness? (Jer. 30:6)

If end times 'Jacob' is a symbolic father-type to Jesus, the manchild born supernaturally to the 'Daughter of Zion' in the book of Revelation (Chapter 12), then we might think of the parallels to Joseph and Mary, Jesus' original earthly father and mother. Joseph and Mary kept Mary's holy, supernatural pregnancy secret. Once Jesus was born, they had to flee from Herod.

Would 'Jacob' and the 'Daughter of Zion' in the end times have an understanding of the upcoming end times "birth" of Christ and feel a need to conceal it? Might they need to flee once he is "born"? To at least address the latter question, the second verse above is the sign of the beginning of "Jacob's trouble," which he and the 'Daughter of Zion'- both held as captives in 'Babylon'-U.S., appear to be delivered out of and are forced to flee, or at least chased into hiding in the "wilderness" at this time.

In addition, like the 'Daughter of Zion' as described in the section above, 'Jacob' is also a father to a remnant of 'Israel's children (including "sons of Jacob") that are attributed or "born" to him. It appears that his children- the remnant "birthed" to him as a Patriarch of the nation of Israel- can likely be considered to be the same as those of the 'Daughter of Zion.' As is the case for the 'Daughter of Zion,' there is much in scripture about a holy, royal family for 'Jacob,' with one being God's promise to the "original" Jacob (via his forefathers Abraham and Isaac). This is the first verse below followed by God's direct promise to end-times 'Jacob':

And God said unto him, I am God Almighty: be fruitful and multiply; a nation and a company of nations shall be of thee, and kings shall come out of thy loins. (Gen. 35:11)

But when he sees his children, the work of my hands, in the midst of him, they shall sanctify my name, and sanctify the Holy One of Jacob, and shall fear the God of Israel. (Is. 29:23)

End times 'Jacob's purpose as God's end times servant, as we know through Isaiah, is to bring light and truth to his people, be an intercessor for them, and liberate them. He then raises up the tribes of Israel and becomes a vessel through which God calls his remnant to return. So, he *re*-births God's people, 'Israel,' spiritually speaking.

End times 'Jacob's own "birthing"

Now that we know about end times 'Jacob' as a father-figure to the coming, newly-birthed 'Israel,' do we know anything about 'Jacob's *own* "birth"? We are told in scripture that 'Jacob' is a part of the holy, royal end times Judah remnant. He comes out of the "waters of Judah"

(Is. 48:1). Given this, it would stand to reason that he *could* be "born" spiritually as a prince into the House of David via the 'Daughter of Zion.' It also stands to reason that end-times 'Jacob' would be the 'Daughter of Zion's "firstborn" (in sequence). This *appears* to be the case for several reasons: 'Jacob' is a leader of the last days 'Jacob army'-Judah remnant that raises the warning to the rest of the world about the anti-Christ Chaldeans; 'Jacob' is a father figure to other sons of Israel who are "spiritually" born throughout the end times; and finally, 'Jacob' ('Israel') is called God's firstborn in the old scripture. In God's people's pre-exodus situation of captivity in Egypt- a prophetic picture of God's people's captivity in last days 'Babylon'- God instructed Moses to tell Pharaoh:

Thus says the Lord, Israel is my son, even my firstborn: And I say unto thee, Let me son go, that he may serve me. (Ex. 4:22-23)

So, God calls 'Israel' (prophetically representing 'Jacob' in these end times) his "firstborn." As we will see in Part 2, being "birthed" or "brought forth" can sometimes symbolically mean being delivered out of captivity. And we have also seen, and will again, that "travailing" many times is a sign of troubled times, even for an entire nation. Scripture says that both 'Jacob' and the 'Daughter of Zion' will be delivered out of their own captivity and these troubled times. This will be similar to a deliverance (of at least an initial remnant) of God's people from their captivity and persecution in ancient Egypt.

At this time when 'Jacob' is initially delivered it appears to be the beginning of the Day of the Lord. This is a time when world leaders will be saying 'peace' but there will be no peace. And it will be the time at which God begins to bring about his punishment in order to destroy 'Jacob's and the 'Daughter of Zion's enemies. The following verse, used earlier in this passage, describes this time of coming war when the 'Daughter of Zion' is in anguish and in travail to give birth to her *first child*:

For I have heard a voice as of a woman in travail, and the anguish as of her that bringeth forth her first child, the voice of the daughter of Zion, that bewaileth herself, that spreadeth her hands, saying, Woe is me now! for my soul is wearied because of murderers. (Jer. 4:31)

This appears to represent the *timing* of the "birth" of end times 'Jacob.' The wars that will begin are those that I address in *Writings of Lion's Lair, Volume 2*, pertaining especially to the United States ('Babylon') and to the country of Israel. The deceived house of Israel within will have been one of those parties engaged in spiritual war against their own anointed remnant.

'Jacob's spiritual birth largely unknown to the world?

Prior to or alongside his own spiritual "birthing," or being brought forth, we know from Chapter 5 that 'Jacob' is held captive and persecuted in 'Babylon.' We are also told in scripture that God keeps 'Jacob' "hidden" (Is. 49:2-3) for a time. 'Jacob's eventual "birthing" described above happens during a tumultuous time in these last days. Like Jesus' end times birth described earlier, 'Jacob's birth may only be known to very few. This is due to anti-Christ Chaldean rulers who control news and messaging in our society and have always prevented this type of information about God's people from being discussed, even from church pulpits in the 'Babylon'-U.S. Their goal is to have the world prepared to accept world Babylon's rulers and their government.

'Jacob's spiritual birthing

Although 'Jacob's own end times spiritual "birthing" may be unknown at the time it happens, it is still certain, and there is much scriptural evidence to support this. There are quite a few verses that speak to this event. In fact, I describe in *Volume 3* how in many cases the Prophet Jeremiah can be considered as a "type" or picture of end times 'Jacob' and also representative of the end times righteous Judah remnant who are spared but taken and held captive in 'Babylon'-U.S. prior to exodus. In his day, prior to God's judgment on the country of Israel at the hands of world Babylon's coalition, Jeremiah lamented his predicament as a righteous, God-anointed messenger stating his opposition to the corrupt rulers of Judah. This is exactly last days 'Jacob's predicament. In Jeremiah's lament in his own time he remarked:

Woe is me, my mother, that thou hast borne me a man of strife and a man of contention to the whole earth! I have neither lent on usury, nor men have lent to me on usury; yet every one of them doth curse me. (Jer. 15:10)

Here, Jeremiah was referring to being "birthed," spiritually-speaking, and being assaulted for his righteous, God-inspired opposition. In unison, God spoke to him in a prophetic context, assuring Jeremiah that it would be well with him and his remnant in the *"time of evil and time of affliction"* (Jer. 15:11). God also reassured Jeremiah about the *final prophetic day of deliverance* when the "Gentiles shall come unto thee from the ends of the earth" (Jer. 16:19). Jeremiah sure appears to be a 'type' and foreshadow of last days 'Jacob' here.

Additionally, end times 'Jacob' is many times addressed directly in scripture by God himself. God "births" 'Jacob' for his own purpose, telling him how he is called with the particular purpose of re-establishing the nation and people of 'Israel.' God refers directly to 'Jacob' as: "my servant"; "my elect"; and "my called." The following verses further demonstrate that 'Jacob' is *spiritually* "birthed" as an end times servant of God:

Behold...I have put my spirit on him... (Is. 42:1)

I have called thee by name; thou art mine. (Is. 43:1)

('Jacob') Whom I have chosen- thus saith the Lord that made thee from the womb, which will help thee... (Is. 44:2)

He that gives breath unto the people...I the Lord have called you in righteousness and will hold your hand... (Is. 42:5-6)

Consider end times 'Jacob's *spiritual* birth, his transformation, along with his spiritual family discussed above. Then, in further consideration of the earthly versus the heavenly, consider Jesus' words in response to his being made aware that his earthly family was standing beside him in his day. Jesus said:

Who is my mother? and who are my brethren? For whosoever shall do the will of my Father which is in heaven, the same is my brother, and sister, and mother. (Matt. 12:48,50)

'Jacob' is clearly an end times servant who is "birthed" to do the will of Jesus and the Father. Jesus will be surrounded in his Kingdom with those fellow-servants he calls his brothers.

~

These key distinguishing factors of, and events surrounding, the "birthing" of the end times holy children of Israel (i.e. those who are spiritually born) will be addressed in additional detail in Parts 2 and 3. I also describe the Lord's anointed remnant in detail in my book, *Biblical End Times, Volume 1.*

9.2 Children of Israel "Birthed" in the End Times (Part 2)

In Part 1, I discussed the 'Daughter of Zion' as Israel's Kingdom queen and mother figure from whom the Kingdom's children will be "birthed." She is referred to in scripture as the "mother of all" and the "mother of nations." I also described how she is the symbolic "mother" to Jesus himself in the book of the Revelation (Chapter 12) story and is also a mother- or sister-type to end times 'Jacob.' And in addition to Jesus and 'Jacob,' it appears that there will be other holy children of Israel's remnant who are "birthed" to her in the last days prior to the Millennial Kingdom.

In this and the following passage (Part 3), I will address the prophetic significance of travails with, and spiritual "birthings" of, God's holy children as far as how these relate to last days events and the general timing of those events. I will present this information within the following sections:

- Initial travails and pains
- The time period of travailing and "birthing" in the last days
- Travails, "birthing" and the war on the country of Israel
- Travails, "birthing" and the war on 'Babylon'-U.S.

In order to discern end times events, we must keep an eye on happenings with God's people, 'Israel.' Travailing and "birthing" processes that involve Israel's children give us key indications about these. As a prophetic 'type' of father-figure, the Prophet Isaiah in some instances represents end times 'Jacob.' Isaiah refers to his own children, a topic that I will address in Part 3 of this series. Meanwhile, what Isaiah says as follows about his children has more broad meaning applicable in a last days context such as that which can also be applied to end times 'Jacob.' Isaiah said:

Behold, I and the children whom the Lord hath given me are for signs and for wonders in Israel from the Lord of hosts, which dwelleth in mount Zion. (Is. 8:18)

In this passage, I will address how travailing with and the spiritual "birthings" of God's children are indicative of last days signs, wonders, events, etc. This will cover the first two items listed above. In Part 3, I will address "birthing"-related signs and Israel's children who are "birthed" as these apply to the coming wars on the countries of Israel and 'Babylon'-U.S., respectively.

Initial Travails and Pains

In the book of Romans, the Apostle Paul tells us that our "whole creation" has been travailing and "groaning" in childbirth pains, even until now (Rom. 8:22). The apostles during Jesus' time on earth surmised how we were already in the "last days." Most verses in scripture referring specifically to pains and "sorrows" associated with "birthing" of Israel's children are an important sign for prophetic events in the *last of the last* days.

Recall in my passage, the 'Daughter of Zion' (Part 2), how her birth pains in scripture are linked directly with last days trouble, even that of entire nations. They are a sign about the anti-Christ Chaldean army coming out into the open in the kingdom war that will manifest worldwide. The Chaldeans' powerful, organized cabal with its lawless and corrupt leaders will heavily impact societies around the world. This will cause social unrest and division not only *within* nations, but also *between* nations. This is a direct consequence of the Satanic dialectic model that Chaldean leaders perpetuate to keep themselves in power and their citizens deceived. It is *designed* to invoke conflict, fighting and destruction. Do you recognize this process in place today?

I show in *Writings of Lion's Lair, Volume 2*, that both 'Babylon'-U.S. and the country of Israel, in particular, are nations that will first be destroyed from within and then attacked and plundered from without. This is a result of the anti-Christ Chaldean kingdom's war that has first and foremost targeted the Lord's faithful servants, with the U.S. and the country of Israel being nations where relatively large populations of them have resided.

"Before all these things..." - Persecution

The general prophetic time period of "travailing" aligns with the "beginning of sorrows" (i.e. birth pains) that Jesus described as *not yet* the end. Jesus described quite a few signs of this last days time period (Matt. 24, Mark 13, Luke 21) that will manifest worldwide. The signs he gave included great deception, including the appearing of many false christs and false prophets along with other signs such as lawlessness, famines, pestilences, earthquakes and the strife and division between nations such as that which I mentioned above.

In relation to his *people* (i.e. last days sheep), specifically, Jesus pointed to heavy spiritual warfare and persecution. This will come at the hands of world Babylon's powers who will cause true Christ-believers to be betrayed, "delivered up," and "handed over to be persecuted." Jesus also spoke of betrayal by friends and family amidst intense persecution at this time. All of these are consistent with the 'Jacob army's resistance in the unconventional war versus the Chaldeans that happens very quietly, behind the scenes, during this time. Interestingly, in one account of Jesus' explanation of last days travails and sorrows he *appeared* to indicate that this heavy persecution of his sheep will happen even prior to the time of sorrows. Note that Jesus said:

But before all these (sorrows), they shall lay their hands on you, and persecute you, delivering you up to the synagogues, and into prisons, being brought before kings and rulers for my name's sake. (Lk. 21:12)

Again, the important point here is that severe persecution of God's people will very likely already be underway once we witness events associated with the *beginning* of "sorrows." This time will be symbolized by the personal travails of the 'Daughter of Zion.'

Then, at the time 'Zion's holy children are actually "birthed," spiritually speaking, they will be fiercely pursued by the enemy in this spiritual war. This will be somewhat analogous to the time when Pharaoh ordered firstborn Israelite baby boys to be killed in ancient Egypt or when Herod ordered babies to be killed at the time around when Jesus was born. Last days events related to persecution will continue to intensify throughout the Day of the Lord. (I describe the Day of the Lord in detail in *Volume 2*).

'Zion' not able to bring forth children for a period of time

'The Daughter of Zion's extreme travailing, birth pains and subsequent symbolic "birthing" of children are a clear sign of a raging spiritual kingdom war in the last days. In fact, the highly tumultuous environment in which she travails is the reason that we are shown in scripture examples of prophecies about bereavement, the inability to deliver, or a lack of strength in giving birth. This represents the time of last days 'Israel's children that God promised to Eve that she (in part, as a foreshadow of the last days 'Daughter of Zion') would have "sorrows" in bringing forth.

Indeed, we know that 'Israel's mother, the 'Daughter of Zion,' will be heavily persecuted herself in the last days and looking for sons to "guide her" or "take her by the hand" (Is. 51:18). However, the following verses show the condition of children, some of whom appear to be "birthed" yet are described as "desolate." They are also held captive. In other words, they are not *fully* "birthed" yet:

Thy sons have fainted, they lie at the head of all the streets, as a wild bull in a net: they are full of the fury of the Lord, the rebuke of thy God. (Is. 51:20)

Arise, cry out in the night: in the beginning of the watches pour out thine heart like water before the face of the Lord: lift up thy hands toward him for the life of thy young children, that faint for hunger in the top of every street. The young and the old lie on the ground in the streets: my virgins and my young men are fallen by the sword; thou hast slain them in the day of thine anger; thou hast killed, and not pitied. (Lam. 2:19, 21)

The ways of Zion do mourn, because none come to the solemn feasts: all her gates are desolate: her priests sigh, her virgins are afflicted, and she is in bitterness. And from the daughter of Zion all her beauty is departed: her princes are become like harts that find no pasture, and they are gone without strength before the pursuer. (Lam. 1:4,6)

The language about Zion's children fainting, fallen, desolate, etc. in scripture is indicative of bereavement of children or of children *not* "brought forth." The 'Daughter of Zion's and her children's captivity in the last days is God's plan. They are being disciplined, both for themselves as well as for prior generations of Israel' who have been disobedient. God strongly and prophetically warned his people and promised in ancient scripture (Deuteronomy, Chapter 28) about the coming consequences and hardships of persecution on them as a result of their disobedience.

God's children sold into captivity in the last days

One major consequence given for God's disobedient people is that they would eventually be scattered "among the nations." As a general principle, we have seen before that when God's sheep are scattered, they are vulnerable. And when they are vulnerable, "wolves" take them captive and persecute them. A couple of specific prophetic promises related to God's people's captivity are as follows:

Thy sons and thy daughters shall be given unto another people, and thine eyes shall look, and fail with longing for them all the day long; and there shall be no might in thine hand. (Deut. 28:32)

Thou shalt beget sons and daughters, but thou shalt not enjoy them; for they shall go into captivity. (Deut. 28:41)

As for being held captive, this applies to both Israel's "spiritual" children as well as its actual children especially in the last days. God tells the righteous 'Daughter of Zion' herself, "you were sold for nothing" (Is. 52:2). She is held and is persecuted by the anti-Christ Chaldeans. 'Zion's *spiritual* children including end times 'Jacob,' who we know will be "in bonds," are also "sold" into captivity. This is a fulfillment of God's prophetic promise from the book of Deuteronomy. Speaking further about this last days time period God confirmed his people's (i.e. 'Judah' and 'Jerusalem') captivity "in those days and in that time" (Joel 3:1) and foretold:

And they have cast lots for my people, and have given a boy for an harlot, and sold a girl for wine, that they might drink. (Joel 3:3)

Here, through the Prophet Joel we are told that the children of 'Judah' and 'Jerusalem' have been sold to the Grecians and "scattered." In the end times, as explained in the curse in the book of Deuteronomy, God warned his people that they would not be able to hold onto their own children due to captivity. In 'Babylon'-U.S. this could translate, practically speaking, to God's people "losing" their children as a result of anti-Christ Chaldean-arranged, planned-marriage-followed-by-planned-divorce schemes. This is likely at least one reason we learn in prophetic scripture that it will be better to be "barren" than with children in the last days. It is also likely a reason that we are told the following about 'Israel's final regathering:

Thus saith the Lord God, Behold, I will lift up mine hand to the Gentiles, and set up my standard to the people: and they shall bring thy sons in their arms, and thy daughters shall be carried upon their shoulders. (Is. 49:22)

'Israel's broken families, will ultimately be reunited upon their final "birthing" as a people and their subsequent regathering in the holy land at the beginning of the Millennial Kingdom.

Ezekiel's prophetic vision of royal lions taken captive

Additional indications of the captivity of God's holy children not fully "birthed" in the last days may remind some of the Judah remnant that was spared by Nebuchadnezzar but was taken back to 'Babylon' in captivity. This is the remnant that the Prophet Ezekiel lived among and addressed in his day with clear end times implications and meaning.

In one of Ezekiel's visions (Chapter 19), there is a prophetic lament for Israel's princes and their royal mother- the latter likely referring to the 'Daughter of Zion.' (Note: She is referred to as a "lioness," rearing her whelps. The lioness reference is likely pointing to her Judah tribal lineage. She is also referred to later in the same chapter as a "vine in the blood"; it is described as one that is "fruitful" and has strong branches for the "scepters of them that bare rule." This appears to be further reference to her association with the end times holy, royal Judah-'house of David' remnant).

Ezekiel's vision shows how the 'Daughter of Zion's vine and tree gets "plucked up in fury" by God and that her branches ("rods") become "broken and withered." Both the 'Daughter of Zion' and her royal house are devoured in this last days vision. Ezekiel's vision shows how a couple of her whelps "learn(ed) to catch prey," likely meaning exposing anti-Christ Chaldean criminal activities, but that both of these whelps are taken captive and quieted in the "land of Egypt." One is quieted directly by the king of 'Babylon.' In a last days context, these are likely a couple members of the 'Jacob army,' possibly even 'Jacob' himself, learning to fight in the unconventional surveillance war in 'Babylon'-U.S. but were identified as such, taken hostage, and quieted by the anti-Christ Chaldeans. ('Egypt' in the last days is sometimes symbolic and is a subset of world Babylon). This is consistent with the last days time period Jesus referred to when God's people will be "delivered up." (For more about the last days quieting of God's message and his people, see my passage entitled, *God's people and message silenced in the last days*, in *Volume 2*.

Overall, spiritual "travailing" and the awakening of God's holy children is very dangerous in the last days anti-Christ Chaldean-controlled world. In Ezekiel's vision and lament, the 'Daughter of Zion's hope is lost, at least temporarily, when she sees (possibly symbolically) that her end times' whelps are captured. To the extent that any of God's spiritual children are discovered by world Babylon's "all seeing eye" surveillance system, you can be assured that they will be quieted and persecuted.

Meanwhile, spiritual "travailing" and the subsequent awakening by Israel's holy children in the last days is necessary for God's children to have eyes to see and ears to hear world Babylon's matrix and imprisoning system and is furthermore necessary for *coming to a realization that they are the primary targets*. Certainly, those in the 'Jacob army' have this spiritual awakening. I described in Chapter 8 that members of this army of the Lord are at least given the strength to fight back in this spiritual kingdom war. The Lord's Spirit is with them.

The Time Period of Travailing and "Birthing" in the Last Days

In the last days, birth pains and spiritual "birthings" of God's holy children are signs of very significant worldwide events, both in-progress and still to come. This is due to the ongoing kingdom war that is being waged. In general, the order of events in the last days as they are told relative to "birthing"-related signs is:

1. Heavy persecution of God's people (likely beginning prior to #2 and then ongoing throughout).
2. Pre-Day of the Lord events (i.e. *"not yet the end"*); ("Beginning of sorrows"- i.e. birth pains)
3. First-half of the Day of the Lord events (i.e. actual, spiritual "birthings")
4. Second-half of the Day of the Lord events (i.e. birthing of the nation of 'Israel'- at the end)

I have already addressed the first two time periods (i.e. persecution and travailing) earlier in this passage. These pains and sorrows through the pregnancy cycle culminate in Zion's "birthing" of 'Jacob.' Once 'Jacob' is spiritually born at the general time period at or near the beginning of the Day of the Lord, then Zion's additional children will begin to be "birthed" as the kingdom war more fully commences. These are actual *spiritual birthings* of God's holy, royal children. So, it naturally represents a more intense stage of the spiritual war that is already raging (i.e. "kingdom versus kingdom"). Due to this very dangerous kingdom war, all of these "births" will be largely kept quiet, hidden and unrecognizable to the public. As it is, do you ever hear this topic discussed, even among bible prophecy teachers?

The continuing "birthing" of God's holy children amidst persecution, pains and tumultuous world events will likely happen in the *first half* of the Day of the Lord, generally speaking. In the *second half* God's people will be forced to flee, wander and hide as the Anti-Christ and beast system temporarily take over full power and authority. The

'Daughter of Zion' will return at the end of the Tribulation period to give "birth" to the larger nation of Israel remnant at the time Jesus returns.

I discuss "birthing"-related signs as these apply to approximately the first and the second halves of the Day of the Lord, respectively, in the remainder of this section.

'Jacob's and Jesus' "birthings" as bookends to the first half of the Day of the Lord

It *appears* that end times 'Jacob' will be the first child to be symbolically, spiritually "birthed." I discussed this in Part 1. At this time, significant troublesome events such as those Jesus spoke of as the "beginning of sorrows" (Matthew, 24, Mark 13, Luke 21) will only intensify, similar to birth pains in physical birth that we know increase in frequency and intensity as the baby(ies) come(s) closer to birth. To re-state these signs and events, Jesus instructed us to look for false christs, false prophets, lawlessness, famines, pestilences, earthquakes, wars and rumors of wars, etc. After 'Zion' travails and 'Jacob' is spiritually "birthed," these events and the *ongoing* persecution of God's people will become increasingly noticeable.

Next, I also showed in Part 1 how Jesus, the manchild himself, is likely the *last* child (in sequence) of God's holy, royal sons to be born to the 'Daughter of Zion.' 'Jesus' *re*-birth (Revelation, Chapter 12) we are told in scripture occurs at the mid-point of the final "week of years," coinciding with even more severe events that include God's judgments on earth at this time, not to mention increased occurrences of supernatural signs and wonders, especially those events described in the book of Revelation that will apply to the final 42 months at the end of the age.

So, in terms of time markers, 'Jacob's "birth" and Jesus' "*re*-birth" *appear* to be bookends for roughly the first half of the Day of the Lord (i.e. ~3 ½ years). In between their respective "births," Zion's travailing and "birth" pains continue during this time as other children are spiritually "birthed." These coincide with spiritual kingdom war events Jesus mentioned above that become amplified as the seals are opened and the riders on horses in Chapter 6 of the book of Revelation.

It is not my intent to cover the book of Revelation in this passage, but the general idea about this initial time is that there will be great wars (via the "sword"), famines, pestilences, a great earthquake, and the resulting deaths of those residing in a fourth part of the earth. The "sword" of large-scale war will be particularly troubling and unnerving at this time.

To once again link these events back to the 'Daughter of Zion's travailing and birthings, you will recall that she is a very strong indicator for events in both Zion- the country of Israel- as well as for the nation of 'Babylon'-U.S. I will demonstrate this strong link and association in *Volume 2* about certain war that is coming to both of these countries. Meanwhile, in Part 3 of this series, I will describe more about these wars in terms of how they will be correlated with "birth" pains and the "birthings" of God's children, 'Israel.'

The Daughter of Zion is delivered from travails in the second half of the Day of the Lord

After giving "birth" to Jesus the manchild at the point of mid-Day of the Lord, and before Jesus' return, the 'Daughter of Zion' will flee the dragon. Her holy remnant (God's children who have been spiritually "birthed") will also have to flee the dragon-serpent and seek refuge in the wilderness at this time. (Note: The remnant here are likely symbolized by the stars surrounding the 'Daughter of Zion' in the book of Revelation (Chapter 12) story). This time of fleeing will coincide with the Anti-Christ committing the abomination of declaring that he is God and is to be worshiped.

It appears that Zion continues to travail at this time, even *after* the birth of the manchild as she remains in 'Babylon.' There is scripture in Lamentations that indicates she continues to mourn because of being separated from the one who could comfort her. She will eventually give "birth" to the larger remnant of the nation of 'Israel' that will finally be *re*-gathered at the end of the Day of the Lord. I will address this larger remnant's regathering in *Volumes 2 and 3*. I will briefly address it again in Part 2 as it applies specifically to 'Ephraim' as a proxy for Israel's 'northern kingdom.'

Although scripture related to the regathering of 'Israel' and it being "born in one day" is most commonly applied by bible prophecy teachers to the establishment of the country of Israel in 1948 and its ongoing status as a growing nation of Jewish people, this verse in Isaiah has a *last of the last days* meaning that is not often discussed.

In fact, this refers to the final "birthing" that is done by the 'Daughter of Zion' for the remnant of Israel along with the "glory of the Gentiles" who go into the Millennial Kingdom. Some of 'Israel' will return from the "north" to a holy land of Israel that has been made desolate and in need of rebuilding. This is a time that God tells Zion and his people 'Israel' that their "seed" will remain as the "new heavens and new earth" (Is. 66:22). In terms of this final "birthing" by the 'Daughter of Zion' at the beginning of God's new Kingdom, we are told:

Before she travailed, she brought forth; before her pain came, she was delivered of a man child. Who hath heard such a thing? who hath seen such things? Shall the earth be made to bring forth in one day? or shall a nation be born at once? for as soon as Zion travailed, she brought forth her children. (Is. 66:7-8)

The manchild here appears to refer again to Jesus, the Alpha and Omega, though this time upon his return. Recall that when Zion "births" Jesus at the mid-point of the final week of years (i.e. 7 years) she *is* in travail. Here, she is not. This appears to be the time we are told upon the Lord's return, "Let us be glad and rejoice, and give honour to him: for the marriage of the Lamb is come, and his wife hath made herself ready" (Rev. 19:7). About 'Zion's final deliverance as told through Isaiah (Chapter 66) there is a strong association with and indications for the beginning of the Millennial Kingdom for Israel and all of the nations at this time. I also discuss the story of all nations' final deliverance and return to the Lord's Kingdom in my books, *Biblical End Times, Volumes 1 and 2.*

~

In summary, in the current last days time period in which we are living we should assume that the persecution of God's people (Jesus Christ's sheep) is underway. Just as travails and "birthings" happen quietly and behind-the-scenes, so does Chaldean persecution via a plethora of unseen, undetectable psychological operation techniques that are employed. This is happening currently in 'Babylon'-U.S. as the spiritual kingdom war progresses.

In my next passage, Part 3, I will discuss what will be the very obvious last days sign of large-scale wars and how these are associated with and relate to "birthing" signs.

9.3 Children of Israel "Birthed" in the End Times (Part 3)

In my last passage, Part 2, I discussed the prophetic significance of "travails" with, and "birthings" of, God's holy children as these relate to end time events as well as the general timing of these events.

In this current passage, I will continue discussing the prophetic significance of travails and birthings of God's spiritual children, particularly as these relate to upcoming war (via the "sword") events in the country of Israel and the nation of 'Babylon'-U.S. Accordingly, these events will be addressed in this passage as follows:

- Travails, "birthings," and war on the country of Israel
- Travails, "birthings," and war on the nation of 'Babylon'-U.S.
- Holy children "birthing" events as additional signs of war and necessary exodus from 'Babylon'-U.S.

I will address each of these topic areas in its own respective section below. The country of Israel and the nation of 'Babylon'-U.S. are addressed in detail in *Writings of Lion's Lair, Volume 2*.

Travails, "Birthings" and the War on the Country of Israel

'The Daughter of Zion' is a bellwether, symbolic sign for the end times country of Israel. Her personal situation, having been betrayed and persecuted by former allies is directly analogous to the country of Israel's situation. The country of Israel's so-called "peace" that will soon be declared with other nations will ultimately be discovered to have been a "false peace" among insincere, deceiving, and betraying international anti-Christ Chaldean partners. Do you see these developments potentially transpiring in our current day?

Zion's travails and the "birth" of 'Jacob' will be ominous news for the country of Israel

Recall that Jesus told us that in the last days when Jerusalem is surrounded by armies that its desolation is near. Old Testament prophets also foretold about this coming time. This is the same general time period when the 'Daughter of Zion' will cry out in travail and give "birth" to her firstborn, *'Jacob.'* Upon doing so, she will be "surrounded" just like Jerusalem will be:

For I have heard a voice as of a woman in travail, and the anguish as of her that bringeth forth her first child, the voice of the daughter of Zion, that bewaileth herself, that spreadeth her hands, saying, Woe is me now! for my soul is wearied because of murderers. (Jer. 4:31)

Behold the voice of the cry of the daughter of my people because of them that dwell in a far country: Is not the Lord in Zion? is not her king in her? Why have they provoked me to anger with their graven images, and with strange vanities? (Jer. 8:19)

The country of Israel's punishment that I describe in detail in *Volume 2* will come upon it for all of their activities related to worshiping foreign gods and following occultic practices. The country of Israel's misguided leaders will realize that *they* are the ones who cooperated with those in the "far country" (see second verse above and recall that the 'Daughter of Zion' resides in 'Babylon'-U.S.) who have persecuted their own people's Matriarch. Israel's leaders at this point will realize that they have been deceived and duped all along by the anti-Christ Chaldeans and a false peace process.

I have described before how this coming 'peace' agreement between the country of Israel and other countries will *really* be about a peace process for the 'Daughter of Zion,' 'Jacob,' and the 'Jacob army' who have exposed the powerful anti-Christ Chaldean system as a crime syndicate. And the peace process will fail because the country of Israel's leaders will have been heavily deceived and blinded as to the truth. God says:

For the hurt of the daughter of my people am I hurt; I am black; astonishment hath taken hold on me. Is there no balm in Gilead; is there no physician there? why then is not the health of the daughter of my people recovered? (Jer. 8:21-22)

Behold, their valiant ones shall cry without: the ambassadors of peace shall weep bitterly. (Is. 33:7)

The "health" of God's daughter will not be recovered or resolved by the phony peace process. This will have been a false, Chaldean-led process that, above-board, appeared to be for peace between the country of Israel and other nations. But behind-the-scenes, in secret (which is how the anti-Christ Chaldeans operate), it will merely have been a *symbolic*, ritualistic process for Israel's and Babylon's Chaldeans' ongoing war against the righteous 'Jacob'-Judah remnant bloodline that includes the 'Daughter of Zion.'

The country of Israel's leaders at this time will finally realize that their Chaldean "friends" were actually their enemies and betrayers. At this time, the country of Israel's leaders will also recognize the extent of their own corruption. As I mentioned above, this *appears* to happen at the point when Zion gives "birth" to her firstborn 'Jacob' ('Israel').

In addition to their mistreatment and persecution of the 'Daughter of Zion,' the country of Israel's deceived Chaldean leaders will learn about their role in the persecution and abandonment of 'Jacob' in the events leading to his spiritual "birth." 'Jacob' is also in the same "far country" (i.e. 'Babylon'-U.S.) as the 'Daughter of Zion.' In a reference to the persecution of 'Jacob'-'Israel' via the Chaldean "mob" God says the following in scolding Judah's (country of Israel's) leaders:

Is Israel a servant? is he a homeborn slave? why is he spoiled? (Jer. 2:14)

God's rhetorical question here could have a meaning for several constituents; but at the least there is likely one meaning for the country of Israel that is in bondage as a nation itself to world Babylon as well as a meaning for end times 'Jacob' who is taken into Chaldean captivity in 'Babylon.'

The country of Israel's leaders will be shown to be spiritually bankrupt

The country of Israel's leaders will be shown in front of the world to be spiritually bankrupt and God-less. Think of the irony here. The 'Daughter of Zion,' 'Israel's queen mother will give spiritual "birth" to 'Jacob,' a prince in Israel's Kingdom to come, while she is in a "far country" ('Babylon'-U.S.) and in heavy travail. Meanwhile, the leaders in God's own land, the country of Israel, will be caught in their "treacherous dealings" (Is. 33:1), foreign gods and iniquities that were responsible for the persecution of their people's own royal family members. In Jeremiah (Chapter 2), God chides his people for their "two evils"; put simply, forsaking him and following other gods- i.e. they have "changed their gods" (Jer. 2:11).

The country of Israel's leaders will have been deceived and tricked. In reference to their corruption and resulting failure, God implicates them for not watching out for their own people, their righteous remnant. They will recognize at this time their own deficiency, which is symbolized by being *without* child. Here, God refers to those who will "come from the north" (Jer. 13:20). These will eventually return as the holy, royal and righteous remnant who are able to be spiritually "birthed" and will be among those who inherit the Kingdom. Consider the following as one line of scripture, beginning with God's question to the corrupt country of Israel's leaders and ending with these leaders realizing their folly:

Lift up your eyes, and behold them that come from the north: where is the flock that was given thee, thy beautiful flock? (Jer. 13:20)

Ye shall conceive chaff, ye shall bring forth stubble: your breath, as fire, shall devour you. (Is. 33:11)

We have been with child, we have been in pain, we have as it were brought forth wind; we have not wrought any deliverance in the earth; neither have the inhabitants of the world fallen. (Is. 26:18)

Prior to the final return of God's faithful anointed remnant, the country of Israel will implode from within and then be attacked from without. They will discover that they have been set up and tricked by the anti-

Christ Chaldeans likely going all the way back to their country's inception in 1948. The Chaldeans will have infiltrated *from within* in God's own land. In speaking about God's last days punishment on the country of Israel, with a reference to Zion's labor pains, the Prophet Jeremiah is referring to these infiltrators and traitors within when he says:

What wilt thou say when he shall punish thee? for thou hast taught them to be captains, and as chief over thee: shall not sorrows take thee, as a woman in travail? (Jer. 13:21)

Internal Chaldean traitors in the country of Israel's own leadership ranks will have been instrumental in bringing about their own country's destruction. God meanwhile will subsequently bring punishment via the "sword" onto the country of Israel and its leaders at the time they are in sorrow like a "woman in travail," again signaling 'Zion's upcoming "birthings." This is the point at which they will recognize:

The harvest is past, the summer is ended, and we are not saved. (Jer. 8:20)

While many of Israel's leaders will not be saved, God will protect and eventually save and deliver both 'Jacob' and the 'Daughter of Zion' who are members of his "small flock" remnant. 'Zion's travailing to give birth above is with 'Jacob' and his anointed end times spiritual "birth" very likely coincides with his preliminary deliverance. God has promised that he will ultimately "break the bonds" that enslaved him. The event of 'Jacob's spiritual "birthing" is likely around the beginning of the Day of the Lord. God will also similarly come to the 'Daughter of Zion's defense with "judgment and righteousness" (Jer. 33:5) for what he calls the "hurt of the daughter of my people" (Jer. 8:21).

The 'Daughter of Zion's additional holy children who will be birthed-i.e. 'Babylon's 'Jacob'-Judah remnant- will be saved and delivered as well. This is God's "small flock" remnant of children who will be established and set up along with the whole house of Israel in the Kingdom to come.

Travails, "Birthings" and the War against the Nation of 'Babylon'-U.S.

I described in detail in *Volume 2* how end times 'Babylon' can be considered as home to 'Israel's 'northern kingdom,' or 'Ephraim,' for the purposes of understanding last days prophetic events. I will also show that God's punishment in the last days will come upon 'Babylon'-U.S. including a final destroying invasion.

In this section I will show how travailing, birth pains and spiritual "births" of God's children will correlate with this punishment. Tracking these "birthing"-related signs and events reveals the same story for 'Babylon' that I describe in *Volume 2*. It will also show how the last days story of 'Babylon *will very closely mirror* that of the country of Israel's as just described.

The beginning of the end for the nation of 'Babylon'- Zion's travails and "birthings"

As we saw with the Prophet Jeremiah related to the country of Israel above we learn through Isaiah how "travailing" birth pains followed by spiritual "birthings" of God's end times children by Israel's mother 'Zion' (Isaiah's wife the "prophetess") will correlate with the time of God's punishment. Tracking these "birthing"-related signs and events foretells the same story for 'Babylon'-U.S. This finding is consistent with the notion that last days events in 'Babylon'-U.S. will very closely mirror those that occur in the country of Israel. We are told of several spiritual "birthings" in the book of Isaiah that serve as signs for prophetic events soon to come in the Day of the Lord. Referring to his own children Isaiah said:

Behold, I and the children whom the Lord hath given me are for signs and for wonders in Israel from the Lord of hosts, which dwelleth in mount Zion. (Is. 8:18)

These "birthing"-related signs are direct warnings given by Isaiah for end times 'Babylon'-U.S. Some are described through his vision of the "burden of Babylon." Isaiah's vision involves a "treacherous dealer," which likely has to do with the same fraudulent peace process I described above involving leaders of the country of Israel. As will be the case with Israel's leaders, corruption that is uncovered will bring God's punishment onto his 'northern kingdom' house of Israel in 'Babylon'-U.S. at the hands of the international anti-Christ Chaldeans. Isaiah prophesied about this time that a watchtower and watchman is set, "My heart panted, fearfulness affrighted me: the night of my pleasure hath he turned into fear unto me" (Is. 21:4). This sign of the end for the nation of 'Babylon'-U.S. related to its corrupt leaders and "treacherous" dealers is described through Isaiah's vision of the "burden of the desert of the sea" with references to the familiar sign of a woman who travails as follows:

A grievous vision is declared unto me; the treacherous dealer dealeth treacherously, and the spoiler spoileth...Therefore are my loins filled with pain: pangs have taken hold upon me, as the pangs of a woman that travaileth... (Is. 21:2-3)

Treacherous dealing by 'Babylon'-U.S.'s leaders will coincide with 'Zion's travails that signal the coming spiritual "birthing" of her firstborn 'Jacob,' which is the same event I described above through Jeremiah as it will apply for the country of Israel. Through Isaiah several additional "birthings" and their associated signs unmistakably refer to the Lord's coming judgment events in our last days time period. One prophetic "birthing" is that which was actually fulfilled and retold as the birth of Jesus to Mary the virgin (Matt. 1:23). While fulfilled in Jesus' first coming to earth the following verse in its context spoken through Isaiah could have additional prophetic meaning. It exists within a line of text that says several times "in that day" with clear storyline indicators for our last days time period. You are likely familiar with the following verses:

Therefore the Lord himself shall give you a sign; Behold, a virgin shall conceive, and bear a son, and shall call his name Immanuel. Butter and honey shall he eat, that he may know to refuse the evil, and choose the good. For before the child shall know to refuse the evil, and choose the good, the land that thou abhorrest shall be forsaken of both her kings. (Is. 7:14-16)

While this "birthing" sign had direct relevance for kings of Isaiah's day who were adversaries of Isaiah's Judah society and planned war against it this sign as it applies prophetically to end times events may again be related to modern day kings of today's 'northern kingdom' of Israel in 'Babylon'-U.S. and its close anti-Christ Chaldean allies who are again aligned against Judah. 'Babylon-U.S. has been deliberately engineered as a melting pot of many nations including ancient enemies who perpetuate the same war against Judah royals manifesting in the last days against 'Jacob's Judah-centric "small flock" remnant.

It appears that the spiritual "birthing" of 'Jacob' and the prophetic sign of Immanuel's birthing above will be at a time when crimes and atrocities of the anti-Christ Chaldeans against the Lord's holy, anointed 'Jacob'-Judah "small flock" remnant are revealed, causing corrupt kings to be exposed and caught. Countries around the world will come to realize 'Babylon'-U.S.'s large-scale fraud at this time. This is likely the beginning of the time of "Jacob's trouble" spoken of by Jeremiah at the time he prophetically inquired, "Ask ye now, and see whether a man doth travail with child? wherefore do I see every man with his hands on his loins, as a woman in travail, and all faces are turned into paleness?" (Jer. 30:6).

In the meantime, the phony, corrupt peace process that I described above for the country of Israel will be the same one that 'Babylon'-U.S.'s leaders will participate in and be caught in the process. 'Babylon'-U.S. will be involved because the "land of the Chaldees" is where the Lord's anointed 'Jacob'-Judah "small flock" remnant including the 'Daughter of Zion' have resided. I described in *Volume 1* that they will have been persecuted including being tracked, mocked and made famous in the Chaldeans' underground world network due to an occult-based storyline, vain images, etc. (Have you ever wondered the real reason why the U.S. and the country of Israel have always been so "close"?).

The bloodline, branch, and fig tree of 'Jacob's "small flock" remnant residing primarily in 'Babylon'-U.S. will have been the "submarine" time bomb below the surface that global anti-Christ Chaldean leaders used to establish Israel in 1948 and then followed in their comic book-style narrative that will lead to the house of Israel's deception and subsequent fall. Just as will be the case with the country of Israel's Chaldean-controlled leaders described above, their allies that include the U.S.'s cooperating house of Israel's and Gentile leaders will be caught at this time. This will be a result of the Lord's "trap" that is set for them. This is the time about which we are told through Isaiah that the Day of the Lord is "at hand."

I mentioned earlier the verse spoken by the Apostle Paul indicating destruction that will come when leaders falsely declare 'peace' at a time of a "woman (travailing) with child." A warning from God spoken through the Prophet Hosea also addresses end times 'Ephraim' ('northern kingdom') in 'Babylon'-U.S. likely showing this same event involving corrupt dealmakers. God indicates here that those who attempt to escape their atrocities will be caught and says that, "When they shall go, I will spread my net upon them..." (Hos. 7:12). This event of "sudden destruction" appears to come at the time when leaders in both 'Babylon'-U.S. and the country of Israel will be saying "peace" and attempting to run and "escape" for cover to join the new world order. Instead, they will learn that they have been exposed.

At the time of Ezekiel's prophetic signs (described in detail in *Volume 3*) the Son of man departs his residence with his belongings and digs through Babylon's symbolic "wall" in the sight of his people Israel we are told that a leader of the country of Israel will try to do the same. At this time, he will be caught along with his partners (i.e. "bands") who will fall by the sword. 'Babylon'-U.S.'s own leaders who will be corrupt allies of Israel's leaders in their dealings will finally receive an awakening as to the real war that has been taking place behind-the-scenes but it will be too late. This war will have included tremendous crime and persecution in the U.S. against the Lord's anointed 'Jacob'-Judah "small flock" remnant including the 'Daughter of Zion' along with a larger segment of the Lord's remnant of Israel and all true Christ-believers. Leaders in 'Babylon'-U.S. will realize that they have blindly taken part as perpetrators on the wrong side of a longstanding spiritual kingdom war and that God himself is now involved.

Judgment will begin via siege and war that comes against 'Babylon'-U.S. in a similar manner as it will come upon the country of Israel. At this time, it will be 'Babylon'-U.S.'s leaders who will be in pain "as a woman that travails." Notice the references below to them being in travail when 'Zion' travails as she approaches the time of giving spiritual "birth" to 'Jacob.' These leaders will be in their own "pain" when they hear of a coming invasion according to this sign given through Isaiah's "burden of Babylon" vision that is corroborated by Jeremiah's prophecy as follows:

Howl ye; for the day of the Lord is at hand; it shall come as a destruction from the Almighty....And they ('Babylon's leaders) shall be afraid: pangs and sorrows shall take hold of them; they shall be in pain as a woman that travaileth: they shall be amazed one at another; their faces shall be as flames. (Is. 13:6,8)

They shall hold the bow and the lance: they are cruel, and will not shew mercy: their voice shall roar like the sea, and they shall ride upon horses, every one put in array, like a man to the battle, against thee, O daughter of Babylon. The king of Babylon hath heard the report of them, and his hands waxed feeble: anguish took hold of him, and pangs as of a woman in travail. (Jer. 50:42-43)

The 'Daughter of Zion's travailing in birth pangs when she cries out at the time of the "beginning of watches" will be a very important warning sign for 'Babylon'-U.S. and the Lord's coming judgment against it.

Holy Child "Birthing" Events as Additional Signs of War and Necessary Exodus from 'Babylon' in the Day of the Lord

In scripture, there are specific, spiritual birthings of God's children in the end times that provide additional, corroborating detail about war that will come onto 'Babylon'-U.S. These "birthings" also inform the exodus event of God's people, 'Ephraim,' who will return to the regathering after fleeing 'Babylon.' These birthing signs and events are discussed in this section below.

Signs based on the "birthing" of God's children- Immanuel

To continue with the "birthing" theme, and linking "birthing" signs to end time events, certain prophecies told through Isaiah (Chapter 7) unmistakably refer to our last days time period. As mentioned above, the prophetic "birthing" of Immanuel as retold at the birth of Jesus to Mary the virgin (Matt. 1:23) has *additional prophetic meaning*. It exists within a line of scripture that says several times, *in that day*, with clear storyline indicators for our current *last days time period*.

The kings referred to as "forsaken" in this story of 'Immanuel's birthing that has both historical and prophetic meaning are two kings (i.e. king of 'Israel' and king of 'Syria') who aligned against Judah and its King (Ahaz) at that time in history. Here, the house of David is told, "Syria is confederate with Ephraim" (Is. 7:2). In simple prophetic terms, this represents an alignment of today's 'Babylon'-U.S.'s and its close allies' anti-Christ Chaldeans who have likely identified and misled 'Ephraim' (i.e. today's 'Israel's/'northern kingdom's people who are also living in 'Babylon') to cooperate in their cabal. Thus, 'Ephraim' have joined Chaldean-traitors in the nation of 'Babylon'-U.S. Altogether, this powerful Chaldean alliance comes against and persecutes the righteous 'Jacob army'-Judah-house of David remnant including 'Jacob' himself and the 'Daughter of Zion.' History repeats, only by God's incredible grand design.

In Immanuel's (God *with* us) story, before he knows how to discern between good and evil, symbolically speaking in terms of age, then both end times kings (i.e. kings of 'Babylon' and 'Syria') will be caught. Their capture will happen at the hands of the king of 'Assyria' (not 'Syria'), consistent with the story in *Volume 2* about the 'Assyrian's invasion of 'Babylon.' In this line of scripture through the Prophet Isaiah we are told that the 'Assyrian' will "stretch out his wings and will fill the breadth of thy land, O Immanuel." (I showed in Chapter 3 how the Lord's Spirit, 'Immanuel' (God *with* us), is working in last days Israel's 'northern kingdom' within 'Babylon'-U.S.).

Note to the reader:

Could 'Immanuel' (God with us) here represent the end times 'Restrainer,' 'Comforter' or Holy Spirit who we know has ties to last days 'Babylon' and is "taken out of the way"? Birth to a virgin here implies deity, meaning Immanuel must be a member of the holy trinity. The *person* in the form of the 'Restrainer' or Holy Spirit will be taken out of the way, perhaps somewhat similar to how Joseph and Mary fled to Egypt to hide with their baby Jesus. This last days time when Immanuel is born will be a highly tumultuous time of war when today's 'northern kingdom' and 'Babylon'-U.S., is invaded by the 'Assyrian's coalition armies.

A natural question arises here as to the relationship between the "birth" of 'Immanuel,' which appears at or near the beginning of the Day of the Lord and Jesus the man-child's birth in the middle of the final "week of years." 'Immanuel' is not immediately caught up. Jesus is. We do know from scripture that the Lord's Spirit is in the land ('Babylon'-U.S.) fighting the Chaldean war along with the 'Jacob army' in the last days, but this likely is happening even before the time of 'Immanuel's "birth" in the last days.

Signs based on the "birthing" of God's children- Mahershalhashbaz

In the very next section of Isaiah's scroll (Chapter 8), Isaiah has a vision of his prophetess-wife conceiving and bearing a son whose name is to be called, as instructed by the Lord, Mahershalhashbaz; (a name that means "swift to the spoil, quick to the plunder"). Isaiah recites:

And I went unto the prophetess; and she conceived, and bare a son. Then said the Lord to me, Call his name Mahershalalhashbaz. For before the child shall have knowledge to cry, My father, and my mother, the riches of Damascus and the spoil of Samaria shall be taken away before the king of Assyria. (Is. 8:3-4)

So, before this child of God knows how to cry to his parents, Samaria, the 'northern kingdom's capital and likely a proxy for other end times U.S.'s major cities, will be plundered and looted. (Note here that this is done by the king of Assyria again, *not* the king of Syria. I address the king of 'Assyria-'Pharaoh' in *Volume 2* with additional scripture as the last days leader of the international Chaldean coalition's nations including today's Medes who will invade and plunder 'Babylon.')

It is possible that the virgin mother of Immanuel above is the same mother/prophetess of Mahershalhashbaz. If this is the case, it could be reasonable to assume that there are *approximately* three years between the "births" of these two boys, or almost the length of half of the final seven-year (i.e. week of years) period. *If* this is the case, then Immanuel and Mahershalhashbaz could be bookends for the first half of the Day of the Lord, just as I stated earlier that 'Jacob's and Jesus' "births" could be. When considering my explanation of end times 'Immanuel' in my note to the reader above, you can see that there are possible explanations for parallels or associations *both between and across* these two pairings.

Meanwhile, for our practical purposes here, the combined "birthings" of 'Immanuel' and Mahershalhashbaz *appear* to represent bookends for the approximate time period of the 'Assyrian's attack on 'Babylon,' beginning with 'Babylon's kings being captured on the front end and the invaders looting the nation of 'Babylon'-U.S. on the back end.

Signs based on the births of God's children- 'Ephraim'

In *Volume 2*, I describe that prophetic 'Ephraim' represents a nation (land), a people, and possibly even a particular person. At the top level, 'Ephraim' represents the collective people of God's last days 'northern kingdom' of Israel who live in 'Babylon'-U.S. Last days 'Ephraim' is described as an "unwise son." The very likely reason that 'Ephraim' is "unwise" was given earlier in this passage. That is, his people are Chaldean traitors within 'Babylon,' confederate with end times 'Syria's ('Babylon's close allies') Chaldeans. Again, related to "birthings" as a sign, we are told about 'Ephraim':

The sorrows of a travailing woman shall come upon him: he is an unwise son; for he should not stay long in the place of the breaking forth of children. (Hos. 13:13)

In general, scripture tells us that last days 'Ephraim' does not come to "birth." 'Ephraim' is in fact not *spiritually* birthed because he and his people are blinded by their Chaldean associations. In parallel to the country of Israel's Chaldeans, 'Ephraim' will realize that their Chaldean associations (foreign gods and idols) were actually their enemies and deceivers. (Sound familiar?)

As a result, prior to the 'Ephraim' remnant's return to the Lord and spiritual "birth," they must be saved while in 'Babylon' when the 'Assyrian' invades. In a line of scripture (Hosea, Chapter 11) that has God reflecting fondly on 'Ephraim' when he "was a child" before he backslid and was blinded by Chaldean iniquities, God promised that he will save 'Ephraim.' God promises through the Prophet Hosea:

How shall I give thee up, Ephraim? How shall I deliver thee Israel?...my heart is turned within me, my repentings are kindled together. I will not execute the fierceness of my anger, I will not return to destroy Ephraim... (Hos. 11:8-9)

Prior to 'Ephraim's deliverance, its people will be forced to flee and will be scattered in the last days. We are told:

My God will cast them away, because they did not hearken unto him: and they shall be wanderers among the nations. (Hos. 9:17)

Ephraim will flee 'Babylon'-U.S., largely during the time the 'Assyrian' invades and comes to plunder. 'Ephraim' is indicative and representative of Israel's worldwide remnant that will wander throughout the Day of the Lord at a time when God has hidden his face and asks in scripture, "Is there no king in you?" It should be noted that 'Ephraim's people probably begin to wander even in the first half of the Day of the Lord because of the trouble that will come upon 'Babylon'-U.S. at this time.

Recall that the Prophet Isaiah- a 'type' of end times 'Jacob'- as I mentioned at the beginning of this passage, tells us that the children given to him are for prophetic "signs and wonders." Above, we saw his son 'Mahershalhashbaz's name means "to plunder." Meanwhile, Isaiah's other son named Shearjashub, about whom we are told earlier in the same story (Chapter 7) is with Isaiah when they consult with King Ahaz of Judah about the kings of 'Israel' and 'Syria' who were aligned against him. Isiah's son Shearjashub's name means, "a remnant shall return."

I will address Israel's larger remnant that will return in *Volume 2.* Although still "unbirthed" at the time of the anointed remnant's "birthing" due to their rejection of Jesus, there will be an 'Ephraim' remnant that will ultimately be saved and "birthed" at the final regathering that I described earlier when a nation is "born in a day." This will be after God hides his face and they wander and seek him. Scripture says:

Therefore will he give them up, until the time that she which travaileth hath brought forth: then the remnant of his brethren shall return unto the children of Israel. (Mic. 5:3)

Upon their wandering, Jesus' Spirit of truth, the 'Comforter,' the two witnesses and the 144,000 anointed ones will help his sheep who seek him in the midst of their persecution and the terrors of the Day of the Lord. Remember the prayers of Jesus' sheep who were the mothers of Jesus and the prophets such as Mary, Elizabeth and Hannah (see Part 1) who prayed for the coming Messiah, Jesus, to be birthed so that the humble would be exalted and the proud and mighty oppressors would be put down.

Many of God's sheep-saints will find themselves praying this identical prayer in the Day of the Lord. And their prayers will be answered with Jesus' *re*-birth and subsequent defeat of the adversary.

~

Ultimately, the prayers of God's sheep will be answered and the answer to the rhetorical question asked by God to his people, "Is there no king in you?" will be good news. The final answer will be that they do indeed have a King. The very next chapter of Isaiah (Chapter 9) shows us the *re*-birth of Jesus, which I addressed in Part 1 of this series. In Part 1, I described how this line of scripture refers to both Jesus' first coming on this earth as well as to his return *again* in the *last days*. People in the "land of the shadow of death" ('Babylon') will get a preview in the midst of the Day of the Lord:

The people that walked in darkness have seen a great light: they that dwell in the land of the shadow of death, upon them hath the light shined. (Is. 9:2)

This *appears* to be a preview of Jesus in the Day of the Lord for his people like 'Ephraim' who are wandering and seeking him, although we do not know how "visible" he will be yet. We know that Jesus will be *re*-birthed to the 'Daughter of Zion' (Revelation, Chapter 12), which may not be initially visible or readily apparent either. Meanwhile, continuing in this same part of Isaiah, and from my last passage, you will recall the following verses:

For unto us a child is born, unto us a son is given: and the government shall be upon his shoulder: and his name shall be called Wonderful, Counsellor, The mighty God…Of the increase of his government and peace there shall be no end, upon the throne of David, and upon his kingdom, to order it, and to establish it with judgment and with justice from henceforth even for ever… (Is. 9:6-7)

While this is commonly attributed to his first earthly coming, I showed that it also carries obvious descriptors about Jesus' *re*-birth, his revealing and his *ultimate return* to establish his Kingdom. Everyone will see him at his return!

Jesus' return is the greatest hope we can possibly have in these end times. I describe the path back to his Kingdom in my books, *Biblical End Times, Volumes 1 and 2.*

Chapter 10.

The Significance of the Time Period of '3'

Passages from Lion's Lair provided in this chapter include:

10.1 The Number '3' as it applies to prophetic end times and the last days remnant (Part 1)

10.2 The Number '3' as it applies to prophetic end times and the last days remnant (Part 2)

10.1 The Number '3' as it Applies to Prophetic End Times and the Last Days Remnant (Part 1)

You are likely aware that certain numbers used in scripture carry additional, significant meaning beyond just our immediate understanding. The frequency of use of these numbers and the patterns associated with them can be helpful in understanding the context of particular stories and lessons that we read.

The number '3' is one that is used across scripture with high frequency. In general terms, it is considered a number that represents completeness. Most notably, it is seen in the Trinity of God represented as three persons; the Father, Son and Holy Spirit. Also recall that Jesus said, "The kingdom of heaven is like unto leaven, which a woman took, and hid in *three* measures of meal, till the whole was leavened" (Matt. 13:33).

There is much study that could be done about the number '3' as it appears in scripture. For our purposes, I will discuss the primary themes and patterns we see as this number applies to end times prophetic events. More specifically, I will associate its meaning to last days events happening with the 'Jacob'-Judah "small flock" remnant whose story I described in detail in Chapters 4-8.

Within this scope, in this passage I will look at '3' as a *period of time* as it may apply for this remnant in the last days. Since many prophecy teachers see the Prophet Daniel's '70th week' and what is referred to as the "Tribulation period" as a final 7-year period, we know that as we approach the *end of the end times* and the Day of the Lord as these are addressed in much scripture that we are considering time in merely a matter of years. (I address the Day of the Lord in detail in *Writings of Lion's Lair, Volume 2*). My personal opinion is that the 'Jacob'-Judah remnant represents the "fig tree generation" about which Jesus said would see all end times events come to pass.

For all of these reasons, when it comes to discussing these very last days it is most practical to examine the time period associated with the number '3' in terms of a period of years. Those familiar with the use of numbers in scripture realize the significant meaning of this particular number as it is used in expressions such as "in 3 days," "on the third day," "after three days," "three days and three nights," etc. We might also consider time periods given in scripture that are equivalent or roughly equivalent to 3 ½ years as these are seen in the prophetic books of Daniel and Revelation.

All of these are useful for attempting to understand the period of '3' in terms of a period of years as it will apply to events of the last days. Upon review of this time period in scripture, the following general themes are observed, especially as they apply for the Lord's people Israel:

- Escaping and journeying
- Deliverance, hiding and rest
- Sacrifice, offerings, teaching, etc.
- Conflict and judgments
- Blessings and restoration

In this and the following passage (Part 2), I will address each of these events commonly seen happening as it relates to a time period of '3.' (In this current passage I will cover the first two events above and in Part 2 I will cover the remainder). Within each section, I will address how the same event might apply to the 'Jacob'-Judah "small flock" remnant's last days story.

Escaping and Journeying

To begin, the number '3' appears several times in the context of time periods associated with the people of Israel's escaping and journeying. The original Patriarch Jacob signaled a division between him and his father-in-law Laban in his preparation to leave Syria and return back to his homeland. This was initially symbolized by Jacob separating his cattle. We are told at this time Laban set "*three days* journey between himself and Jacob" (Gen. 30:36). Shortly thereafter, Jacob gathered his wives, children and possessions to return to the land of Canaan. We are told, "And it was told Laban *on the third day* that Jacob was fled" (Gen. 31:22). Jacob felt the need to hastily escape a hostile situation and return to the land where his father Isaac remained.

Another well-known exodus situation in which we see the number '3' is in Moses leading Israel out of Egypt. God told Moses to approach the king of Egypt and say, "The Lord God of the Hebrews hath met with us: and now let us go, we beseech thee, *three days* journey into the wilderness, that we may sacrifice to the Lord our God" (Ex. 3:18). When they repeated their intent to go on a *three day* journey, Israel realized the importance of being released from Pharaoh so that they could go worship and "sacrifice to the Lord our God" (Ex. 8:27) and furthermore so that they would not be subjected to judgments of pestilence or the "sword." After their eventual release by Pharaoh, he and his army pursued them after *three days*, somewhat similar to Laban pursuing Jacob above. Overall, from the time Israel departed Egypt, we are told that it was in the *third month* that they came into "the wilderness of Sinai" (Ex. 19:1).

Another *three day* journey of Israel's tribes and armies later on was when they departed Mt. Sinai, "journeying unto the place of which the Lord said, 'I will give it to you,'" as spoken by Moses to his father-in-law (Num. 10:29). Upon departing, they carried the ark of the covenant and followed a "cloud of the Lord" by day. Their initial, short-term goal was to "search out a resting place" (Num. 10:33). They needed rest from enemies and strangers while they journeyed in the wilderness. In addition to the cloud overhead, another supernatural sign of receiving assistance from God was how the enemy would be staved off upon Moses merely raising his arms.

As another, final example of and precedent for a *three day* journey of Israel while amidst enemies, when their tribes were newly traveling through the promised land in Joshua's day they found themselves among peoples living in the land who deceived Joshua into making a covenant to live among them. This was at the time we are told, "And the children of Israel journeyed, and came unto their cities on the *third day*" (Josh. 9:17). Joshua, his troops and subsequent Judges of Israel would have to fight many battles to assume the holy land.

Escaping and journeying of the last days 'Jacob'-Judah "small flock" remnant

It is clear that Israel remnants, both the 'Jacob'-Judah "small flock" and the larger house of Israel will be forced to escape, "flee," and "come out of" last days 'Babylon.' The 'Jacob'-Judah "small flock" remnant in 'Babylon'-U.S. will flee from 'Babylon's kings and princes. They will escape into the wilderness (i.e. 'Jacob' goes into the wilderness, the 'Daughter of Zion' is instructed to go to "the field," etc.), somewhat analogous to ancient Israel's trip into the wilderness after escaping the Pharaoh and his armies. In some ways, it will also be similar to the original Patriarch Jacob escaping Laban while in Syria. (There is a last days 'Syria' or 'Kingdom of Damascus' alongside 'Ephraim' represented within the mingled people groups in 'Babylon' overall).

For the "small flock" remnant's initial escape, however, we are not given in scripture a direct indication of a time period of '3' (years, months, etc.) for their removal. I surmise that they will likely be removed suddenly at or near the beginning of the Day of the Lord. This will be due to the nature of the approximate onset of the coming of the Son of man that Jesus warned would be like the Days of Lot and the Days of Noah. This also appears to be the approximate time period when the 'Restrainer' will be "taken out of the way," or when 'Jacob' will be "saved out of" the time of "Jacob's trouble." In the book of Hosea, where the Lord indicates that he will "return to his place" in the end times, he says that he will be "as a lion" to Ephraim and "as a young lion" to Judah and will "tear and go away" when there is no one else to deliver this remnant that he rescues. Similarly, the Lord says in the book of Amos:

As the shepherd taketh out of the mouth of the lion two legs, or a piece of an ear; so shall the children of Israel be taken out that dwell in Samaria in the corner of a bed, and in Damascus in a couch. (Am. 3:12)

While this deliverance for the "small flock" remnant will be sudden, it is *possible* that it could happen in a literal three day time period based on precedent although we do not have direct indication of this in scripture.

I will discuss the necessity for the "small flock" remnant's deliverance to a safe place of hiding in the next section, particularly due to their spiritual "birthings." In the meantime, their deliverance will be for reasons similar to those for Israel coming out of ancient Egypt; that is, realizing the need to be delivered out of God's impending judgments. In the last days, these will again include famine, pestilence, the "sword" of war, etc. along with many others. I have described that partial judgments will come at the hands of the 'Assyrian' and his armies who will besiege, invade and plunder 'Babylon'-U.S. The 'Assyrian' and his partners will have been an adversary aligned against the 'Jacob'-Judah "small flock" remnant who reside therein.

'Jacob's anointed remnant's initial removal will be a sudden escape representing merely the beginning of their long journey back to the holy land. Within this journey, I discuss a time period of '3' associated with their deliverance and hiding in the following section. It is after they have been delivered and been in hiding that there will come *another* need for journeying. In this case, we are given a *period of '3.* This is the sign in the book of Revelation (Chapter 12) of the woman "clothed with the sun," with the "moon at her feet," and she is surrounded by 12 stars while giving birth to the man-child. The man-child is "caught up" to his throne and the woman and her remnant flee ("fly") away from the dragon that will be expelled out of heaven. We are told that her remnant flees to the wilderness to be "nourished" for a period of days equivalent to *3 ½ years*. This is the same time that the dragon will give power to the beast (i.e. 42 months).

This latter escape and journeying in the final time period at the end of the age can be seen as similar to the last *period of 'three'* applying to Moses' people's journey after departing Mt. Sinai described above.

With their armies, Moses and his people were told to travel *three days* with the ark and to search out resting places. There is a hint in scripture and then a subsequent fulfillment of increased conflict with surrounding enemies once they left from the Sinai wilderness and traveled near or through neighboring lands. This post-Sinai conflict might be at least roughly considered as a parallel to the increased conflict in the last part of the Day of the Lord when the beast system is on full-display. In a multitude of ways, God will fight for and protect his faithful servants in the last days as they journey and come closer to the doorstep of the "land of milk and honey." Of course, Israel's larger remnant around the world will be fleeing the enemy and wandering during this latter time period amidst heavy turmoil and persecution.

Deliverance, Hiding and Rest

As I addressed above, the history of Israel's need to escape, journey and flee enemies to move closer to their final resting place occasionally required stops along the way. Periodic stops will be the result of deliverance, and for the purpose of both rest and preparation in order for them to continue.

Practically speaking, first and foremost, Israel's people historically had to be hidden to find refuge from their enemies. We have notable examples of this in scripture. At the time the Pharaoh of Egypt set his sights on killing firstborn Hebrew children, Moses' Levite mother hid him for *three months*. In Joshua's day, Rahab the harlot in Jericho helped Israel's spies by advising them to hide themselves from the king. She told them to go and abide in a nearby mountain for *three days*. Many are also familiar with David's flight from King Saul. He planned with his ally Jonathan, Saul's son, to go to a predetermined hiding place in a field to wait for further instructions. David would do this *after three days*. Ironically, later on after King Saul, Jonathan and Israel's armies were defeated by the Philistines, a self-identified escapee out of the "camp of Saul" came to David seeking refuge. We are told that this took place *on the third day* (1 Sam. 30:1). In one more irony, when David's rebellious son Absalom fled from David and his armies, we are told that he went to a place called Geshur and was in refuge there for *three years* (2 Sam. 13:38).

Once Israel had been delivered or they were at rest, then they were able to regroup and plan to move forward in their journey. A good example of this was the Joshua-led Israelites who were at the doorstep of the Promised Land. After Joshua was commissioned by God, he told the people, "Prepare you victuals; for *within three days* ye shall pass over this Jordan, to go in to possess the land, which the Lord your God giveth you to possess it" (Josh. 1:11). After *three days*, the officers commanded the people to proceed after the Ark of the Covenant of the Lord and cross the Jordan.

As an individual example, prior to his own journey to Nineveh, Jonah was in the belly of a large fish for *three days and three nights*. This was a deliverance from a boat on the stormy seas and his position as an Israelite who had rebelled against God and found himself among fearful Gentile mariners who decided to cast him overboard in an attempt to still the seas. Jonah returned to God at this time. After the fish spit him out, God reiterated his instructions for Jonah to travel to Nineveh. Jonah's journey in this Gentile city was *three days*.

We see a few other individual examples of Israelites using a period of '3' to prepare themselves to meet adversaries or Gentile rulers. I mentioned Moses being hidden as a baby in the last section; we are told that during this *three month* period he was "nourished," and we know that he was shortly thereafter delivered out of the river by Pharaoh's daughter. In another example, Daniel and his friends Shadrach, Meshach and Abednego, seen as knowledgeable, wise Judah-tribe children of exiled Israel were "nourished" for *three years* by the king of Babylon so they would be prepared to stand before him. In the following kingdom of the Medes and Persians, Esther asked Mordecai to gather Jews in the town to fast without food or drink for *three days and nights* while she did the same prior to the dangerous act of approaching the Gentile king.

Given examples above, the period of '3' appears to be a time during which one can contemplate or prepare one's mind. The Apostle Paul, several times in his journeying, stayed at a place for a period of *three days*. As an enemy of the Jews, a couple of times he waited out of sight from them for this same *time period of '3'* (days, months).

When ancient Judah King Rehoboam was asked by northern tribes to re-consider his father Solomon's heavy-handed governing style, he asked them to approach him again after *three days* so that he could consult with others. In another example of respite, the northern kingdom's wicked King Ahab who was strongly rebuked by the Prophet Elijah was granted a period of peace without war with Syria for *three years* because God saw that he had humbled himself.

Deliverance, hiding and rest of the last days 'Jacob'-Judah "small flock" remnant

In the first section of this passage I discussed the initial, sudden escape of the 'Jacob'-Judah "small flock" remnant out of the theater of direct conflict in the Day of the Lord. It appears that they will go into a wilderness setting or a "field" to get out of harm's way. Their deliverance may be represented as follows:

Come, my people, enter thou into thy chambers, and shut thy doors about thee: hide thyself as it were for a little moment, until the indignation be overpast. (Is. 26:20)

Their escape will be after their fighting in the unconventional spiritual kingdom. I have surmised how it will likely be the results of their resistance and exposure of the adversary's tactics that will kick off events of the Day of the Lord. They will have fought in the 'Babylon'-U.S. theater of conflict. This is the 'west' (relative to the land of Israel) where the sun sets, and where Ephraim was located among the tribes around the Tabernacle. Last days 'Ephraim' is within 'Babylon'-U.S. and 'Jacob's Judah-centric "small flock" remnant are also in the midst. The meaning behind the sun's setting in scripture is associated with saving, release and rest from enemies. The sun's setting turns into the moon's rising. A deeper Hebrew meaning of the moon in Hebrew is associated with resting, silence and quietness as well as repairing and renewing.

While events of Israel's remnant's end times deliverance and hiding will be very similar to those in the biblical past that were associated with a time period of '3,' a period of '3' is again not explicitly stated in scripture for these last days events. There is one particular period of '3,' however, that might be of interest. When asked about the end times, Jesus talked about a "wicked generation" that will only be given one sign; he described the sign of Jonas and referred to the end times Son of man who will spend *three days and three nights* in the "heart of the earth." *If* this is a sign about the end times, then we might consider whether this hiding occurs prior to or after the onset of the Day of the Lord. Regardless, the end times Son of man who Jesus is referring to here will be as the Spirit of truth, about whom we are told the world (i.e. unbelievers) "cannot receive, because it seeth him not, neither knoweth him…" (Jn. 14:17). It *could* be that Jesus was also referring to this last days Son of man when he said, "The days will come, when ye shall desire to see one of the days of the Son of man, and ye shall not see it" (Lk. 17:22). Overall, any last days individual who represents the Holy Spirit will be hidden. A common theme observed in scripture is the Lord warning that he will "hide his face" from his people Israel in particular in the end times. (I address this topic in detail in *Volume 2*)

Otherwise, for the hastily delivered 'Jacob'-Judah "small flock" remnant who will go into some wilderness setting at or near the beginning of the Day of the Lord, there are no definitive periods of time given in scripture. However, their surrounding environment and human needs will be the same as those of ancient Israel while in a similar situation of exile and semi-captivity. I will discuss the need for this remnant's sanctification as well as God's surrounding judgments in Part 2. In the meantime, this remnant will be coming out of conditions of "hard bondage" in 'Babylon'-U.S. They will likely be looking for a place of rest from enemies such as Moses and his people. They will also be looking for "nourishment" such as baby Moses was given, and later Daniel and his friends, as described above. This will help as they find themselves in a holding pattern at or near the beginning of the Day of the Lord, and will certainly be looking for the Lord's guidance for future direction in their journey. This will be their state of affairs in the first part of the highly tumultuous Day of the Lord. The first part of the Day of the Lord *could be* approximately three (or 3 ½) years in length.

One other, similar event we might consider for this remnant in the Day of the Lord has to do with their "spiritual birthings" and possible actual birthings, as their Judah-centric remnant "takes root downward" as in King Hezekiah's remnant's day. As to "birthings" as they may apply to or be symbolic for end times events, I described this in detail in Chapter 9. Recall that the Prophet Isaiah said about these:

Behold, I and the children whom the Lord hath given me are for signs and for wonders in Israel from the Lord of hosts, which dwelleth in mount Zion. (Is. 8:18)

In prophetic language in the book of Isaiah (whose name means 'Yahweh is salvation') applicable for the end times, his persona as a kind of last days 'Jacob' describes his children as signs. The sequential birthings of his latter two sons, Immanuel and Mahershalalhashbaz are of special interest. According to the text in Isaiah (Chapters 7 and 8), these birthings occur at a time that kings (of Israel and Syria) Isaiah abhors will be forsaken in Immanuel's infancy and "the land" will be plundered by the 'Assyrian' during the time Isaiah's next son Mahershalalhashbaz is still a baby. (Note: I explained previously that, while Jesus' life fulfilled Immanuel, the Lord's presence in the end times suggests a re-birthing of Immanuel (God with us) based on scripture including this part of text in Isaiah).

This brief summary of birthings of Isaiah's children and their signs, assuming both occur in succession to the same woman (the "prophetess"), possibly suggest or symbolize that the 'Jacob'-Judah "small flock" remnant's birthings may occur over an approximate *3-3 ½ year* timeframe. The apparent capture of kings and plundering of the land of 'Babylon'-U.S. where this last days remnant resides as signaled by Isaiah is consistent with much other scripture about these same events that will occur in the land during this general time.

Furthermore, as it applies to the hiding of this remnant and their "taking root," it would be practical to assume that the Lord's enemies in the spiritual kingdom war would want to discover any "spiritual birthings" of his children. Recall that the adversary fundamentally desires their own kingdom apart from the God of Israel and his people. Also recall that Moses had to be hidden from Pharaoh who went after Israel's firstborn. Later, Mary and Joseph had to flee Herod who was after Hebrew children two years or younger and take baby Jesus to Egypt. We can assume that the last days 'Jacob'-Judah "small flock" will be sought in a similar manner.

In summary of this current passage, the strong historical pattern of the Lord's people needing to escape, journey and hide from adversaries is apparent. In prophetic scripture related to the end times, they will do this again. While these events commonly occurred historically in a time period of '3,' as they will occur in the end times we can only refer to them in very general terms with respect to a time period. For example, the 'Jacob'-Judah "small flock" remnant's initial deliverance into the wilderness and their time of respite will occur in the first part of the Day of the Lord, which may generally equate to the first half of what many refer to as the final seven-year Tribulation period. Their second "fleeing and journeying" event will begin according to the sign of the woman described above based on Revelation, Chapter 12, which leaves 3 ½ years remaining in the Day of the Lord.

Meanwhile, during this same time period, some of Israel's remaining larger remnant around the world will begin to awaken, flee and wander. For this larger remnant, they will especially awaken as the beast system becomes openly aligned and committed against them. This escape and journey of the larger remnant of Israel will also generally align with the last (3 ½ years) of the Day of the Lord.

Gentile believers over the course of the Day of the Lord will also awaken, albeit quite a bit earlier than Israel's large remnant. It is possible that there may even be Gentiles among the Christ-believing 'Jacob'-Judah "small flock" remnant's initial gathering. Regardless, many Gentiles will come to understand the story of the "small flock" remnant of these Jesus Christ-faithful early on. The anointed remnant's plight and message that becomes known will reassure Gentiles in their faith. In *Volume 2*, especially, I provide scripture that assures Christ-believers that the Lord knows who they are and will protect many saints during the Day of the Lord. (See Appendix A in this book entitled *Personal Salvation in Jesus Christ Alone*). Having said this, however, we are also told that there will be martyred saints during this last time, presumably including both Gentiles and those of Israel.

In Part 2, I will cover the remainder of events occurring in a time period of '3' and how these may apply to Christ-believing remnants in these last days. I describe both believing Israel's and Gentiles' return to the Kingdom in my book, *Biblical End Times, Volume 2.*

10.2 The Number '3' as it Applies to Prophetic End Times and the Last Days Remnant (Part 2)

In Part 1, I described the frequency and significance in scripture of the number '3' and the common events associated with Israel where this number occurs, especially as '3' refers to a period of time. Since we commonly see patterns of events in scripture that will reoccur in the end times, in Part 1 I showed where the number '3' as a time period will again be significant in its application to last days events. More specifically, I examined the number '3' as it will apply to the 'Jacob'-Judah "small flock" remnant's last days: 1) escape and journeying, and 2) deliverance, hiding and rest. In this current passage, I will repeat this process for the final three events occurring in a time period of '3' most often observed in scripture. These include:

- Sacrifices, offerings and teaching
- Conflict and the Lord's judgments
- Blessings and restoration

As I did in Part 1, I will look at the time period of '3' as it applies to each of these biblical events, first historically, and then subsequently how each will apply to the 'Jacob'-Judah "small flock" remnant again in the end times.

Sacrifices, Offerings and Teaching

One pattern or theme observed with a time period of '3' in scripture is related to sacrifices and offerings. In Jewish law, sacrifices were typically offered on the first day. An offering of animals "without blemish" was made. In some cases, this began a *three day* period of fasting or abstaining. Any sacrifice that remained *on the third day* was burned in the fire and considered to be abominable if eaten.

Particularly notable, an unblemished male lamb was offered at Passover. As the ultimate holy, righteous fulfillment as a sacrifice and atonement, Jesus was crucified. In Isaiah, Chapter 53, which refers to Jesus, we are told, "the Lord hath laid on him the iniquity of us all" (Is. 53:6). Much can be said about Passover, but Israel's first adherence to this feast day in Egypt marked the saving and redemption of their firstborn and their "release" as a people.

As a "firstborn" himself, Jesus' fulfillment of the Passover was for the saving and redemption of his people. He was also a fulfillment of the goat that was sacrificed as part of the sin offering that Aaron the priest was instructed to do by God through Moses after the death of his two sons as described in the book of Leviticus (Chapter 16). This was an atonement for Israel before the Lord; one goat was sacrificed, but the other was released and freed into the wilderness as the scapegoat that carried away all of the iniquities of the people of Israel.

Of course, after his sacrificial, atoning death Jesus was then raised *on the third day*. Jesus had already instructed the Pharisees before this time to tell Herod of his activities including casting out devils, healing disease and then he said that, *"on the third day* I shall be perfected" (Lk. 13:32). Jesus was the perfected offering, a fulfillment of commands in the law for Jews to purify themselves on this day. He no longer "remained" on the third day because he was holy and had been resurrected.

Passover was celebrated just prior to *both three day* journeys of Moses and his people Israel that I described in Part 1. After their initial release out of Egypt they arrived in the wilderness of Sinai after their journey of *three months*. Moses was then told that the Lord would come down and appear on the mountain in the sight of Israel. After Moses heard a word from the Lord, he instructed his people to be ready "*against the third day*." And to the men he said, "Come not near your wives." After Moses came back down from the mountain he then "sanctified the people and washed their clothes" (Ex. 19:14).

Similarly, while on the run from King Saul, David on his journey approached a priest who only had holy bread to offer. For the bread, David had to assure the priest that, "Women have been kept from us about these *three days*" (1 Sam. 21:5). Jesus, of course, we know represents the true, eternal bread of life and the water that "springs up into everlasting life." I will describe below how we should expect to be similarly clean as was David approaching the priest prior to Jesus' return.

In another act of purifying the people of Israel, at the time Ezra the priest had led them back to the homeland from Babylon, he and other priests observed and lamented that they and those remaining in the land had rebelled against God and that many had taken "strange wives." They made a proclamation throughout the land that all "children of captivity" should gather at Jerusalem. They were to arrive *within three days*. At this time Israel was commanded to "separate yourselves from the people of the land and from strange wives" (Ezra 10:11).

With regard to Jewish law, there were also several instances we are told that *on the third day* there was a requirement of tithe or offering. One notable example of an Israeli society-wide "tithe of the land" offering was when righteous King Asa of Judah renewed the altar of the Lord, put away abominable idols in the land, and *in the third month* of the 15th year of his reign gathered Judah and Benjamin as well as Manasseh and Ephraim of the northern kingdom. He called them to return, re-commit to the Lord and bring their spoil as a great offering. At the time, they entered into a covenant that all should seek him.

~

Finally, in addition to sacrifices and offerings to the Lord occurring in a time period of '3,' there is a teaching and disciple-ing component that is seen several times. Jesus himself was found by his parents *after three days* sitting amidst others in the temple while "all that heard him were astonished at his understanding and answers" (Lk. 2:47). At Ephesus, the Apostle Paul taught of the Holy Ghost and baptism based on belief in Christ. We are told, "And he went into the synagogue, and spake boldly for the space of *three months*, disputing and persuading the things concerning the kingdom of God" (Acts 19:8). It was at the *end of three years* Paul finally reminded the Ephesians how he had strongly warned that after he departed "grievous wolves" would enter among them and would even deceive some disciples.

In more ancient days, the son of King Asa, King Jehoshaphat, in the *third year* of his reign instructed his princes and Levites to teach throughout "all the cities of Judah" about the Lord's law. This happened and the "fear of the Lord" fell upon all of the kingdoms of the lands around Judah.

Sacrifice, offerings and teaching of the last days 'Jacob'-Judah "small flock" remnant

I have explained in previous chapters that end times 'Jacob' and his remnant represent a kind of atoning sacrifice for the people of Israel in these last days. While Jesus was the ultimate sacrifice as Israel's Messiah and the world's Savior many will only understand more about him as their God after they see how he delivers his last days "small flock." As the initial sacrificial lamb without blemish, Jesus was the sin offering for all, and this allowed the opportunity of grace that 'Jacob' and his last days remnant will receive. Jesus was also the type of sacrifice that allowed 'Jacob' and his remnant to become as the scapegoat that is "released into the wilderness" in the last days. This is their escape that I addressed in Part 1.

As ones who will have to go through the Lord's purging and refining process *prior to* the time of "Jacob's trouble," 'Jacob's anointed remnant will be like those of Israel who were brought forth out of Egypt's "furnace of affliction." I have described how end times 'Jacob' himself is as a kind of atoning sacrifice on behalf of Israel. In a similar although much less significant manner as Jesus, last days 'Jacob' is ascribed with both the sins of Samaria and the "high places of Judah" (Mic. 1:5); these represent the last days 'northern kingdom' within the U.S. and those in the country of Israel. The Lord says that he gives last days 'Jacob' as a "spoil" (Is. 42:24) because of the house of Israel's sin and disobedience.

As an outcome of his own personal battle versus the spiritual kingdom adversary, 'Jacob's own personal iniquity will be atoned for because he will make, "All the stones of the altar as chalkstones that are beaten in sunder, (and) the groves and images shall not stand up" (Is. 27:9). When 'Jacob' and his remnant (i.e. house of Jacob) are delivered, they will rely solely upon and will wait for the Lord in the wilderness. The following instructions from the Prophet Isaiah will apply:

Sanctify the Lord of hosts himself; and let him be your fear, and let him be your dread. And he shall be for a sanctuary; but for a stone of stumbling and for a rock of offence to both the houses of Israel, for a gin and for a snare to the inhabitants of Jerusalem. (Is. 8:13-14)

This remnant will be alone yet still surrounded by great turmoil in the Day of the Lord, a time period I address in detail in *Volume 2*. They will be forced to rely only on the Lord. They will be recovering from many wounds and in need of cleansing, sanctification and spiritual renewal. Recall that immediately following Passover, a time signaling the beginning of a couple of Moses' peoples' ancient journeys, there was a seven-day Feast of Unleavened Bread during which no leavened bread could be eaten. 'Jacob' and his newly freed remnant will need to remain clean upon their escape and journey. They will need to be found without what Jesus referred to as the leaven of hypocrisy.

Even so, we are told that the Lord will have to plead with his "backsliding" people to repent and turn to him. The following verse will apply: "Like as I pleaded with your fathers in the wilderness of the land of Egypt, so will I plead with you, saith the Lord God" (Ez. 20:36). The 'Jacob'-Judah "small flock" remnant will be coming out of a 'Babylon'-U.S. system of false, foreign gods and their associated idolatrous and abominable practices. I described the Prophet Isaiah's last days persona in Part 1 of this series. Recall that Isaiah said, "Woe is me! for I am undone; because I am a man of unclean lips, and I dwell in the midst of a people of unclean lips: for mine eyes have seen the King, the Lord of hosts" (Is. 6:5).

Isaiah was renewed, but the Lord will have to plead with his people who come out of this land of a "strange language" in the last days once they are delivered into the wilderness. Not all will be righteous, and we are told that the Lord will not leave 'Jacob' and his "small flock" altogether unpunished. We are told that their sins will be uncovered. They will need to be sanctified. God will have to "wash away" the "filth" of the daughters of Zion and the bloodshed of 'Jerusalem' (Is. 4:4). The following verse from Isaiah will apply: "Wash you, make you clean; put away the evil of your doings from before mine eyes; cease to do evil" (Is. 1:16). As this applies to a time period of '3' there is not an explicit indication in scripture, but based on the historical pattern it could be that this remnant will be "fasting" or abstaining in obedience, at least in a spiritual sense, for approximately three days (or translated to three *years*).

Upon their escape, the 'Jacob'-Judah "small flock" remnant will also be coming directly out of a 'Babylon'-U.S. society where the Lord's scattered sheep have mingled within, thereby resulting in what he calls his "speckled" inheritance. Perhaps the original Patriarch Jacob's cattle foreshadowed these last days sheep. This remnant will come out of 'Babylon'-U.S., a scenario symbolized in ancient times by Israel retreating after their Jericho victory but were instructed by God not to touch any of its spoil and keep themselves from any "accursed things." In this ancient day of Joshua, a man of Judah was stoned for carrying out a 'Babylonian'-type artifact. Similarly, recall that upon Jacob's escape out of Syria his wife Rachel secretly carried away an idolatrous possession of her father Laban, unbeknownst to Jacob. Possessions of 'Babylon' and any accompanying idolatrous practices will need to be completely removed from and left behind by the last days remnant. This will be the beginning of their own purification process.

The 'Jacob'-Judah remnant's sanctification process will also require separation. In addition to being physically delivered out of and separated from 'Babylon's society, its idols and into the wilderness they will need to be separated as a people. This is likely the time about which we are told in scripture that "none will want her mate," and possibly the last days time described when "one will be taken and the other left." Their separation will be similar to that described above when Ezra and his other priests exhorted the captive people of Israel to, "separate from the people of the land." The question will be who among this remnant can finally and completely separate themselves, spiritually speaking, so that they can be cleansed, sanctified and found wearing "white garments" as Jesus instructed will be necessary. If this remnant properly uses the first *three day* period after their deliverance and release to separate and abstain then they will be spiritually prepared for when the Lord appears, which I discuss below.

~

Finally, I mentioned above a teaching or disciple-ing component associated with the Lord's historical servants as it occurred in a *three day* period. In the last days, we have another *three year* (3 ½ year) period during which the Lord's 'Two Witnesses' will testify. These will be Elijah- or John the Baptist-types who will exhort people to repent of their transgressions, serve Jesus Christ, and prepare for his soon-coming Kingdom. The extent to which the 'Two Witnesses' may have personally encountered the Lord themselves in the last days or whether they will be affiliated with the 'Jacob'-Judah "small flock" remnant in the wilderness is unknown. It is also unknown whether the 'Two Witnesses' will be related to the 'Comforter' or 'Spirit of truth' whom Jesus referred to who will: Serve as a teacher and reminder of his words (Jn. 14:26); demonstrate the sin of the world (and unbelief in him) in contrast with true righteousness (Jn. 16:8); and take from what is his of Jesus (and the Father) and make it known (Jn. 16:14-15). Regardless, these witnesses will be among others (e.g. John the Revelator, 144,000 witnesses, 'Jacob,' etc.) who will prophesy and teach to the world in the Day of the Lord.

Conflict and the Lord's Judgments

In scripture, we also see the number '3' as it will apply to a time period of conflict or judgment. Out of all of the judgments that came onto Pharaoh and ancient Egypt, for the ninth judgment scripture says, "…there was a thick darkness in all the land of Egypt *three days*" (Ex. 10:22). This occurred prior to the Lord's tenth and final judgment at the time, which was the slaying of Egyptian firstborn sons. During this time that darkness came over the land it, "came between the camp of the Egyptians and the camp of Israel." Israel's camp was given light at this time.

Darkness that descends signaling the coming of the Day of the Lord will be associated with the Lord's judgments. These judgments will be similar to ancient ones, especially familiar ones such as famine, pestilence and the "sword" (of war). As one historical indication, when David transgressed by conducting a census in the land, God offered him his choice of punishments; these included either famine, pestilence or the sword of the enemy. In each case, the punishment on his kingdom was to be for a *time period of '3.'* In another instance, the judgment of famine came upon David's Kingdom that was attributed to King Saul's prior transgressions. This was a judgment that lasted for *three days* in the "days of David."

In Israel's northern kingdom, in speaking through the Prophet Amos to his rulers about their transgressions of foreign god worship and oppression of others, God told of his judgments of the sword and pestilence against them and then also reminded them that he gave them hunger and withheld rain for *three months* prior to the harvest in some cities. Of course, you likely recall how the Prophet Elijah prayed that it might not rain in the northern kingdom due to its idolatry, and we are told, "It rained not on the earth by the space of *three years and six months*" (James 5:17).

Among God's ancient judgments the "sword" was a particularly common one occurring on or just after the third day. The "sword" is mentioned on several occasions as it relates to a time period of '3.' When Jacob came to reside in the city of Shechem in Canaan his daughter Dinah was defiled in the land by the son of its prince. *On the third day*, Jacob's sons Simeon and Levi slew all the men of the city with the sword.

While in the land of the Philistines, while staying away from King Saul, David and his fighting men had returned *on the third day* to Ziklag where their families resided. The town had been burned with fire and their wives and children had been taken captive. David enquired of the Lord and was assured that he would, "overtake them, and without fail recover all" (1 Sam. 30:8). David's troops found the Amalekite enemy and slew them all, took the spoil, and recovered all.

In another instance, King David gave his commander *three days* to prepare his troops for war against the tribe of Benjamin who had declared separation from his kingdom due to the children of Belial within. Later, the tribe of Benjamin was again identified by the rest of Israel as being associated with the wicked acts of the "children of Belial." When Benjamin would not turn them over Judah and Israel's tribes came against them with the sword, beginning on the *third day*.

Rehoboam's son Abijah, King of Judah, who we are told reigned for *three years* went to war against King Jeroboam. God delivered wicked Israel into his hands. This caused the end of idolatrous Jeroboam's reign. Not long after, in the *third year* of King Asa of Judah, the northern kingdom's King Baasha slayed Jeroboam's son and successor King Nadab. Later, during the reign of King Jehoshaphat of Judah, when he went to visit the King of Israel he was invited to join in war versus Syria because its people remained residing in the northern kingdom's land. Israel's king observed at this time that there had not been war with Syria for a period of *three years*.

~

While we find that the number '3' is associated with and signals these kinds of overt events of conflict and judgment, it is also associated with God's people's collective captivity over time according to a longstanding, ancient promise of his. God promised that his people would suffer captivity at the hands of their enemies for their rebellion in ancient times. This began not long after with Gentile kings who besieged them. In the latter days of Israel's northern kingdom, the king of Assyria besieged Samaria and at the *end of three years* conquered it. Nebuchadnezzar King of Babylon made King Jehoiakim of Judah his servant for *three years* before Jehoiakim rebelled. Judah was then destroyed by Nebuchadnezzar.

Conflicts and the Lord's judgments surrounding the last days 'Jacob'-Judah "small flock" remnant

As their own punishment, I described that the 'Jacob'-Judah "small flock" remnant will have gone through a purifying and refining process of the Lord's judgment early on in the last days prior to being delivered at or near the beginning of the Day of the Lord. Although they will be delivered from the theater of God's judgments and extreme conflict 'Jacob's semi-captive remnant will still be surrounded by many judgments at this time.

Symbolic of the onset of the Day of the Lord at night, darkness will be part of God's end times judgments. Many times in scripture we are told about darkness that will occur in the Day of the Lord similar to God's ninth judgment on ancient Egypt described above. Darkness in the last days is referred to as: "darkness that shall cover the earth"; "thick darkness"; "no brightness"; the sun "becomes black as sackcloth" etc. This darkness is directly associated with the time that God will bring "destruction among the nations" (Ez. 32:9).

As it will be associated with the sun's setting and the eve of judgment, both of which coincide with darkness, I described in Part 1 the 'Jacob'-Judah "small flock" remnant's sudden deliverance and escape into the wilderness. I also described events of the sun's setting and the moon's rising as carrying meaning of rest, hiding, concealment, etc. The "small flock" remnant who represent some of the "children of the light" referred to by the Apostle Paul will likely be given light during this time that they are separated from their enemies.

Perhaps as in the ancient days of Moses and his people, darkness in the Day of the Lord will again provide a means of separation from their enemies. We are prophetically told, "The Lord sent a word into Jacob, and it hath lighted upon Israel" (Is. 9:8). Otherwise, in the book of Matthew's version of Jesus' *Parable of the Lamp,* Jesus talked about light that will shine and cannot be hidden. He did this after his Sermon on the Mount where he links those who will inherit the Kingdom (i.e. poor in spirit, persecuted, peacemakers, meek, etc.) to those who are the "salt of the earth," "light of the world," and a city on a hill that "cannot be hid."

While somewhat delivered and separated at this time this remnant will likely remain in a semi-captive state, likely somewhere in their homeland of 'Babylon'-U.S. This will be somewhat of a continuance of siege and captivity conditions they will have experienced prior to the Day of the Lord. We have indications from the prophetic personas of Major Prophets Ezekiel and Isaiah about the continuing end times captive state of the "small flock" remnant. 'Ezekiel's persona is laying on his side, in bands, unable to talk, etc. Isaiah's persona walks "naked and barefoot" as an apparent sign of his captivity.

Meanwhile, in contrast, as a result of Israel's larger remnant's own part in being complicit with the adversary in the spiritual kingdom war, and their own rebellion, familiar judgments of famine, pestilence, the sword and "wild beasts" in the time leading into the Day of the Lord will first come onto the whole house of Israel. Just as we saw the ancient northern kingdom besieged and conquered, and then Judah's final king was besieged and his society conquered, the last days house of Israel's primary lands of residence- the U.S. and the country of Israel- will face the same fate. We see these kinds of judgments among those Jesus referred to as they will possibly occur at the time of the "beginning of sorrows." These will likely coincide with or lead into the time period of the riders on the horses carrying very similar judgments when the first four seals are opened in Chapter 6 of the book of Revelation. Wars and a multitude of other judgments will then come onto the entire world in the Day of the Lord as God turns his attention to the worldwide 'Babylonian' adversary. In one of the Prophet Daniel's visions, *in the third year* of the reign of King Belshazzar, Daniel prophesied of these kinds of large-scale kingdom wars that will come.

Judgments that will only intensify during the Day of the Lord will surround the semi-captive 'Jacob'-Judah "small flock" remnant in 'Babylon U.S. As I described is the case with some other events this remnant will experience that have commonly been historically associated with a time period of '3,' there is no explicit time period given for particular judgment events that will surround them while they are in the wilderness. We do know that the Pharaoh-'Assyrian' and his armies will invade and plunder 'Babylon'-U.S. And as a leader of the spiritual kingdom adversary against the Lord and his anointed 'Daughter of Zion' and "small flock," he will be aware of their presence in the land.

Otherwise, we have a couple of clues as to a time period of *three years* of war within 'Babylon'-U.S. 'Babylon'-U.S. is a nation of many different "peoples" including Israel's last days 'northern kingdom' that the 'Assyrian' has had prior affiliation with. In *Writings of Lion's Lair, Volume 2,* I describe the many different *people groups* that support or partner with the 'Assyrian.' End times 'Moab' (note Moab no longer exists as a land) is just one people group that has been a partner with the 'Assyrian,' yet at least some reside in 'Babylon'-U.S. where the 'Assyrian' has had significant prior influence. While they will have been complicit with this kingdom adversary aligned against Israel they will be in the crossfire when the 'Assyrian' invades. Recall the general principle Jesus spoke of which is that Satan's kingdom fights against and destroys itself. In his Word, God warns in more than one place that last days 'Moab' will be condemned and destroyed within a time period as that of a *three year-old* heifer or hireling.

In an ancient signal of this kind of future judgment, in an offering to the Lord, Abraham took a heifer of *three years old* among other offerings and sacrificed it at the time God gave him the eternal land promise. God also told him that Israel's people in the interim would come into bondage but that their enemy would ultimately be destroyed. Although much of the last days house of Israel has been deceived and compliant in their own bondage, the meaning behind Abraham's sacrifice is a "picture" of God's "rod of judgment" destroying 'Babylon'-U.S. for the way it will be found to have treated and held captive its own people of Israel within. About this last days time period of 'Babylon'-U.S.'s judgment at the hands of the 'Assyrian' in the book of Micah, an ancient prophet to both the northern kingdom and Judah, God says that he will "cut off the cities of thy land, and throw down all thy strong holds" (Mic. 5:11). Generally speaking, it will be a process of destruction that will come onto both 'Babylon'-U.S. and the country of Israel that could take approximately the *first few years* leading into the Day of the Lord.

The 'Jacob'-Judah "small flock" remnant in the wilderness will be surrounded at the time of the 'Assyrian's and his armies' invasion but I have described that they will be protected. Just as they will have had a "supernatural"-assisted rescue to go into the wilderness they will be protected by God. We are told, "And the remnant of Jacob shall be in the midst of many people as a dew from the Lord" (Mic. 5:7). This is the time mentioned when this remnant will rely directly on the Lord as a sanctuary and that he will be as a "rock of offense" when the 'Assyrian' enemy enters their land. We are also told that at this time the Lord will make this remnant that includes "seven shepherds and eight principal men" as a "lion among the beasts of the forest," and furthermore, we learn that their "hand will be lifted up upon (their) adversaries."

The 'Jacob'-Judah "small flock" remnant will continue to see chaos and fighting around them at the time leading into the Day of the Lord. They will continue to be surrounded by enemies and conflict, just as it was in ancient days in Canaan for their early fathers Abraham, Isaac and Jacob. After they are surrounded in the first part of the end of the age by the 'Assyrian' and his armies, then as time progresses both the adversary's persecution of saints and God's judgments on the world will become more severe. I described in Part 1 a kind of second *three year* phase of journeying, hiding, and fighting enemies that 'Jacob' and his remnant may go through, similar to that of Moses and his people Israel's post-Sinai journeying. This second phase will begin when they "flee" the dragon and go into the wilderness at the time the woman who is described in Revelation, Chapter 12, gives birth to the "man-child" and the dragon is cast down to earth. During this 42-month phase, it is not clear the extent to which this remnant will have to "fight" enemies like Moses and his people did. But their salvation and protection in the Day of the Lord is implied because we know that they will finally return at the time when 'Jacob' raises up all of the tribes of Israel and the isles will "wait for his law."

Blessings and Restoration

Finally, blessings and restoration in scripture are many times associated with a *three year* time period. First and foremost are supernatural or spiritual blessings. After Israel's *three month* escape from Egypt into the wilderness the Lord came down on Mt. Sinai in their sight. Of course, the ultimate fulfillment of God coming to earth in the person of Jesus included his resurrection *on the third day* after his crucifixion. It was Jesus, speaking of the temple of his body, who said, "destroy this temple and *in three days* I will raise it up" (Jn. 2:19). Recall from above that Jesus said that he would be "perfected" *on the third day* after his work of healing and casting out devils. Through Jesus' work when he came to earth then the "holy temple" that he represented was completed and his Spirit became available to all believers. We are restored through our faith in him.

Perhaps as a foreshadowing of Jesus' first coming the second temple in Jerusalem was restored and completed *on the third day of the month* of Adar according to the decree of Persian King Artaxerxes, Mede King Cyrus, and as prophesied by the Prophet Haggai. It was Nehemiah who originally arrived at Jerusalem during this time and he remained there for *three years*. With plans to restore the temple, he inspected the remains of the original temple, encouraged the people to support re-building it and spoke with local corrupt rulers and priests to demand a release of the people who they had taken captive and taken over their land by usury and likely with other heavy-handed tactics. They agreed to provide a release or a kind of "restoration" for the people.

Additional examples in scripture show that Gentiles and their kings were sometimes used by God for blessings according to a *three day* pattern or cycle. Recall that it was an Egyptian man who approached King David and his troops after he had been cast out by his camp and been without food or water for *three days and three nights.* David replenished him and the Egyptian led David and his people to the enemy's location. It was King Ahasuerus who in the *third year* of his reign showed off the "riches of his glorious kingdom and the honor of his excellent majesty" and then heard Queen Esther's plea for her people. Later, this king issued a decree in the *third month* that granted the Jews a right to "stand for their life" and fight back against their enemies.

In yet another example Joseph interpreted his fellow prisoner's dream according to his fate at the hands of Pharaoh who had cast both of them into prison. Joseph assured this other prisoner who was Pharaoh's chief butler that he would be restored *within three days.* Interestingly, part of the butler's dream included a vision of a vine with *three branches* that budded, blossomed and brought forth clusters of ripe grapes. Perhaps the butler's dream had some prophetic meaning of blessing and restoration for beyond himself and also for Joseph and the people of Israel. Related to this, see my passage in Chapter 11 related to the *Parable of the Mustard Seed.*

In addition to these examples involving Gentiles, Israel of course did experience its share of restoration or replenishment in time periods of '3.' Recall after their initial *three day* journey from Egypt into the wilderness the Israelites at first found no food or water. Then, they were replenished by 12 wells of water and quails and manna for food. Also recall the Prophet Elisha went away from the sons of prophets of the northern kingdom in Jericho as a sort of hiding his face. He then returned *after three days* and healed the waters of the "dry, barren" land, proclaiming that there would be "no more death or barren land" (2 Ki. 2:21). On another occasion, when the Prophet Samuel was led to appoint Saul as the first king of Israel, after Saul was brought to him he made a point to assure Saul that the asses his father lost *three days prior* had been recovered. This was the original intended purpose of Saul's journey. Finally, Joseph placed his brothers in a holding place of captivity in Egypt for *three days* under the auspices that they were spies; at their release he restored them with grain and gave their money back in this ancient time of famine.

Not too long after the early days split-off of Israel from Judah, Solomon's son Rehoboam's Judah kingdom was restored and "made strong." This was after God's commands that Rehoboam held his peace and not fight against Israel. Instead, under his direction in fortifying cities of Judah many Levites and priests returned to his kingdom including those from Jeroboam's idol-worshiping northern kingdom. These assisted Rehoboam in making his kingdom "strong" for *three years*, thereby walking in the ways of his fathers Solomon and David. Speaking of, King Solomon's kingdom had been replenished with various riches *every three years* by his ships of Tarshish.

Later, Judah's King Hezekiah who was told by Isaiah that he would soon die of illness repented to God and begged for extended years. God granted him these. God told the Prophet Isaiah for Hezekiah, "Turn again…I have seen thy tears, behold I will heal thee: *on the third day* thou shall go up to the house of the Lord" (2 Ki. 20:5). It was also in Hezekiah's day that the Lord saved a remnant of Jerusalem from the king of Assyria's attacks. This remnant we are told was the "escaped of the house of Judah." God said to them:

*And this shall be a sign unto thee, Ye shall eat this year such things as grow of themselves, and in the second year that which springeth of the same; and in the **third year** sow ye, and reap, and plant vineyards, and eat the fruits thereof. (2 Ki. 19:29)*

This remnant's saving, blessing and subsequent growth as a vineyard reminds one of the butler's dream above but is a continuation of God's original promise to Israel through Abraham, Isaac and Jacob. It was Abraham who was on his journey to sacrifice his son Isaac according to God's instructions about whom we are told: "Then *on the third day* Abraham lifted up his eyes, and saw the place afar off." (Gen 22:4). Of course, the Lord provided a sacrifice in Isaac's place. And it was at this place that the Lord told Abraham because of his faith:

That in blessing I will bless thee, and in multiplying I will multiply thy seed as the stars of the heaven, and as the sand which is upon the sea shore; and thy seed shall possess the gate of his enemies. (Gen. 22:17)

I mentioned earlier how Jesus fulfilled this kind of sacrifice in our place. His sacrifice will allow the last days remnant of Israel to be released and carry forward his own original promise to Abraham. Perhaps there is a chance that on the *third day* (or year) after the 'Jacob'-Judah "small flock" remnant's initial deliverance into the wilderness they will be provided a vision of the coming kingdom as Abraham was or possibly even experience the presence of the Lord. I describe in the section below the *possible* blessing of the Lord himself appearing in some form at around the three year mark into their deliverance. There is certainly a strong pattern in scripture for blessings given by God at a time period of '3'; this assumes obedience and commitment to him.

Blessings and restoration of the last days 'Jacob'-Judah "small flock" remnant

It goes without saying that for all believers in the end times, the ultimate blessing will be Jesus' return and the establishment of his Kingdom. I just mentioned above the possibility that the 'Jacob'-Judah "small flock" remnant may experience an early or supernatural appearance of the Lord in some form. For an idea, we might begin by recalling some of the ways in which the Lord was continually present with his ancient people when they came out of Egypt and were in the wilderness (i.e. pillar of fire/cloud of smoke, in the Tabernacle, on top of the Mount Sinai, etc.). It is likely that this kind of supernatural presence of God among his remnant people will continue throughout the Day of the Lord. At the least, we know that the Lord has promised last days 'Jacob' and his Judah-centric remnant: "I will hold your hand" (Jer. 30:10); "I am with you" (Jer. 42:11); "I am in the midst" (Jer. 14:9); etc. This remnant may also wait for an actual appearance of the Lord such as that I describe below.

Meanwhile, this remnant will come out of an environment in 'Babylon'-U.S. where they had been targeted, oppressed and persecuted by the anti-Christ Chaldeans. The Lord prophetically admits to this remnant that he has, "given (them) the bread of adversity, and the water of affliction…" (Is. 30:20). They will essentially be escapees; they will be part of God's people who are "left of the sword." Recall how Israel escaped from Pharaoh out of the valley of the shadow of death. Also, recall how both Job and King David walked through and were delivered out of this same "valley."

In a world of turmoil that will experience the Lord's judgments coming onto it, as well as a very powerful adversary aligned against 'Israel' and all Christ-believers, a blessing for the "small flock" remnant will be the deliverance, protection and comforting that they receive. These semi-captive escapees and refugees will become isolated from the world and alone in the wilderness. As the true plumbline of righteousness in the last days the Spirit of the Lord Jesus Christ will remain the cornerstone among them. He is the rock of righteousness and justice this remnant will continue to rely on all the way through the Day of the Lord described as: "a tried stone"; "a rock of offense"; and a "snare." I showed above how the last days remnant is instructed, "Let (the Lord) be your sanctuary." They will indeed return directly "unto the mighty God" (Is. 10:21). This is explained as follows:

And it shall come to pass in that day, that the remnant of Israel, and such as are escaped of the house of Jacob, shall no more again stay upon him that smote them; but shall stay upon the Lord, the Holy One of Israel, in truth. (Is. 10:20)

Of course, the blessing of the light among them will be first and foremost attributed to the Lord's Spirit being in their midst. Recall Jesus saying, "I am the light of the world: he that followeth me shall not walk in darkness, but shall have the light of life" (Jn. 8:12). 'Jacob' and his remnant will also be led and provided for at this time in a world of famine and dried up waters. As in the day Israel entered the wilderness and God provided for them, the Lord will be their pathmaker once again:

And I will bring the blind by a way that they knew not; I will lead them in paths that they have not known: I will make darkness light before them, and crooked things straight. These things will I do unto them, and not forsake them. (Is. 42:16)

In *Volume 3*, I describe this Judah-centric remnant's likely temporary "holding pattern" situation in the wilderness in 'Babylon'-U.S. under some form of protected captivity, I described that this will be a time when God is doing a "new thing" and is: "making a way in the wilderness"; giving "waters in the wilderness and rivers in the desert"; and providing "fountains in the midst of valleys." The Lord promises:

For I will pour water upon him that is thirsty, and floods upon the dry ground: I will pour my spirit upon thy seed, and my blessing upon thine offspring. (Is. 44:3)

In that day sing ye unto her, A vineyard of red wine. I the Lord do keep it; I will water it every moment: lest any hurt it, I will keep it night and day. (Is. 27:3)

Again, there is no definitive time period of '3' attached to this phase of the "small flock" remnant's provision in the wilderness. It will continue throughout the Day of the Lord. However, I mentioned above that in the *third year,* or just after (~3 ½ years), this would be a point in time based on precedent when the Lord *could* appear in a more visible manner to his "small flock" remnant of refugees in the wilderness. The first three year period after their deliverance will have allowed them a time to separate, abstain, sanctify, worship and prepare for his appearance. This timing of his appearance would be consistent with precedent in Moses' day and in Jesus' day (i.e. *after the third day*). There may be other indications in scripture such as the following verse:

After two days will he revive us: **in the third day** *he will raise us up, and we shall live in his sight. (Hos. 6:2)*

In fairness, this particular verse is most often referred to by prophecy teachers to mean that it will be after two days (meaning 2,000 years since Jesus' resurrection, with a day equal to 1,000 years), and in the third day we will join Jesus and his Kingdom. And this view is consistent with what is known as the 7th day of creation that has the Millennial Kingdom beginning after 6,000 years of human history. It is possible that both interpretations are the case. You might recall those who were close to Jesus and were lamenting *on the third day* after his crucifixion about his promise to redeem Israel. Jesus immediately appeared to them and soon after to many others who experienced his post-resurrection presence.

Similarly, consider that it will be *3 ½ years* (42 months) into the final week of years when the 'Two Witnesses' who have prophesied to this point are killed. They will then be supernaturally raised for all to see and resurrected to heaven *after 3 ½ days*. This will be similar to Jesus' crucifixion and his raising on the third day. Interestingly, after the 'Two Witnesses' are raised we are told that seven trumpets will sound with voices in heaven saying, "The kingdoms of this world are become the kingdoms of our Lord, and of his Christ; and he shall reign for ever and ever" (Rev. 11:15).

Meanwhile, "birthing" signs of Immanuel ("God with us") and subsequently the "Wonderful, Counselor, the mighty God" signal the Lord being in the midst of his remnant in Babylon's wilderness *in some form*. The latter refers to the Lord himself likely *at a time period approximately half way through the Day of the Lord.* This is the time when the archangel Michael will stand up and everyone who is written in the book of life will be delivered. A strong theme pronouncing the re-beginnings of God's Kingdom at this time is also observed in the following verses: "Of the increase of his government and peace there shall be no end, upon the throne of David, and upon his kingdom, to order it, and to establish it with judgment and with justice from henceforth even forever" (Is. 9:7); and, "And she brought forth a man child, who was to rule all nations with a rod of iron" (Rev. 12:5). In some form Jesus Christ himself will appear among his anointed remnant in the wilderness during this highly tumultuous time. Recall that it was at the fourth watch of the night when Jesus appeared to his disciples in the ship during a storm.

Altogether, all of this is to say that at *approximately 3 ½ years* into the beginning of the Day of the Lord (i.e. *around* the mid-point of the last '7'-year period), this will be a "high watch" period for an appearance of the Lord himself.

At this point, Israel, as symbolized by the woman and her remnant will flee into the wilderness for the remaining time period of 3 ½ years. This is the same time (i.e. 42 months) the beast is given to reign over the world and that we are told the *third* 'Woe' of judgment comes. It will be this second and final *3 ½ year* phase in the Day of the Lord during which the 'Jacob'-Judah "small flock" remnant and the newly awakened, greater house of Israel believers will flee and hide, waiting for the Lord's return. In the meantime, the holy land of Israel will be in too much turmoil for this return until the end of the age.

We know that at the end of the Day of the Lord 'Jacob' will finally raise up the tribes of Israel. Gentile believers will be among them. This will be the time about which we are told:

That thou ('Jacob') mayest say to the prisoners, Go forth; to them that are in darkness, Shew yourselves. They shall feed in the ways, and their pastures shall be in all high places. (Is. 49:9)

It will be at this time we are told that the Lord will "stretch out his hand a second time." The Lord will gather a second harvest when he recovers his larger house of Israel remnant from the "four corners of the earth" (Is. 11:11-12) and from "all the ends of the earth" (Is. 45:22). He says:

And it shall come to pass, after that I have plucked them out I will return, and have compassion on them, and will bring them again, every man to his heritage, and every man to his land. (Jer. 12:15)

The "small flock" remnant, the larger remnant of Israel believers, and believing Gentiles will all return to the Lord's Kingdom together. I describe this process in more detail in *Volume 2*.

~

In conclusion, there is a strong pattern of common events that occurred historically in a time period of '3' that will repeat in the end times. While this particular time period is not always explicitly indicated for these events we can generally see how they may repeat in periods of '3' or '3 ½' along with what will be a clear midpoint in the final "week" of highly significant events described above. Events including Israel's escape, journeying, sanctification, and blessings will generally occur in periods of '3' while they are surrounded by the Lord's judgment events.

It should be mentioned that these kinds of events will be underway in the time of the "beginning of sorrows." Thus, there could be events with time periods of '3' that occur *prior to* the onset of the Day of the Lord. These are not clearly indicated in scripture but I briefly mentioned a couple. For example, I mentioned the possibility of an end times Son of man being hidden in the "heart of the earth" for 3 days and 3 nights. I also mentioned the pattern we see of initial siege that occurs in a time period of '3' prior to invasion. This kind of siege may very well precede initial invasions that we will see come upon 'Babylon'-U.S. and the country of Israel that I describe in *Volume 2*. Events like these may not be readily recognizable and trackable in terms of time period, however, because we know that the Day of the Lord will come as a "thief in the night."

Of course, the ultimate blessing will occur at the end of the Day of the Lord when the Lord establishes his eternal Kingdom and all believers return. I describe all believers' return to the Kingdom in my book, *Biblical End Times, Volume 2*.

Chapter 11.

Kingdom Prophecy and Parables

Passages from Lion's Lair provided in this chapter include:

11.1 Prophecy in the Psalms

11.2 End Times Prophecy in Jesus' Parables

11.3 Prophecy in Jesus' Parable of the Mustard Seed

11.1 Prophecy in the Psalms

Scripture in the Psalms contains several important prophetic themes including those which are very significant for our current last days time period. Of course, one major theme that runs throughout is that of King David's battle versus his enemy, the anti-Christ spirit of his day, which I address in more detail in *Writings of Lion's Lair, Volume 3*. His story and battle is a very relevant prophetic picture of the battle of last days 'Jacob' and the Judah remnant against the Chaldeans. King David's battle also foretold the story of end times 'David' who I addressed in detail in Chapter 6.

In this passage, I will cover additional major prophetic themes in the Psalms, which strongly foretell the central storyline of the spiritual battle between God's Kingdom warriors versus the anti-Christ spirit and its attempt of a new world order and kingdom apart from God's.

Speaking of God's Kingdom, it is readily apparent in King David's psalms that he possessed an incredible heart and spirit for God's eternal Kingdom. King David's head was "in the clouds," so to speak, but I mean that sincerely, and in the most respectful and admirable of terms. He constantly meditated upon and prayed on those things that were eternal and outside of his immediate purview. Of course, it didn't hurt that he had been made aware directly by God that it would be his royal throne and house that would be established on God's holy hill forever.

King David's words, not surprisingly, are a large influence on the prophetic topics that are covered in the Psalms, overall, and that I will cover herein. Major prophetic topic areas that I will address in this passage include:

- The (initial and final) coming Messiah, Jesus Christ
- God's heavenly Kingdom as seen through King David's eyes
- God's heavenly inheritance through the Davidic line

Each of these areas is addressed in its respective section below.

The Messiah who Came to Earth and will Return- Jesus Christ

While there are many prophecies in scripture about Jesus' eventual coming to the earth it is interesting that the ones told about him in the book of Psalms also happen to be a good representation for what his people also go through (on a smaller scale) on their figurative pilgrimage back to the holy land. Jesus, in particular:

1. Gained initial victory by his death (and especially his resurrection), which proved him as God and his persecutors as being of the evil, world kingdom
2. Sits enthroned at the right hand of God
3. Has inherited the Kingdom from God, his Father
4. Will return again to defeat his enemies
5. Will reign over the Kingdom as the King of Glory

I will address each of these areas in more detail; I have also shown in Chapters 4-8 at least a somewhat similar story for the Lord's faithful remnant: They are persecuted for their faith in Jesus Christ; they (will) gain victory over their enemies as a result of their proven faith; they will inherit their own place in the coming Kingdom; and they will get to serve with and worship Jesus Christ. Their vineyard will include a royal remnant who serve him on his holy hill.

Meanwhile, the progression of Jesus Christ as the King of Kings and Lord of Lords in scripture in the book of Psalms is as follows.

Initial victory

First is the picture of what was to be his coming persecution along with his crucifixion at the hands of the false god-, false idol-worshiping anti-Christ spirit- Pharisee/Roman variety- of his day. Initially, in Psalm 22, we are given a key marker as King David prophetically used Jesus' own eventual words, "My God, my God, why have you forsaken me?" (Ps. 22:1). King David then offered what appeared to be an accurate description of Jesus' treatment in his day:

But I am a worm and not a man, scorned by everyone, despised by the people. All who see me mock me; they hurl insults, shaking their heads. (Ps. 22:6-7)

David further called these enemies of his and of Christ like "roaring lions" who tear their prey and "open their mouths wide" against him. Then, in what many believe to be a prophetic description of Jesus' crucifixion, King David wrote:

For dogs have compassed me: the assembly of the wicked have inclosed me: they pierced my hands and my feet. (Ps. 22:16)

Other scripture in God's Word tells us and proves that Jesus was subsequently resurrected following his death on the cross.

Enthroned at the right hand of God

As just mentioned, there is plenty of biblical evidence for Jesus' resurrection and then his subsequent transfiguration and ascension. Furthermore, according to the Psalm verses below we know that he remains enthroned in heaven at the moment:

Yet their (the heavens') voice goes out into all the earth, their words to the ends of the world. In the heavens God has pitched a tent for the sun. (Ps. 19:4) ('Sun' here refers to "Son").

The Lord said unto my Lord, Sit thou at my right hand, until I make thine enemies thy footstool. (Ps. 110:1)

So, the highly-revered King David, who was a God-chosen, God-anointed prophet, priest and king in his own right, here (in the last verse above) refers to "my (his) Lord," in a sign of Jesus Christ as Lord on the heavenly throne. And we know when Jesus eventually came, he referred back to this same verse in speaking with the Pharisees in making a point about who he was.

Jesus inherits the Kingdom

In the Psalms we see plenty of prophetic scripture that demonstrates that God has given Jesus the Kingdom to come and that he is in fact the "Great King" of Zion. Thus, he will leave his heavenly throne and return to us again and be in our midst here on earth for his Millennial reign. The following verses indicate this:

Yet have I set my king upon my holy hill of Zion. I will declare the decree: the Lord hath said unto me, Thou art my Son; this day have I begotten thee. (Ps. 2:6-7)

Lift up your heads, O ye gates; and be ye lift up, ye everlasting doors; and the King of glory shall come in...Who is this King of glory? The Lord of hosts, he is the King of glory. Selah. (Ps. 24:7,10)

When Jesus returns we are told in the Psalms that he will be like a "bridegroom coming from his Chamber, like a champion rejoicing to run his course" (Ps. 19:4).

Returns to defeat his enemies

As we know, prior to the coming Millennial Kingdom there will be a final battle that must take place to defeat the worldwide anti-Christ Chaldean army. Satan and his minions in the last days will be obsessed with Jerusalem and the temple since the Anti-Christ will strive to set up his counterfeit kingdom. In the following verse, the "mountains of many peaks" essentially represent the anti-Christ Chaldean leaders who are part of Satan's evil, oppressive kingdom that is aligned against God's Kingdom to come.

Why do you gaze in envy, O mountains of many peaks? This is the mountain God chose for His dwelling, where the Lord will surely dwell forever. (Ps. 68:16)

So, the anti-Christ Chaldean power and spirit will still be entrenched until the very last days and must be defeated. This is why scripture in the book of Psalms (and elsewhere in God's Word) says many times about Jesus that he, "crushes kings," "judges nations," and "crushes rulers of the whole earth" (Ps. 110:1). Other psalm verses describe his coming battle cry such as:

Thou shalt break them with a rod of iron; thou shalt dash them in pieces like a potter's vessel. (Ps. 2:9)

Who is this King of glory? The Lord strong and mighty, the Lord mighty in battle. (Ps. 24:8)

These verses are obviously consistent with others elsewhere in the Bible such as: (with the) "breath of his lips," he will slay the wicked (Is. 11:4); he will "rule the nations with an iron scepter" (Rev. 12:9); and he will be the stone that strikes the statue "on its feet of iron and clay" (Dan. 2:34), and crushes them. (The latter is the statue of successive kingdoms described by the Prophet Daniel with the feet made of iron and clay representing the last days mingled anti-Christ Chaldean-controlled kingdom).

Jesus reigns as King of glory

Once Jesus returns and defeats the adversary representing all evil and wickedness here on this earth then he will reign in the Millennial Kingdom. People in the whole earth will finally rejoice and worship him as the one, true God. "Many nations" will come to Zion to worship and to learn the Lord's "ways" and his "paths" (Mic. 4:2). We learn further in Psalm 72 as follows how Jesus will be glorious and highly exalted in his reign:

He shall have dominion also from sea to sea, and from the river unto the ends of the earth. (Ps. 72:8)

His name shall endure forever: his name shall be continued as long as the sun: and men shall be blessed in him: all nations shall call him blessed. Blessed be the Lord God, the God of Israel, who only doeth wondrous things. And blessed be his glorious name for ever: and let the whole earth be filled with his glory; Amen, and Amen. (Ps. 72:17-19)

Yea, all kings shall fall down before him: all nations shall serve him. For he shall deliver the needy when he crieth; the poor also, and him that hath no helper. He shall spare the poor and needy, and shall save the souls of the needy. He shall redeem their soul from deceit and violence: and precious shall their blood be in his sight. (Ps. 72:11-14)

God's Heavenly Kingdom

As I mentioned earlier, King David had a true, single-focused heart and mind for the heavenly Kingdom and God's royal throne. Of course, it was David, upon coming to Jerusalem, who was foremost concerned with establishing God's temple. Those in his house commented about David:

How he sware unto the Lord, and vowed unto the mighty God of Jacob; Surely I will not come into the tabernacle of my house, nor go up into my bed; I will not give sleep to mine eyes, or slumber to mine eyelids, Until I find out a place for the Lord, an habitation for the mighty God of Jacob. (Ps. 132:2-5)

Accordingly, it is not surprising that some of David's psalms described his longings for and visions of God's heavenly Kingdom. In exploring them, we find some prophetic insights. To begin, in several of his psalms, David envisioned and described a liturgical procession marching through the gates of the temple in a last days picture or context at the time when Jesus assumes his throne. This is after Jesus defeats his and his people's enemy, thereby saving his righteous remnant and his servants with justice, setting them free. In these psalms, David prophetically described singing, music, and praise amidst "shouts of joy and victory." David pronounced, "This is the day that the Lord has made…" and, "The stone the builders rejected has become the cornerstone" (Ps. 118:22). So, this celebration will punctuate the last phase of the prophecy of Jesus Christ in the Psalms in the section above. That is, Jesus will assume his heavenly throne in glory with his saints at his side. We read:

Let us go to his dwelling place, let us worship at his footstool, saying, 'Arise, Lord, and come to your resting place, you and the ark of your might. May your priests be clothed with your righteousness; may your faithful people sing for joy.' (Ps. 132:7-9)

King David in God's heavenly Kingdom

While King David remarkably wrote about the very day Jesus Christ will begin his reign it is apparent that he longed to be there in the Kingdom himself. He repeatedly emphasized the righteousness and holiness of Jesus and his saints, the beauty of God's palace, and in his prayers and visions he practically transported himself to be among them. Recall that he concludes his famous Psalm 23 with, "…and I shall dwell in the house of the Lord forever." Also consider the following:

How amiable are thy tabernacles, O Lord of hosts! My soul longeth, yea, even fainteth for the courts of the Lord: my heart and my flesh crieth out for the living God…Blessed are they that dwell in thy house: they will be still praising thee. Selah. Blessed is the man whose strength is in thee; in whose heart are the ways of them. (Ps. 84:1-2,4-5)

O send out thy light and thy truth: let them lead me; let them bring me unto thy holy hill, and to thy tabernacles. Then will I go unto the altar of God, unto God my exceeding joy: yea, upon the harp will I praise thee, O God my God. (Ps. 43:3-4)

Open to me the gates of righteousness: I will go into them, and I will praise the Lord: This gate of the Lord, into which the righteous shall enter. I will praise thee: for thou hast heard me, and art become my salvation. (Ps. 118:19-21)

So, there is no question that David is intimately connected to his promised eternal throne and God's Kingdom. His strong, near obsessive (in a good way) focus on Jesus Christ's ultimate righteous reign and eternal kingdom show why he is referred to in other scripture as, "a man after God's own heart" (1 Sam. 13:14). We shall ultimately get to see how King David's spirit manifests in heaven. Meanwhile, David recognized his own mortality in his day and envisioned the time "when he awakes" and is with the Lord. The following verses show firsthand what he expects to see and experience:

As for me, I will be vindicated and will see your face; when I awake, I will be satisfied with seeing your likeness. (Ps. 17:15)

You make known to me the path of life; you will fill me with joy in your presence, with eternal pleasures at your right hand. (Ps. 16:11)

I remain confident of this: I will see the goodness of the Lord in the land of the living. (Ps. 27:13)

Because of my integrity you uphold me and set me in your presence forever. (Ps. 41:12)

Not surprisingly, given King David's character he associated the principles of righteousness, "goodness," and "integrity" with God's Kingdom to come- those things he always desired and longed for.

House of David- Inheritance

King David was not solely focused on himself with regard to God's coming Kingdom. He was extremely aware of and thoughtful about his Davidic line to follow, which may be referred to as his "house" (of David) or inheritance. The covenant promise that God made to him for his eternal family throne was no doubt influential in David's thoughts for himself and his future royal family's throne in the heavenly Kingdom.

Through his anointing King David appeared well-aware of the nature of his inheritance and family line to come, including how they will be "preserved forever," blessed (i.e. "will flourish in the courts of God" – Ps. 92:13), and will represent his house to serve Jesus Christ in the heavenly Kingdom. As the Millennial Kingdom's royalty, King David's "house" is considered to be a big part of God's inheritance. (See Chapter 4). Meanwhile, several of the following psalm verses highlight King David's certain awareness about the coming blessing for his future eternal heavenly Kingdom inheritance:

The Lord hath sworn in truth unto David; he will not turn from it; Of the fruit of thy body will I set upon thy throne. If thy children will keep my covenant and my testimony that I shall teach them, their children shall also sit upon thy throne for evermore. (Ps. 132:11-12)

Then our sons in their youth will be like well-nurtured plants, and our daughters will be like pillars carved to adorn a palace. Our barns will be filled with every kind of provision. Our sheep will increase by thousands, by tens of thousands in our fields; our oxen will draw heavy loads. There will be no breaching of walls, no going into captivity, no cry of distress in our streets. (Ps. 144:12-14)

The righteous shall flourish like the palm tree: he shall grow like a cedar in Lebanon. Those that be planted in the house of the Lord shall flourish in the courts of our God. They shall still bring forth fruit in old age; they shall be fat and flourishing… (Ps. 92:12-14)

Blessed are those who dwell in Your house; They will still be praising You. Selah. Blessed is the man whose strength is in You, Whose heart is set on pilgrimage. (Ps. 84:4-5)

Other psalms along these lines describe the eternal existence of the Davidic line who will have "years without end," "seed (that) endures forever," and children who sit upon the throne "forever more."

In fact, it appears as if King David was deliberately and consciously writing some of his psalms for a future generation of his family line to come. David, in his wisdom and thoughtfulness, prayed, "I will make thy (God's) name to be remembered in all generations," (Ps. 17:1); and when he recognized he was in older age with few days left he requested of God, "…do not forsake me until I declare your power to the next generation, your mighty acts to all *who are to come*" (Ps. 71:18). David showed that he was truly in-tune with his family/"house" in generations to come and communicated to them through his psalms.

King David's prophetic psalms about his people's deliverance

It is clear through King David's additional psalms and prayers that he had been given insight and prophetic knowledge of the last days battle between his and Jacob's descendants versus the end times anti-Christ Chaldean army. In their prayers/psalms it is clear that King David and those in his house of his day could tell that his future inheritance would experience an "evil time," "years wherein we have seen evil," and that this remnant would need to be saved and rescued at the hands of God himself. The following verses demonstrate this amazing prophetic foreknowledge:

Deliver me; rescue me from the hands of foreigners whose mouths are full of lies, whose right hands are deceitful. (Ps. 144:11)

The Lord is the strength of his people, a fortress of salvation for his anointed one. Save your people and bless your inheritance; be their shepherd and carry them forever. (Ps. 28:8-9)

For the Lord loveth judgment, and forsaketh not his saints; they are preserved for ever: but the seed of the wicked shall be cut off. The righteous shall inherit the land, and dwell therein forever. (Ps. 37:28-29)

(Note: There is much more in the prophetic psalms referring to God's end times deliverance of Israel and Gentile believers in the midst of his judgment to come. I will address this in *Writings of Lion's Lair, Volumes 2 and 3*).

Last days 'Davidic Prince' servant

Given that the house of King David in his day had prophetic foresight and concern into his last days inheritance, as discussed in the section above, it stands to reason that they had similar prophetic foresight for God's individual end times house of David's saints and servants.

In Chapter 6, I addressed the last days Millennial Kingdom's 'Davidic Prince' who King David appears to refer to several times in his psalms. This 'Prince' is sometimes prophetically referred to in the context and background of a (future) "day of trouble." King David almost appears to be writing about a future mirror image of himself- which is the 'Davidic Prince' figure. Just like King David, I described how end times 'David' goes through his own last days' battle with the same ancient foe that his forefather David was so familiar with. The 'Prince' is a victorious warrior figure who leads the exodus of his people back to their land and is a major influencing force behind the building of the Millennial Kingdom temple. This happens as a second fulfillment of the original event of King David entering Jerusalem and planning for God's temple to be built.

Below, I provide some additional prophetic scripture and justification from the psalms that show support and prayer in King David's day for the end times 'Davidic Prince.' Just as for other end times biblical characters that I have referred to, his experience can be thought of as generally representative in a lot of ways of other servants of Jesus Christ in these last days.

The 'Davidic Prince' in scripture

It is possible that the 'David Prince' is the one who is prophetically referred to in various ways in the psalms. While he is generally referred to as a servant, he also appears to be referred to with other terms such as: "the horn of David"; "the horn of his people"; "the anointed one"; "the Lord's right hand"; and "the son you (God) have raised up." The latter term was used by King David's Levitical servants at the time in relation to this future servant being a leader of the "vine" God has planted but has then since been "broken down" and "burned with fire" (See *Volume 2*). In the prophecy of their calling out to God in their distress, God's people ask:

Let your hand rest on the man at your right hand, the son of man you have raised up for yourself. (Ps. 80:17)

This prophecy in context *appears* to be referring to a last days, non-deity, servant of Jesus Christ. The 'Davidic' Prince may also be prophetically referred to, at least in a loose sense, in some other areas of the Psalms. Some examples of verses that certainly seem to fit the 'Davidic Prince's character given what we know about him include:

Who shall ascend into the hill of the Lord? Or who shall stand in his holy place? (Ps. 24:3) (In Chapter 4, I explained the answer to this question is likely the 'Davidic Prince')

Praise the Lord! Blessed is the man who fears the Lord, Who delights greatly in His commandments. His descendants will be mighty on earth; The generation of the upright will be blessed. (Ps. 112:1-2)

(He who dwells in the shadow of the Most High) ...because he loves me, I will rescue him; I will protect him; for he acknowledges my name. (Ps. 91:1,14)

There (Zion) will I make the horn of David to bud: I have ordained a lamp for mine anointed. His enemies will I clothe with shame: but upon himself shall his crown flourish. (Ps. 132:17-18)

I provided additional scripture from the Psalms about the Lord's deliverance of his end times 'Davidic Prince' servant in Chapter 6.

~

In summary, through King David and other psalmists we learn prophetically about Jesus' future comings, including his initial coming and subsequent death and resurrection. We also learn about Jesus' final triumphant return to his righteous throne. And we learn somewhat about the heavenly Kingdom as described by King David who also informs us about his end times inheritance and his protégé, the 'Davidic Prince,' for the Millennial Kingdom. I write more about this in my book, *Biblical End Times, Volume 1*.

11.2 End Times Prophecy in Jesus' Parables

A lot that we can learn about end times prophecy is related to the last days lost sheep of the house of Israel including those I have addressed to this point in this book. Given that Jesus himself said that he was not sent to anyone but these, we might consider his words as they apply in today's end times. In fact, Jesus had many words directly about the end times from which all nations and believers who take heed will ultimately benefit.

In this passage I will focus on Jesus' parables in an attempt to ascertain possible meaning for the biblical story that is likely currently playing out. This story involves a core, yet very small remnant who I described in earlier chapters of this book and have written about in my book,

Biblical End Times, Volume 1. These will help to bring Jesus' Light to Gentiles of the world as well as to the house of Israel. Their lost sheep remnant is likely part of the last days fig tree generation that Jesus said in his *Parable of the Fig Tree* will witness "all these things" that come to pass. He also said that the sign of this fig tree would indicate that the "Kingdom of God is nigh at hand."

In order to bring forth truth and light to others in the last days, the Lord's anointed remnant fights in the spiritual kingdom war with his assistance to expose the lies and wicked ways of the adversary. What the adversary had attempted to suppress and keep hidden will finally come out at a time when all things are revealed. In the context of the ancient kingdom war that comes to a final conclusion and division of good and evil recall that Jesus told his disciples (with application for us) that he spoke in parables so that, "you (can) know the mysteries of the kingdom of heaven, but to them it is not given" (Matt. 13:11).

The lack of discussion about the end times anointed remnant in our churches, seminaries, etc. along with the fact that they are kept hidden (as I will discuss herein) are strong signs that they are at least part of the "mysteries" of the Kingdom that Jesus refers to. Because of their story leading up to the final harvest and judgment referred to in several of Jesus' parables we might consider them according to the following categories:

- The *Parable (of the Sower)* that helps understand all parables
- Harvest work parables
- Parables about redemption through repentance and forgiveness
- Parables about Jesus' Light and revealing
- Parables about the beginnings of a new Kingdom

I will describe each of these parable categories in separate sections below followed by the last days anointed remnant's expected fulfillment of these.

Parable of the Sower

It makes sense to consider the *Parable of the Sower* first in order to understand the bigger story of which all parables are a part. In the version from the book of Mark Jesus taught, "And he said unto them, Know ye not this parable? and how then will ye know all parables?" (Mk. 4:13). In short, Jesus described the seed sown on good ground as one that yields abundant fruit for the kingdom in contrast with the seed sown on stony ground or among thorns. In this parable in the book of Luke Jesus explained, "But that on the good ground are they, which in an honest and good heart, having heard the word, keep it, and bring forth fruit with patience" (Lk. 8:15). Perhaps Jesus was repeating an idea from prophetic words spoken by King David, "And he shall be like a tree planted by the rivers of water, that bringeth forth his fruit in his season; his leaf also shall not wither; and whatsoever he doeth shall prosper" (Ps. 1:3).

'Jacob's last days anointed remnant

As I describe in this book as well as in the story given in my books *Biblical End Times, Volumes 1 and 2,* 'Jacob's "small flock" remnant are a part of those who fit the definition for the seed sown on good ground. As a seed of the "blessed of the Lord" (Is. 65:23) God also refers to them as a "branch of (his) planting" and the "shoot I have planted, the work of my hands." Although not perfect, 'Jacob,' 'David,' and the 'Daughter of Zion' as leading figures in this remnant are recognized in scripture individually for their faith and righteousness. Their remnant will be part of the collective fulfillment of the following:

For as the earth bringeth forth her bud, and as the garden causeth the things that are sown in it to spring forth; so the Lord God will cause righteousness and praise to spring forth before all the nations. (Is. 61:11)

Here, we might recall Jesus' *Parable of the Mustard Seed* as a tree that grows from a small seed and becomes great in the Kingdom. (I discuss this parable below). Perhaps 'Jacob's remnant are also one measure of leaven out of the three Jesus mentions in his *Parable of Yeast* that make up and complete the Kingdom of heaven. In the meantime, in the midst of the kingdom war 'Jacob's anointed remnant with the Holy Spirit are ones who have faith as Jesus taught in another part of scripture, "If ye have faith as a grain of mustard seed, ye shall say unto this mountain, Remove hence to yonder place; and it shall remove;

and nothing shall be impossible unto you" (Matt. 17:20). The mystery of their behind-the-scenes spiritual war where mountains are indeed moved is consistent with Jesus' *Parable of the Growing Seed* in that such a seed shall "spring and grow up" but a man should not know how. We are told further about their growth:

The wilderness and the solitary place shall be glad for them; and the desert shall rejoice, and blossom as the rose. It shall blossom abundantly, and rejoice even with joy and singing: the glory of Lebanon shall be given unto it, the excellency of Carmel and Sharon, they shall see the glory of the Lord, and the excellency of our God. (Is. 35:1-2)

'Jacob's "small flock" remnant are planted by God, given growth by him, and ultimately yield fruit of the Kingdom that all belongs to Jesus (the "vine" or the "root"). Their growth is consistent with teaching in God's Word about how such a seed on good ground will yield an abundant crop of "fruit" that is multiplied exponentially (Mk. 4:20). Thus, we might rightly assume that their seed is planted on the good ground of faith in Jesus described in the *Parable of the Sower* above. Their resulting Kingdom "tree" will fulfill God's promise all over again to Abraham for Israel to become as numerous as the "sand of the sea" as well as his promise to King David that his descendants would become as "countless as the stars of the sky."

Harvest- and Servant-Worker Parables

The *Parable of the Wise Builders* conveys the message that God's Kingdom is like a house that is built on a firm, deep foundation or rock. This is similar to the good ground described above that is necessary to bring about the end times harvest for the Kingdom. Related to this harvest, we might next consider parables about workers in the vineyard who bring about the Kingdom. It is the same continuing ancient harvest about which Jesus remarked, "The harvest truly is plenteous, but the labourers are few; Pray ye therefore the Lord of the harvest, that he will send forth labourers into his harvest" (Matt. 9:37-38).

The *Parable of the Vineyard Workers* is the one where Jesus explains that the pay is the same for all workers regardless of the time they spend. All earn the Kingdom of heaven because they are apparently the "chosen" who work to bring about the "full ear of corn" that gradually grows as a result of their small seed that is planted. At the time the corn is ready for harvest their remnant of believers is culled from the chaff. In this parable Jesus also makes a point to say that the "last shall be first and the first last" (Matt. 20:16). There are several possible interpretations of this but one could indicate that the last days anointed remnant of a final generation who usher in the final harvest will be the first into the new heavenly Kingdom on earth. On a related note, I describe the concept of "new wine" in the Kingdom as spoken by Jesus later in this passage. Of course, Jesus is the owner and the Alpha and Omega of all.

Meanwhile, the general 'servant-worker' theme is also observed in several other parables spoken by Jesus. Servants in these who do his (the Master's) work as a necessary job (*Parable of the Master and his Servant*) have a variety of duties. These include: Watching for the Son of Man's return from a "journey" or a wedding (*Parables of the Watchful Servants* and *10 Virgins*); feeding his sheep (*Parable of the Faithful and Wise Servant*); investing their resources to yield fruit for the Kingdom (*Parable of the Talents*); and being good and faithful stewards and servants, even of little things, including the "unrighteous mammon" (*Parable of the Shrewd Manager*) that we live in the midst of today. It is clear, however, that a true servant in the midst of the spiritual kingdom war will forsake or lose all of his possessions- this is also according to Jesus (*Parables of the Cost of Discipleship* and *the Rich Fool*).

'*Jacob's last days anointed remnant*

'Jacob's anointed remnant in the last days are directly tied to doing work for the end times harvest. In practical terms their work is resisting the kingdom adversary's continuous warring and persecution tactics and fighting back. This is the adversary about which we are told, "the lords of the heathen have broken down the principal plants thereof...," as well as the pastors that have "destroyed" and "trodden" on the Lord's vineyard. 'Jacob's remnant described in Chapters 4-8 are "held fast" and "oppressed together" in last days 'Babylon.' In resisting this onslaught, the following verses in scripture are clear indications of their "small flock" remnant fighting back to assist in bringing about the end times harvest:

And Ephraim is as an heifer that is taught, and loveth to tread out the corn; but I passed over upon her fair neck: I will make Ephraim to ride; Judah shall plow, and Jacob shall break his clods. (Hos. 10:11-12)

Arise and thresh, O daughter of Zion: for I will make thine horn iron, and I will make thy hoofs brass: and thou shalt beat in pieces many people: and I will consecrate their gain unto the Lord, and their substance unto the Lord of the whole earth. (Mic. 4:13)

Fear not, thou worm Jacob…Behold, I will make thee a new sharp threshing instrument having teeth: thou shalt thresh the mountains, and beat them small, and shalt make the hills as chaff. (Is. 41:14-15)

In this war for justice and righteousness sake, partially represented by the *Parable of the Persistent Widow*, their remnant who are part of God's "own elect" resist with "righteousness as the plumbline." God assures 'Jacob' that he has called him in righteousness. 'David' represents a "righteous branch." God tells the 'Daughter of Zion,' "the nations will see your righteousness…" (Is. 62:11). They are righteous stewards and servants in the unrighteous "mammon" of last days 'Babylon.'

As Jesus warned would happen to his servants, because of their stand for righteousness 'Jacob' and his habitations become "devoured" and "consumed"; the house of David is brought to "ruins"; and the 'Daughter of Zion' becomes "barren," "deserted" and an "outcast" without comfort. In this refining process 'Jacob' takes on and pays debt in atonement for the house of Israel's transgressions overall. God asks:

Who gave Jacob for a spoil, and Israel to the robbers? did not the Lord, he against whom we have sinned? for they would not walk in his ways, neither were they obedient unto his law. (Is. 42:24)

Is Israel a servant? is he a homeborn slave? why is he spoiled? (Jer. 2:14)

A consequence and outcome of the anointed remnant's battle is that 'Jacob' becomes a messenger to the nations. Therefore, 'Jacob' or others in this remnant *may* be as those who qualify as watchmen-types who Jesus says he (the Master) puts in charge of giving servants their "food" at the proper time or in "due season." In the last days season of spiritual battle 'David' of this remnant as a "standard" (or "banner") and the 'Daughter of Zion's "travails" signal and warn of upcoming separation and judgment at the time of the harvest that I will address in a separate section below. Judgment at the harvest will be an answer to the ancient Psalmist's appeal, "Let all be confounded and turned back that hate Zion" (Ps. 129:5).

Parables about Redemption through Repentance and Forgiveness

Several of Jesus' parables are centered around the lesson of repentance and forgiveness. Jesus makes the point in the *Parable of the Two Debtors* about the one who is forgiven the most will be the most appreciative. Of course, in *Parables of the Prodigal Son* and the *Lost Sheep* where one goes astray there is much rejoicing over the one who is "found" and recovered. And in the *Parable of the Lost Coin* that is recovered Jesus says this lost one represents "one sinner that repenteth" (Lk. 15:10). Altogether, these parables are indicative of Jesus' words of his time to his disciples about the will of his Father that he "should lose nothing," speaking of the sheep he was sent to save through his grace and mercy. Jesus prophetically said about these that he "should raise it up again at the last day" (Jn. 6:39).

On the other hand, there are those who must *offer* the kind of forgiveness Jesus has instructed to the ones who repent. In the *Parable of the Shrewd Manager*, on behalf of his Manager the servant forgives debt by offering grace and accepting partial payments. Recall in his day Pharisees were confused by what means Jesus could forgive debts-they didn't understand who he was. It is ultimately only through his grace offered and power for healing that a remnant of Israel and others who are found complicit with the adversary can come to redemption in the last days.

Otherwise, a couple of Jesus' parables describe and contrast the principle of *unforgiveness*. The *Parable of the Pharisee and the Tax Collector* demonstrates this difference with the tax collector finally begging for mercy with a contrite heart. On the other hand, in the *Parable of the Unforgiving Servant* he did not extend the same mercy to his debtors as he received. Jesus remarked in this parable about how judgment will come upon those who continue to hold grievances and warned of consequences, "if ye from your hearts forgive not every one his brother their trespasses" (Matt. 18:35).

'Jacob's last days anointed remnant

Those who understand the state of the last days house of Israel and the atonement that 'Jacob' makes on their behalf will be ones who understand Jesus' parables involving forgiveness. It will be necessary for 'Jacob's atoning remnant who go through unjust persecution to forgive fellow believers who did not understand that they were complicit with the adversary. Yet even 'Jacob's remnant who are afforded imputed righteousness through their faith must do work in the vineyard described above because they are not perfect and have their own 'debts.' In the *Parable of the Two Sons* the one who repented was the one who went to work in his father's vineyard.

'Jacob's remnant's last days persecution by the adversary is an initial microcosm of and early warning for Christ-believers and the larger house of Israel's vineyard that will be extended no mercy by the adversary at the time they go through a purging and refining process. Regardless of their level of righteousness, individually, all true Christ-believers and those in the house of Israel must still go through a similar harvesting process at a time when the rain will fall on the just and the unjust alike.

As it is, keep in mind that aforementioned shepherds and priests who destroy the Lord's vineyard include Israel's own shepherds who were charged with looking out for the flock. (I address these in more detail in *Volume 2*). They are the last days representation of the *Parable of the Householder* (vineyard owner) who gave his husbandmen stewardship but then they killed his servants. Scripture about these kinds of corrupt leaders reminds of Jesus' *Parable of the Good Samaritan* describing one in need of help but is bypassed by a Pharisee and a Priest. God forewarns these last days shepherds that he will "overturn" their reign and there "shall not be a crown" for them.

Yet it is possible that even a corrupt remnant of Israel will be among those the Apostle Paul says for whom it is possible as the original, natural part of the Kingdom tree to be put back as compared with a "wild" olive branch including Gentile believers who are grafted in. Applying to original Israel one might be reminded of the *Parable of the Unfruitful Fig Tree* representing unrepentance and had not produced fruit for three years; Jesus instructed waiting another year to give more time. At least some in the last days house of Israel who do not know their Messiah will come to understand the "better law" that he represented in a world held in bondage by the accusing and persecuting enemy.

As it is, scripture indicates that there will be intra-Israel war in the last days. For the 'whole house' of Israel to return as described in several parts of scripture the last days 'northern kingdom' and Judah must be reassembled. Two sticks in the Son of man's hand described in Ezekiel 37 will represent this re-beginning of the Kingdom. Also symbolic of this is the story told through the Prophet Hosea where Gomer the harlot representing unclean idols and riches is betrothed to Hosea as a signal of God's forgiveness to last days 'Israel.' This will be an example of God's words describing that he will have mercy on those he chooses to have mercy. This is represented in Gomer's particular case as follows:

And I will sow her unto me in the earth; and I will have mercy upon her that had not obtained mercy; and I will say to them which were not my people, Thou art my people; and they shall say, Thou art my God. (Hos. 2:23)

Whereas Israel's last days idolatrous 'northern kingdom' will have participated in 'Babylon's delicacies as well as in an occult-based war against 'Jacob's righteous Judah-centric remnant they will eventually relent as they learn truth about 'Jacob's remnant's cause as Christ-believers. Many of these will finally understand Jesus as their Messiah and the grace that they have been extended. We are told that, "The envy also of Ephraim shall depart" (Is. 11:13).

However, even within Judah there will be reconciliation that is necessary. The previous "unforgiving" branch of shepherds and rulers above likely include "Men of Judah" who align with 'Babylon' against their own Matriarch ('Daughter of Zion'), 'Jacob' and even "vex" or oppress some of Ephraim. And within Judah the house of David is described as having "many breaches" that will need to be restored. It is likely that 'Jacob's righteous remnant including the aforementioned "righteous branch of David" will be "repairers of the breach" (Is. 58:12) due to their resting on the grace of the Lion of Judah (Jesus) themselves.

God promises that he will, "raise up the tabernacle of David that is fallen, and close up the breaches thereof; and I will raise up his ruins" (Am. 9:11). Applying to their last days anointed remnant God says, "Open ye the gates, that the righteous nation which keepeth the truth may enter in" (Is. 26:2). In the process of establishing 'Jacob's and house of David's previously "forsaken and hated" lost sheep remnant God justifies this move and reassures greater 'Israel':

Yet, behold, therein shall be left a remnant that shall be brought forth, both sons and daughters: behold, they shall come forth unto you, and ye shall see their way and their doings: and ye shall be comforted concerning the evil that I have brought upon Jerusalem, even concerning all that I have brought upon it. And they shall comfort you, when ye see their ways and their doings: and ye shall know that I have not done without cause all that I have done in it, saith the Lord God. (Ez. 14:22-23)

In one caveat, I explained above that 'Jacob's righteous remnant will not be altogether "clean." They will have made the decision by strong faith to come out of 'Babylon's system where they had been immersed in a culture of foreign and false gods and idols. At the time of their awakening they will collectively identify with the Prophet Isaiah's words, "I am a man of unclean lips, and I dwell in the midst of a people of unclean lips" (Is. 6:5).

I have also previously touched on how their reassembled remnant will have a last days wilderness experience prior to returning to the land of Israel during which many among them will seek forgiveness as well as sanctification, purification and cleansing. The Son of man will have to plead with Israel's remnant because not all will be righteous. For example, we are told that God will have to "wash away" the "filth" of the daughters of Zion and the bloodshed of 'Jerusalem' (Is. 4:4). This will be necessary because Jesus instructed that his servants should be found wearing clean garments in anticipation of his return.

Parables of Light and Revealing

Another category of Jesus' parables includes those related to light and revealing. I believe that these are relevant to any who are awake and searching for it in the last days. The Apostle Paul said that "children of the light" will understand the time of the final season. Otherwise, in the book of Matthew's version of Jesus' *Parable of the Lamp,* Jesus talks about light that will shine and cannot be hidden. He does this after his Sermon on the Mount where he links those who will inherit the Kingdom (i.e. poor in spirit, persecuted, peacemakers, meek, etc.) to those who are the "salt of the earth," "light of the world," and a city on a hill that "cannot be hid." He said:

Neither do men light a candle, and put it under a bushel, but on a candlestick; and it giveth light unto all that are in the house. (Matt. 5:15)

Is a candle brought to be put under a bushel, or under a bed? and not to be set on a candlestick? (Mk. 4:21)

In this particular chapter of Matthew, Jesus went on to repeat the principles of forgiveness, mercy, peacemaking, reconciliation, etc. discussed above and re-emphasized maintaining righteousness in the midst of the adversary.

'Jacob's last days anointed remnant

I described the Lord's anointed "small flock" remnant's battle versus a cruel enemy in the last days spiritual kingdom war in my book *Biblical End Times, Volume 1.* The outcome of this battle where evil is called good and good-evil will be revealed, likely at a time when all things are revealed. In Mark's version of Jesus' parable about light and revealing above, Jesus said, "For there is nothing hid, which shall not be manifested; neither was any thing kept secret, but that it should come abroad" (Mk. 4:22). 'Jacob' and the Lord's anointed remnant will be shown as overcomers in their victory that exposes the adversary and its tactics. 'Jacob' is described as a "light" to the Gentiles in a last days context- he will obviously testify of Jesus as his Savior.

In the process of last days revealing the "small flock" remnant's own revealing as servants who will proceed into the beginnings of the heavenly Kingdom will be revealed. In a couple places in scripture they are described as inheritors of the Lord's Kingdom and the "desolate heritages." In the continuing theme of their remnant as a growing seed that is planted on good soil and brings about the harvest, through Zechariah the Lord says:

For the seed shall be prosperous; the vine shall give her fruit, and the ground shall give her increase, and the heavens shall give their dew; and I will cause the remnant of this people to possess all these things. (Zech. 8:12).

My personal belief is that *Parables of the Hidden Treasure* and *Hidden Pearl* refer to these inheritors who we know had previously been "hidden." In Proverbs, Chapter 3, Solomon reminds us that the Lord's "secret is with the righteous" and that the lady "Wisdom" is a "tree of life" who is "more precious than rubies" and that she must be sought and found. This is likely the 'Daughter of Zion' about whom scripture tells us the Lord "finds" and delivers. The last days 'Son of man' himself as one who the world will not know and "cannot receive" will be revealed at some point; 'Jacob' is hidden as an "arrow" in God's quiver but eventually becomes a light; (The Daughter of) 'Jerusalem' is told to "awaken"; etc. These servants will eventually "bud" and "spring up as among the grass" to be recognized and go into the Kingdom as leaders who inherit the ancient covenant promises for ruling of the land and the people.

Consistent with this is in meaning of parables such as the *New Wine* and *New Cloth*. Jesus described each of these being of the nature that they are not meant to be combined with their former state (i.e. old wineskins or old garments). Along these lines, in the *Parable of the Owner of a House* Jesus says this owner brings forth things both old and new. It is possible that the last days anointed "small flock" remnant that the Lord says he "preserves" represents the "new." Because of their battle we are told in scripture that 'Jacob's law will go forth to the isles. Israel and citizens of the Kingdom will also be given a new heart and new spirit. We know at the same time, however, that ancient servants such as the disciples of Jesus' time as well as Israel's original fathers Abraham, Isaac and Jacob representing the "old" will also be present in the Kingdom.

Parables about the Beginnings of a New Kingdom

End times meaning in Jesus' parables is punctuated by those that show a separation between evil and good at the time of the final harvest. *Parables of the Rich Man and Lazarus*, the *Wheat and Tares*, the *Sheep and Goats*, and *Casting a Net into the Sea* illustrate or foretell of this separation. In addition, the aforementioned *Parable of the Householder* as well as the *Parables of the Wedding* or *Great Feast* in the books of Matthew and Luke, respectively, are those that clearly indicate the beginnings of a new Kingdom and include Jesus' words earlier about many who are called (or "invited") but few are chosen. Not surprisingly, those who inherit the Kingdom in these parables have qualities consistent with inheritors mentioned in Jesus' Sermon on the Mount. These are like the ones who Jesus described choose the "lowest seat at the feast" in his parable of the same name or possess qualities of poor, lame, widows, fatherless, etc. They are moved to the front of the ceremony when the others do not attend.

Those who are "invited" but do not attend due to remaining hard-hearted, without forgiveness, stiffnecked, or too involved in other affairs or worldly "mammon" are described in several parables as going to a place where there will be "outer darkness" and "wailing and gnashing of teeth." It should be mentioned that this separation process as described begins *on earth*. The timing of separation in several of these parables is very likely the beginning of a process that occurs on or around what will be just the *beginning* of the Day of the Lord. The meaning of terms in a couple of these parables (i.e. outer darkness, wailing, gnashing of teeth, etc.) can be associated with living in a condition that is likely torment, heavy affliction and the kind of "hell-on-earth" scenario that is expected to occur once God's wrath on the earth arrives. (I describe the Day of the Lord in detail in *Volume 2*).

In his *Parables of Wheat and Tares* and the *Sheep and the Goats* Jesus appears to add a little more finality to this kind of judgment. In the former, Jesus said that the harvest (this separation) represents the "end of the world." He further said the Son of man will send forth his angels to throw out of the Kingdom "all things that offend, and them which do iniquity, and shall cast them into a furnace of fire…," a fire that he also described as "everlasting." In terms of the harvest narrative described thus far in this passage we are told that these tares will be "as stubble" in the Day of the Lord so that, "…the day that cometh shall burn them up…that it shall leave them neither root nor branch" (Mal. 4:1).

This final division illustrates the "great gulf fixed" as described in the *Parable of the Rich Man and Lazarus.* In contrast with the fire, Jesus foretold that the remaining righteous who are the sheep separated from the goats will shine forth as the sun in the "Kingdom of their Father." (Note the reference to their light shining again as described above). This Kingdom they inherit is one described as being, "prepared for you from the foundation of the world."

'Jacob's last days anointed remnant

Indeed, it will be the poor who enter the Kingdom. We are told that it is they who will trust that the "Lord has founded Zion." The 'Daughter of Zion' of the last days anointed remnant will be a Matriarch-Queen in the coming heavenly Kingdom. We are told that all of her sons will "marry" her, but she is the bride of the Lord. Events signaled through the *Parable of the Wedding Feast* as well as the *Parable of the 10 Virgins possibly* allude to the marriage between the 'Daughter of Zion' and the Lord. The signal for this marriage is also given in the story of the Song of Solomon. Other prophetic verses about such a last days wedding tell us that the bridegroom will be "taken away" (Lk. 5:35), the bride will go "out of her closet" (Joel 2:16), etc. Believers have instructions to be watching for the moment when the Son of Man *returns* from this wedding (Lk. 12:36).

Unfortunately, for the wicked, this marriage or union will signal the beginning of a process for separation between the two spiritual kingdoms. Language about "midnight" used in two of Jesus' parables suggests the *beginning* of judgment for the adversary's kingdom that includes some of his people, 'Israel.' Of course, the division between the 10 virgins (5 ready, 5 not ready) at the time of the midnight wedding occurs with the latter group being told by the Lord, "I know you not." Meanwhile, one uninvited guest at the wedding in this same parable is identified as the adversary and is thrown out. The *Parable of the Friend at Midnight* also suggests division at this time when calamities escalate. In this parable the friend asking for food corroborates other prophetic scripture indicating that there will be food shortage (i.e. famine) at this time. "Midnight" or night time on several other occasions in scripture signals this time of the Lord's judgment. I have written in my books, *Biblical End Times, Volumes 1 and 2*, that the Lord removing himself or "hiding his face" (i.e. the time at which the bridegroom is "taken away") is a sign that calamities will come upon the people.

Altogether, Jesus' parables tell the integrated prophetic story that is apparent throughout scripture. That is, a last days anointed remnant of his believers will point to His light, lessons and ability to provide salvation for the benefit of a previously blinded 'Israel' and any Gentiles who seek the true God of the universe and his Kingdom to come.

11.3 Prophecy in Jesus' Parable of the Mustard Seed

The *Parable of the Mustard* Seed spoken by Jesus is a Kingdom parable. This means that it can be seen as having meaning for God's upcoming Millennial Kingdom and beyond. The following is the actual *Parable of the Mustard Seed* as it was spoken by Jesus in the book of Mark:

> *And he said, Whereunto shall we liken the kingdom of God? or with what comparison shall we compare it? It is like a grain of mustard seed, which, when it is sown in the earth, is less than all the seeds that be in the earth: But when it is sown, it groweth up, and becometh greater than all herbs, and shooteth out great branches; so that the fowls of the air may lodge under the shadow of it. (Mk. 4:30-32)*

(Note to the reader: In this same parable as given in the book of Matthew, we are told that this seed becomes a tree. I will use "tree" in this passage as compared with "herb" for the purposes of easier comparison, interpretation and understanding).

The small mustard seed that Jesus spoke about develops great branches and becomes a great tree. In the big picture, we can look at this as a tree that God will establish for reclaiming his inheritance for his Kingdom; they are represented by the birds that flock to this tree and its fruit.

In some ways, God's people in the Millennial Kingdom will be starting anew; albeit still with God's original promise to Abraham, Isaac and Jacob; that is, for his people to grow and become as the "sand of the sea." In this passage, I will discuss how the *Parable of the Mustard Seed* relates to this; in the meantime, as background, recall what God said to Adam and Eve when they represented the beginning of human life in the Garden and then to Noah and his sons when they were beginning again post-flood. These instructions are seen in respective verses below:

And God blessed them, and God said unto them (Adam and Eve), Be fruitful, and multiply, and replenish the earth, and subdue it: and have dominion over the fish of the sea, and over the fowl of the air, and over every living thing that moveth upon the earth. (Gen. 1:28)

And God blessed Noah and his sons, and said unto them, Be fruitful, and multiply, and replenish the earth. (Gen. 9:1)

After the last days "vine" of the house of Israel has been stripped because of their disobedience, and after much of the world's population has been reduced because of events in the Day of the Lord (See *Writings of Lion's Lair, Volume 2*), Israel's remnant will eventually be regathered from across the world. This will represent a reuniting of the kingdom of Judah and the 'northern kingdom' of Israel. Then, they will multiply in the Kingdom once again just as God had originally instructed Adam and Eve.

The mustard seed comes directly from God

In his *Parable of the Mustard Seed*, it is God (Jesus) himself who can be seen as the one who plants the seed. From other scripture, we can infer that it is Jesus who "ministers the seed" just like the husbandman who watches over the "vineyard of red wine," saying, "I the Lord do keep it; I will water it every moment: lest any hurt it, I will keep it night and day" (Is. 27:3). Jesus is the Son of man who not only "ministers" the mustard seed but he keeps the tree and through it he "gives (its) increase" and "gives bread" (2 Cor. 9:10).

When considering this mustard tree, we might consider that every good thing comes from God above and is of God's sovereign domain. The following ancient verses remind us about this and how the mustard tree is the property of God's Kingdom:

For every beast of the forest is mine, and the cattle upon a thousand hills. I know all the fowls of the mountains: and the wild beasts of the field are mine. If I were hungry, I would not tell thee: for the world is mine, and the fullness thereof. (Ps. 50:10-12)

Surely the mountains bring him forth food, where all the beasts of the field play. He lieth under the shady trees, in the covert of the reed, and fens. The shady trees cover him with their shadow; the willows of the brook compass him about. Behold, he drinketh up a river, and hasteth not: he trusteth that he can draw up Jordan into his mouth. (Job 40:20-23)

Jesus sows and plants the mustard seed, and of course Jesus' Holy Spirit can be seen as the root or the vine from which its branches grow. Then, the fruit of this mustard tree includes the fowls of the air who come to nest in it. This resulting "fruit" is God's inheritance. It is Jesus who ultimately claims these fruits for himself as follows:

The husbandman that laboureth must be first partaker of the fruits. (2 Tim. 2:6)

Who goeth a warfare any time at his own charges? Who planteth a vineyard, and eateth not of the fruit thereof? Or who feedeth a flock, and eateth not of the milk of the flock? (1 Cor. 9:7)

You may recall from Chapter 3 that in these last days the Lord himself labors and wars against his anti-Christ enemy on behalf of his Kingdom and servants.

Contents of this passage

Given the short story of the *Parable of the Mustard Seed* and the background above, I will address the concepts of this parable according to four simple components:

- A very small seed
- A good, righteous seed sowed on good ground
- Growth that makes it become very large
- Fruit of the Kingdom

The second component- an assumption that the small seed is a righteous one and is planted on good ground- is not found explicitly in the words of the parable but can be easily inferred in the course of its interpretation. In fact, in scripture that includes Jesus explaining faith, he mentions that one must have "faith as a grain of mustard seed" in order to move a mountain, which appears to be at least partially related to this parable when considering its entire interpretation that I will provide herein. Jesus' words about having faith like a mustard seed include:

And Jesus said unto them, Because of your unbelief: for verily I say unto you, if ye have faith as a grain of mustard seed, ye shall say unto this mountain, Remove hence to yonder place; and it shall remove; and nothing shall be impossible unto you. (Matt. 17:20)

Faith such as that which is associated with the mustard seed is highly and positively correlated with righteousness, and we can easily assume that its resulting tree is a good one. Otherwise, in contrast, we certainly have many examples in scripture of trees of God's house of Israel people that are corrupt, unrighteous and that are cut down as a result. This contrast is put most simply in the words of Jesus as follows:

Even so every good tree bringeth forth good fruit; but a corrupt tree bringeth forth evil fruit. A good tree cannot bring forth evil fruit, neither can a corrupt tree bring forth good fruit. (Matt. 7:17-18)

Given that the tree in this parable at hand grows from a tiny mustard seed, becomes very large, and produces good fruit and the fowls of the air that come to nest in it, it certainly is not one that is a candidate to be cut down due to a lack of good fruit.

A Very Small Seed

The mustard seed itself in this parable might be seen as the seed of a servant(s). In the *Parable of the Wheat and Tares*, Jesus likened the good seed planted as to the "children of the kingdom." This may generally be assumed to be the case for the mustard seed. "Children of the kingdom" are described by the Apostle Paul in the book of Second Timothy as those who are persevering soldiers who are in bonds, persecuted, yet remain faithful and suffer for the elect's (i.e. God's chosen ones') sake.

Jesus makes a point in the *Parable of the Mustard Seed* to say that this seed is the "least of all seeds." While this seed may be seen as representing the children of the kingdom, it may also represent an individual servant of the Lord who is small and insignificant in stature, yet who likely has a house of Israel bloodline at the least. This servant's small stature is in obvious contrast to the last days "great men" and "mountains" of Israel who are referred to in the book of Ezekiel and are likely very powerful rulers and shepherds in God's land with distinguished house of Israel bloodlines.

I described earlier in this passage how this small mustard seed turns into a very large tree that houses God's inheritance, 'Israel,' who proceed into the Millennial Kingdom. Therefore, this tiny seed represents the beginning of what God refers to as the "branch of my planting" in the end times. Its tree produced in its infancy may then be seen as the "low tree" that God exalts or as the "dry tree" referred to by Jesus that God eventually causes to "flourish." This is a seed that is chosen by God that turns into his branch about which he refers, "A little one shall become a thousand, and a small one a strong nation: I the Lord will hasten it in his time" (Is. 60:22).

End times small seed

We might think about this small seed and its infancy in growth in terms of God's chosen end times servants who I described in Chapters 4-8 of this book. At a time period that God prophetically refers to as the "day of small things" (Zech. 4:10), end times 'David' ('Zerubbabel') is instrumental in bringing back God's people and ultimately prepares the Millennial Kingdom temple for God with the "eyes of the Lord" who roam the earth.

In the Prophet Amos' vision of these same last days, he saw a vision of a 'David-versus-Goliath'-type battle with end times 'Jacob' at the helm, representing 'Israel' versus world Babylon's anti-Christ soldiers. This battle happens during the current last days when the Chaldeans are devastating God's vineyard. Amos saw 'Jacob' in his vision and inquired of God twice, "By whom shall Jacob arise? For he is small" (Am. 7:2,5). Small and insignificant 'Jacob' is the servant described in detail in the book of Isaiah and *possibly* as follows in Chapter 53:

For he shall grow up before him as a tender plant, and as a root out of a dry ground: he hath no form nor comeliness; and when we shall see him, there is no beauty that we should desire him. (Is. 53:2)

(Note: In Chapter 5 about end times 'Jacob,' I mentioned that he is referred to in chapters of Isaiah (42, 49, 50, 52 and possibly 53, referred to as "servant songs"). This end times servant described through Isaiah will receive a "divided" share of the spoil with the "strong" according to Chapter 53. *All* has already been given to Jesus- the whole Kingdom is his- he does not need anything to be shared. Overall, while this chapter is attributed to Jesus in the New Testament, there is good reason to believe that Isaiah 53 also speaks about an end-times servant. This would represent a double fulfillment).

End times 'Jacob,' who raises up God's inheritance 'Israel' and is a compilation of historical biblical servants, could be a 'type' of Joseph, at least in part, who we know was sold by his brothers into captivity and left behind. Last days "men of Judah" and rulers of the country of Israel come against and "feed themselves" off of their own people, including 'Jacob' and his "small flock" remnant. The following verse refers to an end times 'type' of Joseph in which God is addressing those in Zion who are powerful rulers in Israel called, "mountains of Samaria," whose "palaces" God says that he abhors. God says about them:

(They) drink wine in bowls, and anoint themselves with the chief ointments: but they are not grieved for the affliction of Joseph. (Am. 6:6)

End times 'Jacob,' like Joseph, and like Jesus, for whom Joseph was also a foreshadowing figure, is rejected by his own people. Thus, 'Jacob' is small.

Similarly, King David in his day was not the obvious choice among his brothers as king, but he was God's choice. His crowning as king did not come easy. Then, he had defectors and many enemies including some in his own house. Nevertheless, King David went on to multiply his own family "tree" of inheritance in his day and beyond within Judah. While the last days house of David suffers a "breach," God's promise that can be seen as an extension of King David's original small house includes:

As the host of heaven cannot be numbered, neither the sand of the sea measured: so will I multiply the seed of David my servant, and the Levites that minister unto me. (Jer. 33:22)

A small seed from the ancient shepherd boy David will turn into a Kingdom of God's people.

A Good, Righteous Seed and Good Ground

It is not a big leap to assume that the mustard seed in this prophetic parable given by Jesus is a good and righteous one. In fact, God's end times anointed remnant are referred to elsewhere in scripture as "the seed of the blessed of the Lord" (Is. 65:23) and more than once by God as "the work of my hands." Those among his last days remnant who are persecuted and mourn are furthermore referred to as "trees of righteousness, the planting of the Lord..." (Is. 61:3). Given that the mustard tree is planted by Jesus himself, it becomes great and brings forth great fruit (via fowls that come to nest in it). (I will describe the fruit of this mustard tree in the final section of this passage). In the meantime, the following two verses include King David's words about the tree of a righteous servant followed by God addressing his end times holy people:

…(it is) planted by the rivers of water, that bringeth forth his fruit in his season; his leaf also shall not wither… (Ps. 1:3)

Thy people also shall be all righteous: they shall inherit the land forever, the branch of my planting, the work of my hands, that I may be glorified. (Is. 60:21)

In his teachings that I referred to earlier, Jesus explained about having "faith as a grain of mustard seed," and I remarked about the positive correlation between faith and righteousness. In addition, given this mustard tree's tremendous growth, its righteous seed can be safely assumed to have been planted on good ground as opposed to poor or rocky soil that is described in Jesus' *Parable of the Sower*. The following verses refer to a seed on good ground that is equated with righteousness:

But that on the good ground are they, which in an honest and good heart, having heard the word, keep it, and bring forth fruit with patience. (Lk. 8:15)

But he that received seed into the good ground is he that heareth the word, and understandeth it… (Matt. 13:23)

The small, righteous mustard seed in good soil must first develop a root or vine that is the Spirit of Jesus himself, and who is the vine that makes the righteous branches fruitful. Through God's increase that I will describe in the section below, the righteous seed planted in good soil develops faithful branches that are "beautiful," "glorious," and consist of God's end times remnant inheritance and heritage, 'Israel.' The following verses refer to a seed that is planted on good soil and that grows and develops strong branches:

Thou preparedst room before it, and didst cause it to take deep root, and it filled the land. The hills were covered with the shadow of it, and the boughs thereof were like the goodly cedars. She sent out her boughs unto the sea, and her branches unto the river. (Ps. 80:9-11)

But ye, O mountains of Israel, ye shall shoot forth your branches, and yield your fruit to my people of Israel; for they are at hand to come. For, behold, I am for you, and I will turn unto you, and ye shall be tilled and sown. (Ez. 36:8-9)

If we are looking to an end times servant figure as an example of the righteous mustard seed, we might again consider end times 'Jacob' who God has "called in righteousness" (Is. 42:6). He qualifies according to Paul's aforementioned definition as a "child of the kingdom" since he is among God's chosen end times remnant who is chastened but then afterwards yields the "fruit of righteousness."

Grows to Become Very Large

The tiny mustard seed in Jesus' parable grows to become a very large tree, one that produces a great amount of fruit. Thus, it fulfills the multiplication effect among God's people that was instructed for Adam and Eve, and then for Noah and his sons after the flood. It represents 'Israel' as an inheritance becoming as the "sand of the sea" again as they proceed into his heavenly Millennial Kingdom.

Related to this tree's growth, in various parts of scripture, we are told that God's remnant in the last days: "sprout"; "spring up"; "flourish"; "blossom and bud"; "grow as the lily," etc. God's last days inheritance mustard tree can also be seen as existing in the "garden (that) causeth the things that are sown in it to spring forth; so the Lord God will cause righteousness and praise to spring forth before all the nations" (Is. 61:11).

The "fruit" produced by this end times mustard tree will likely be seen by people across the world. In Jesus' *Parable of the Sower*, we learn about the good seed that is planted on good ground, which then grows tremendously and yields its fruit as follows:

And other fell on good ground, and sprang up, and bear fruit an hundredfold. And when he had said these things, he cried, He that hath ears to hear, let him hear. (Lk. 8:8)

But other fell into good ground, and brought forth fruit, some an hundredfold, some sixtyfold, some thirtyfold. (Matt. 13:8)

We know that any tremendous "growth" of life that happens such as that seen with the mustard seed is an increase that comes only from God, who is the original planter and sower. Recall that it was the Apostle Paul in his own plant growth analogy who said that it is God who "gives the increase."

The supernatural growth process of God's Kingdom is something that we do not understand and that may be considered a mystery. In fact, in speaking about the time leading up to the harvest, and right before he spoke the *Parable of the Mustard Seed*, Jesus said the following about the Kingdom of God:

And he said, So is the kingdom of God, as if a man should cast seed into the ground; And should sleep, and rise night and day, and the seed should spring and grow up, he knoweth not how. For the earth bringeth forth fruit of herself; first the blade, then the ear, after that the full corn in the ear. (Mk. 4:26-28)

We might be reminded here about the 'Daughter of Zion,' a Kingdom queen and mother. After she loses her extended royal, earthly "family" and is taken captive and made desolate, she then subsequently and suddenly arises to see her family of Israel return and appear in the holy land for the Millennial Kingdom.

The mustard seed tree represents the growth of God's Kingdom inheritance

In his words about those who already have much and to whom more will be given, it is logical to infer that Jesus may have been referring to God's inheritance, 'Israel' and 'Jacob,' who are beneficiaries of his covenant promise. In his statement that is possibly related to Kingdom growth, Jesus said:

For whosoever hath, to him shall be given, and he shall have more abundance: but whosoever hath not, from him shall be taken away even that he hath. (Matt. 13:12)

So, it appears that part of the prophecy in the *Parable of the Mustard Seed* is that of God's increase and multiplication for his end times inheritance of Israel, just as he instructed for Adam and Eve and then later Noah. Even in the ancient, prophetic *Song of Moses* we are told about God's people, "Thou shalt bring them in, and plant them in the mountain of thine inheritance, in the place, O Lord, which thou hast made for thee to dwell in…" (Ex. 15:17). When his two nations of Israel and Judah come back together, rejoin, and return for the Millennial Kingdom God says:

Moreover I will make a covenant of peace with them; it shall be an everlasting covenant with them: and I will place them, and multiply them, and will set my sanctuary in the midst of them for evermore. (Ez. 37:26)

And out of them shall proceed thanksgiving and the voice of them that make merry: and I will multiply them, and they shall not be few; I will also glorify them, and they shall not be small. (Jer. 30:19)

The result of God's original planting of the small mustard seed, for which he also gives the increase, is his inheritance that flocks to the tree's branches. In terms of relating the increase and multiplication to his end times servants again, we might consider what God says about end times 'Jacob' or similar servants. 'Jacob' and his last days remnant are those who may be seen as branches that bear fruit but are purged so that they may bring forth even more fruit; this is found in the book of John, Chapter 15. The same concept is also found in the book of Hebrews in which we are told by the Apostle Paul that the process of chastening "afterward yieldeth the peaceable fruit of righteousness unto them which are exercised thereby" (Heb. 12:11). God says to chastened and persecuted 'Jacob' and his remnant:

And I will multiply men upon you, all the house of Israel, even all of it: and the cities shall be inhabited, and the wastes shall be builded: And I will multiply upon you man and beast; and they shall increase and bring fruit: and I will settle you after your old estates, and will do better unto you than at your beginnings: and ye shall know that I am the Lord. (Ez. 36:10-11)

And all the trees of the field shall know that I the Lord have brought down the high tree, have exalted the low tree, have dried up the green tree, and have made the dry tree to flourish: I the Lord have spoken and have done it. (Ez. 17:24)

This multiplication is God's fruit of the Kingdom, which I will address in more detail as follows.

The Mustard Seed and its Tree Yield Fruit of the Kingdom

In the case of the *Parable of the Mustard Seed* that grows into a tree, the fruits of the Kingdom can be seen as the birds of the air that come and lodge in its branches and in its shadows. In fact, if we consider the mustard tree to represent God's inheritance he brings through his servant 'Jacob,' given the totality of scripture and this strong theme throughout God's Word, then we might view the birds of this tree to be the fruit of the house of 'Jacob.' The Apostle James described "precious fruit of the earth" as appearing in the time of latter rains and upon the Lord's return, which James said is the fruit that the husbandman waits for. This appears to refer to the same fruit of God's inheritance that is 'Jacob' and his people 'Israel.' They are described as follows:

He shall cause them that come of Jacob to take root: Israel shall blossom and bud, and fill the face of the world with fruit. (Is. 27:6)

The end times infant-stage growth of the mustard tree for God's Kingdom inheritance can be seen as his 'Jacob'-Judah "small flock" remnant who abide in the vine of Jesus Christ. They fit the Apostle Paul's words of exhortation to those in the church of Philippi, saying, "Being filled with the fruits of righteousness, which are by Jesus Christ, unto the glory and praise of God" (Phil 1:11). This remnant includes the "escaped house of Judah" that will likely "take root downward and bears fruit upward" (Is. 37:31) as the remnant of King Hezekiah's day. God's 'Jacob'-Judah remnant will "shoot forth its branches" and will "yield fruit" (Ez. 36:8), which will be the firstfruits of God for the world to see. This is indicated in the following verses:

The wilderness and the solitary place shall be glad for them; and the desert shall rejoice, and blossom as the rose. It shall blossom abundantly, and rejoice even with joy and singing: the glory of Lebanon shall be given unto it, the excellency of Carmel and Sharon, they shall see the glory of the Lord, and the excellency of our God. (Is. 35:1-2)

'Jacob's "small flock" remnant will represent the beginning of the fulfillment of Moses' ancient prophetic vision for the house of 'Joseph' that will be as a "fruitful bough, even fruitful by a well." 'Jacob' will ultimately raise up the tribes of Israel and will be a light to the Gentiles in bringing all of the people in the Kingdom together under Jesus Christ. God tells 'Jacob' that he will establish the earth and cause him to "inherit the desolate heritages" (Is. 49:8). This is the same time about which God says, "And I will multiply the fruit of the tree, and the increase of the field, that ye shall receive no more reproach of famine among the heathen" (Ez. 36:30). God says the following to end times 'Jacob' about the fruit that flocks to God's Kingdom tree:

But when he seeth his children, the work of mine hands, in the midst of him, they shall sanctify my name, and sanctify the Holy One of Jacob, and shall fear the God of Israel. (Is. 29:23)

The remnant shall return, even the remnant of Jacob, unto the mighty God. For though thy people Israel be as the sand of the sea, yet a remnant of them shall return: the consumption decreed shall overflow with righteousness. (Is. 10:21-22)

And they shall spring up as among the grass, as willows by the water courses. One shall say, I am the Lord's; and another shall call himself by the name of Jacob; and another shall subscribe with his hand unto the Lord, and surname himself by the name of Israel. (Is. 44:4-5)

So, it is 'Jacob' and his remnant people who will ultimately grow into the people of God's entire Kingdom. Of course, believing Gentiles will be grafted in. I describe Israel's and Gentile-believers' return to this Kingdom in more detail in *Volume 2.*

Conclusion

In conclusion, consider the following two sets of prophetic scripture which speak about a last days tree of inheritance that effectively summarize the contents of this passage. They speak to the tremendous growth and fruit of God's righteous inheritance tree, 'Israel.' Notice the striking similarity of the following verses to Jesus' *Parable of the Mustard Seed*, which I restated from scripture at the beginning of this passage:

I will be as the dew unto Israel: he shall grow as the lily, and cast forth his roots as Lebanon. His branches shall spread, and his beauty shall be as the olive tree, and his smell as Lebanon. They that dwell under his shadow shall return; they shall revive as the corn, and grow as the vine: the scent thereof shall be as the wine of Lebanon. (Hos. 14:5-7)

Thus saith the Lord God; I will also take of the highest branch of the high cedar, and will set it; I will crop off from the top of his young twigs a tender one, and will plant it upon an high mountain and eminent: In the mountain of the height of Israel will I plant it: and it shall bring forth boughs, and bear fruit, and be a goodly cedar: and under it shall dwell all fowl of every wing; in the shadow of the branches thereof shall they dwell. (Ez. 17:22-23)

Both of these sets of scripture tell of an end times tree of inheritance that is planted by God, given an increase by God, and yields the fruit of his Kingdom. Thus, these verses appear to represent the soon coming fulfillment of the prophecy that is in Jesus' *Parable of the Mustard Seed*.

~

To summarize, this great tree represented in the *Parable of the Mustard Seed* is God's inheritance people, which only come forth as a result of his own planting and through his own power that causes the increase. His end times servants as the branches of this tree may only understand God's tremendous glory, power and Kingdom through their faith, righteousness and abiding in the vine or root of the tree that is Jesus Christ.

Appendix.

Personal Salvation in Jesus Christ Alone

(Ref: The following taken and adapted from the book, Studies in Bible Prophecy, by Thomas E. Lewis, with permission.)

"What must I do to be saved?" (Acts 16:30)

This is the single most important question that every person must answer. The answer to this question is found in the pages of God's Word to mankind, the Bible. The central event of all of human history was the crucifixion of Jesus Christ, two thousand years ago, to redeem mankind back to God. The message of the Bible is that of a Savior and of a loving God who desires that all humans be saved from eternal separation from God in a place called hell. The Bible says that God is not willing that any should perish but that all should come to repentance (2 Pet. 3:9). From God's Word to mankind we can glean the following facts:

All humans are sinners: For all have sinned and come short of the glory of God (Rom. 3:23). In the book of Romans (3:19) we are told that all of the world stands guilty before God. However, we also read:

But the scripture hath concluded all under sin, that the promise by faith of Jesus Christ might be given to them that believe. (Gal. 3:22)

The wages of sin is death: If we were to die in our sins, the Bible says that we will suffer eternal separation from God (Rom. 6:23). As part of the Lord's final judgment this is described as:

And whosoever was not found written in the book of life was cast into the lake of fire. (Rev. 20:15)

The good news is: "…the gift of God is eternal life through Jesus Christ, our Lord" (Rom. 6:23). Eternal life in the presence of God is a free gift offered by a loving God to all mankind. We are told: "Being justified freely by his grace through the redemption that is in Christ Jesus" (Rom. 3:24). Salvation through Jesus Christ is offered to every human being as a free gift. There is nothing that we can do to earn our salvation. We are told:

For by grace are ye saved through faith; and that not of yourselves, it is the gift of God, not of works, lest any man should boast. (Eph. 2:8-9)

<u>Only through Jesus Christ can we be saved:</u> Jesus said: "I am the way, the truth, and the life; no man cometh unto the Father, but by me" (Jn. 14:6). In the book of Acts we read: "Neither is there salvation in any other; for there is no other name under heaven given among men, whereby we must be saved" (Acts 4:12). In the book of Hebrews we read: "Wherefore, he (Jesus Christ) is able to save them to the uttermost that come unto God by him, seeing he ever liveth to make intercession for them" (Heb. 7:25).

What must you do to receive the eternal salvation so freely offered by a loving God? In the book of Romans we are told:

If thou shalt confess with thy mouth the Lord Jesus, and shalt believe in thine heart that God hath raised him from the dead, thou shalt be saved. For with the heart man believeth unto righteousness; and with the mouth confession is made unto salvation...For whosoever shall call upon the name of the Lord shall be saved. (Rom. 10:9-10,13)

It is that simple. You just have to ask. If you will call upon the name of the Lord Jesus Christ to save your soul, He then promises you eternal life. In the book of John we are told, "But as many as received him, to them gave he power to become children of God, even to them that believe on his name" (Jn. 1:12). We are also told:

For God so loved the world, that he gave his only begotten Son, that whosoever believeth in him should not perish, but have everlasting life. For God sent not his Son into the world to condemn the world, but that the world through him might be saved. (Jn. 3:16-17)

And this is the record, that God hath given unto us eternal life, and this life is in his Son. (1 Jn. 5:11)

Making the decision for salvation in Jesus Christ

Would you like to pray, right now, and ask Jesus Christ to save your soul? If you're not sure what to say, you might pray something like the following simple prayer:

Lord Jesus, I know I am a sinner and I ask you to forgive me of all my sins. I'm asking You to come into my life to be my Savior and Lord. Help me to live the Christian life and to turn from my sins and follow you. In Jesus name I pray.

If you prayed this prayer, meaning it as best as you know how, according to God's word you are saved. Jesus does not turn any away. He said, "All that the Father giveth me shall come to me; and him that cometh to me I will in no wise cast out." (Jn. 6:37)

Why is it so urgent that you be saved? We are told: "God now commandeth all men everywhere to repent, because he hath appointed a day in which he will judge the world in righteousness by that man whom he hath ordained; concerning which he hath given assurance unto all men, in that he hath raised him from the dead" (Acts 17:30-31). The good news of salvation through Jesus Christ has been preached for two thousand years. The Bible clearly says that there is an "appointed time" for Christ to judge the world. If you are saved through your faith in Jesus Christ then you can rejoice that your eternal soul will be in heaven.

Salvation in the soon-coming Day of the Lord

We are coming upon the end of the age; an age called the Day of the Lord. Very difficult times will come onto the entire earth and people will be looking for answers in the midst of their own personal turmoil. In a couple of biblical passages within the context of the Day of the Lord we can remain assured that at this time, "Whosoever shall call upon the name of the Lord shall be saved" (Acts 2:21, Joel 2:32). Additional verses associated with salvation through Jesus Christ that we might also keep in mind during upcoming trials and tribulations are as follows.

Being saved from wrath:

For God hath not appointed us to wrath, but to obtain salvation by our Lord Jesus Christ. (1 Thess. 5:9)

Much more then, being now justified by his blood, we shall be saved from wrath through him. (Rom. 5:9)

Being counted worthy and righteous:

Watch ye therefore, and pray always, that ye may be accounted worthy to escape all these things that shall come to pass, and to stand before the Son of man. (Lk. 21:36)

Wherefore, beloved, seeing that ye look for such things, be diligent that ye may be found of him in peace, without spot, and blameless. (2 Pet. 3:14)

Being delivered and hidden:

The Lord knoweth how to deliver the godly out of temptations, and to reserve the unjust unto the day of judgment to be punished. (2 Pet. 2:9)

Seek ye the Lord, all ye meek of the earth, which have wrought his judgment; seek righteousness, seek meekness: it may be ye shall be hid in the day of the Lord's anger. (Zeph. 2:3)

There hath no temptation taken you but such as is common to man: but God is faithful, who will not suffer you to be tempted above that ye are able; but will with the temptation also make a way to escape, that ye may be able to bear it. (1 Cor. 10:13)

(To the angel at the Church of Philadelphia) Because thou hast kept the word of my patience, I also will keep thee from the hour of temptation, which shall come upon all the world, to try them that dwell upon the earth. (Rev. 3:10)

For Jesus Christ-believers living in our current last days time period our true faith is very likely to be tested in the midst of the raging spiritual kingdom war. There are only two sides in this war. This is becoming more apparent every day now. There is: Jesus Christ- the truth; and 2) Everything else that is in an anti-Christ junk pile. The anti-Christ matrix-"machine" that is already in place will force the issue from here on out until Jesus returns to establish his Kingdom. One will be required to make a clear allegiance one way or the other.

As such, true believers should be prepared for troubles and persecution in our current last days time period. No matter what, however, Jesus Christ saves. That is the meaning of his divine name. That is the good news. True, faithful believers who stand for their faith can rest in the comfort of the salvation of their eternal soul. We are told, "The Lord is good, a strong hold in the day of trouble; and he knoweth them that trust in him" (Nah. 1:7). Overall, Christians are to be seeking Jesus' Holy Spirit, not the wrath of God that will consume the earth. For our final resting and living place is in heaven, "from which also we look for coming of our Savior, the Lord Jesus Christ" (Phil. 3:20).

As for how Christ's salvation for his people who are on earth might look in these very last days, this remains to be seen. While there will be martyrs, they will be raised again for his Kingdom. Otherwise, as far as the Lord's timing, methods, ordering/phasing of salvation events, etc. as these apply on an individual basis, only God knows. No matter how these transpire, they will be supernatural and divinely guided by our loving God himself. Again, for all believers who are found in the book of life this is very good news that we can trust.

One theme that I identified in scripture given above in which true, faithful believers can take comfort in these times is that we are told that we can be "saved from wrath" (1 Thess. 5:9, Rom. 5:9) or will have some kind of escape. Again, how this happens is up to God. Meanwhile, believers should maintain simple, strong faith in this promise. Believers should also naturally have a desire in their hearts to supplement their faith in the midst of today's spiritual darkness with the action items listed in the section below. This is so that, in Jesus' words above, we may be "counted worthy" to escape.

If you prayed to receive Jesus Christ as your Lord and Savior, what should you do now?

Read your Bible daily: The Bible says, "As newborn babes, desire the sincere milk of the word, that you may grow by it" (1 Pet. 2:2). Jesus said, "If ye continue in my word, then are ye my disciples indeed; and ye shall know the truth and the truth shall make you free. Jesus also said, "It is written, Man shall not live by bread alone, but by every word that proceedeth out of the mouth of God (Matt. 4:4). The Gospel of John is a good place to begin.

Pray daily: Jesus said that men ought always to pray and not to faint (Lk. 18:1). Christians are instructed to come boldly unto the throne of grace, that we may obtain mercy, and find grace to help in time of need (Heb. 4:16). The Psalmist wrote: "Evening, morning, and at noon, will I pray, and cry aloud, and he shall hear my voice" (Ps. 55:17).

Attend a Bible-believing, Bible-preaching church: The Bible instructs Christians: "Not forsaking the assembling of ourselves together, as the manner of some is, but exhorting one another, and so much the more as ye see the day approaching" (Heb. 10:25). Surely, the day of his return is drawing close.

Obey Jesus' commands: The natural consequence of a contrite heart that is surrendered to Jesus Christ as Lord will desire righteousness. The Holy Spirit will guide one in the difference between right and wrong but the most important words are from Jesus himself:

Thou shalt love the Lord thy God with all thy heart, and with all thy soul, and with all thy mind. (Matt. 22:37)

And the second is like unto it, Thou shalt love thy neighbour as thyself. (Matt. 22:39)

Jesus said on these two commandments of his rests "all of the law and the prophets" (Matt. 22:40). Jesus also summarized the law and the prophets when he spoke what is known as the Golden Rule:

Therefore all things whatsoever ye would that men should do to you, do ye even so to them: for this is the law and the prophets. (Matt. 7:12)

Scripture is clear that nobody is perfect. One other simple instruction of Jesus to keep in mind is his words to the woman caught in adultery; he did not condemn her but said, "Go and sin no more" (Jn. 8:11). Even more so Jesus said that we are to, "Be ye therefore perfect, even as your Father which is in heaven is perfect" (Matt. 5:48).

Avoid being deceived: While Jesus mentioned above that the law is contained and summed up in his commands one specific law that I will bring to attention in these last days is that we are to serve no other gods besides him. This may seem self-explanatory and redundant but therein lies the deception. Jesus said, "Swear not at all," referring to secret oaths or allegiances. These pledges to any organizations or individuals that may in any way distract or hinder one's freedom to study God's Word, speak openly about his Word, or worship him, and him only, are an avenue for deception. These kinds of allegiances are obvious cause for being "blinded" and are a reason even for those who may believe that they have some sort of piety or spiritual righteousness to be ultimately be told by Jesus, "I never knew you" (Matt. 7:23).

There is very good reason we learn in scripture that the "way is narrow" and that "few are chosen." Deception that is rampant in these last days will lead to a very large apostasy even in Christian houses of worship. This is part of a "falling away" from what is true.

As an initial personal test, you might consider if you truly understand the reason that we are told by Jesus that those for whom heaven awaits are those who are: persecuted; poor; lame; poor in spirit; meek; mourning; cast out/desolate; have left homes; etc. If you do not feel persecuted in these last days then you are likely on the wrong side of the war. Recall Jesus' words, "The servant is not greater than his lord. If they have persecuted me, they will also persecute you; if they have kept my saying, they will keep yours also." (Jn. 15:20). Another way of understanding where you stand personally might be to consider Jesus' words:

...For I was hungry and you gave me something to eat, I was thirsty and you gave me something to drink, I was a stranger and you invited me in, I needed clothes and you clothed me, I was sick and you looked after me, I was in prison and you came to visit me. (Matt. 25:34)

Jesus here was speaking on behalf of any of those who become heavily persecuted, especially for his sake. He knew in his day the results of anti-Christ, gang-style persecution and lawlessness that causes an individual to become desolate. When the anti-Christ cabal targets a person, they control and influence others around them in their ability or manner to provide them assistance.

Especially given our current time period that includes heavy spiritual warfare, if you do not fall into the designations above nor understand why/how people end up what might be considered the "last," even in a society like 'Babylon'-U.S., then you would best be advised to find a way to "take up your cross." Sooner or later you will make a clear decision one way or the other. The anti-Christ Chaldeans will force this issue pertaining to one's faith in these last days.

The Bible says: "How shall we escape, if we neglect so great salvation…" (Heb. 2:3). There will be no escape for those who reject, are indifferent or are lukewarm to God's provision for eternal salvation through the shed blood of Jesus Christ. Jesus said:

He that rejecteth me, and receiveth not my words, hath one that judgeth him: the word that I have spoken, the same shall judge him in the last day. (Jn. 12:48)

The horrible fate of those who align against Jesus is recorded in the book of Revelation:

And whosoever was not found written in the book of life was cast into the lake of fire. (Rev. 20:15)

Don't delay. Come to Jesus Christ now while you still have the chance. The Bible says: "Now is the day of salvation (2 Cor. 6:2); tomorrow is promised to no one. Also, "Boast not thyself of tomorrow; for thou knowest not what a day may bring forth" (Prov. 27:1).

About the Author

Leo Lewis is a Bible-believing, salvation-believing Christian residing in the Denver, Colorado area. Mr. Lewis draws on a professional background of leading project-based market research producing data-driven insights for clients. His career in several roles included analyst work on nearly 200 unique projects using diverse work scopes and methodologies. He holds an M.B.A. and a B.B.A. in Finance.

In his books, *Biblical End Times, Volumes 1 and 2*, released in 2024, Mr. Lewis produced the integrated end times story found in scripture that is not told from the Church pulpit nor is discussed even among the bible prophecy community.

These books along with his newly released, *Writings of Lion's Lair, Volumes 1-3*, support the unique story of a last days anointed remnant who will achieve victory in the spiritual kingdom war. This remnant will proceed into the Millennial Kingdom to reside among recognized leadership that serves Jesus Christ.

The path through the tumultuous Day of the Lord to arrive at this Kingdom for Gentile believers and a house of Israel remnant who will return with the Lord's anointed is also discussed in this current book series, *Writings of Lion's Lair*.

All content comprising the *Writings of Lion's Lair* series is also currently freely available online for an indefinite period of time at mysouldoeswait.com.

~

You may access Mr. Lewis' other books, *Biblical End Times, Volumes 1 and 2*, at the same source as this current Volume.